THE CITY OF FALLING ANGELS

Also by John Berendt

Midnight in the Garden of Good and Evil

The City of

Falling Angels

JOHN BERENDT

SCEPTRE

First published in Great Britain in 2005 by Hodder and Stoughton
A division of Hodder Headline

The right of John Berendt to be identified as the Author of
the Work has been asserted by him in accordance with
the Copyright, Designs and Patents Act 1988.

A Sceptre Book

1 3 5 7 9 10 8 6 4 2

Grateful acknowledgement is made for permission to reprint the following selections: 'Fragment (1966)'
from *The Cantos of Ezra Pound.* Copyright © 1934, 1937, 1940, 1956, 1959, 1962, 1963, 1966, 1968
by Ezra Pound. Reprinted by permission of New Directions Publishing Corp.
'Ciao Cara' from *Ezra Pound, Father and Teacher: Discretions* by Mary de Rachewiltz. Copyright © 1971,
1975 by Mary de Rachewiltz. Reprinted by permission of New Directions Publishing Corp.
Excerpts from the diary of Daniel Sargent Curtis. Reprinted by permission of the Marciana Library.
'Dear [Sir]' letter from Olga Rudge to lawyer, April 24, 1988. Reprinted by permission of Mary de
Rachewiltz.
'Dearest Mother' letter from Mary de Rachewiltz to her mother, Olga Rudge, February 24, 1988.
Reprinted by permission of Mary de Rachewiltz.

A CIP catalogue record for this title is available from the British Library

Hardback ISBN 0 340 82498 0
Trade Paperback ISBN 0 340 82499 9

Typeset in Centaur by Hewer Text UK Ltd, Edinburgh
Printed and bound by Clays Ltd, St Ives plc

Hodder Headline's policy is to use papers that are natural, renewable
and recyclable products and made from wood grown in sustainable forests.
The logging and manufacturing processes are expected to conform to the
environmental regulations of the country of origin.

Hodder and Stoughton Ltd
A division of Hodder Headline
338 Euston Road
London NW1 3BH

Endpapers: La Fenice, 1954. Photograph © Hulton-Deutsch Collection/Corbis

For Harold Hayes and Clay Felker

'Beware of falling angels'

– Sign posted outside the Santa Maria della Salute Church in Venice in the early 1970s, before the restoration of its marble angels

Contents

This is a work of non-fiction. All the people in it are real and are identified by their real names. There are no composite characters. For the reader's convenience, a partial list of people and places appears at the end of the book, along with a glossary of Italian words used frequently in the text.

PROLOGUE:

The Venice Effect

'EVERYONE IN VENICE IS ACTING,' Count Girolamo Marcello told me. 'Everyone plays a role, and the role changes. The key to understanding Venetians is rhythm — the rhythm of the lagoon, the rhythm of the water, the tides, the waves . . .'

I had been walking along Calle della Mandola when I ran into Count Marcello. He was a member of an old Venetian family and was considered an authority on the history, the social structure, and especially the subtleties of Venice. As we were both headed in the same direction, I joined him.

'The rhythm in Venice is like breathing,' he said. 'High water, high pressure: tense. Low water, low pressure: relaxed. Venetians are not at all attuned to the rhythm of the wheel. That is for other places, places with motor vehicles. Ours is the rhythm of the Adriatic. The rhythm of the sea. In Venice the rhythm flows along with the tide, and the tide changes every six hours.'

Count Marcello inhaled deeply. 'How do you see a bridge?'

'Pardon me?' I asked. 'A bridge?'

'Do you see a bridge as an obstacle — as just another set of steps to climb to get from one side of a canal to the other? We Venetians do not see bridges as obstacles. To us bridges are transitions. We go over them very slowly. They are part of the rhythm. They are the links between two parts of a theatre, like changes in scenery, or like the progression from Act One of a play to Act Two. Our role changes as we go over bridges. We cross from one reality . . . to another reality. From one street . . . to another street. From one setting . . . to another setting.'

I

We were approaching a bridge crossing over Rio di San Luca into Campo Manin.

'A *trompe l'oeil* painting,' Count Marcello went on, 'is a painting that is so lifelike it doesn't look like a painting at all. It looks like real life, but of course it is not. It is reality once removed. What, then, is a *trompe l'oeil* painting when it is reflected in a mirror? Reality twice removed?

'Sunlight on a canal is reflected up through a window on to the ceiling, then from the ceiling on to a vase, and from the vase on to a glass, or a silver bowl. Which is the real sunlight? Which is the real reflection?

'What is true? What is not true? The answer is not so simple, because the truth can change. I can change. You can change. That is the Venice effect.'

We descended from the bridge into Campo Manin. Other than having come from the deep shade of Calle della Mandola into the bright sunlight of the open square, I felt unchanged. My role, whatever it was, remained the same as it had been before the bridge. I did not, of course, admit this to Count Marcello. But I looked at him to see if he would acknowledge having undergone any change himself.

He breathed deeply as we walked into Campo Manin. Then, with an air of finality, he said, 'Venetians never tell the truth. We mean precisely the opposite of what we say.'

I

An Evening in Venice

THE AIR STILL SMELT OF charcoal when I arrived in Venice three days after the fire. As it happened, the timing of my visit was purely coincidental. I had made plans, months before, to come to Venice for a few weeks in the off-season in order to enjoy the city without the crush of other tourists.

'If there had been a wind Monday night,' the water-taxi driver told me as we came across the lagoon from the airport, 'there wouldn't be a Venice to come to.'

'How did it happen?' I asked.

The taxi driver shrugged. 'How do all these things happen?'

It was early February, in the middle of the peaceful lull that settles over Venice every year between New Year's Day and Carnival. The tourists had gone, and in their absence the Venice they inhabited had all but closed down. Hotel lobbies and souvenir shops stood virtually empty. Gondolas lay tethered to poles and covered in blue tarpaulin. Unbought copies of the *International Herald Tribune* remained on newsstand racks all day, and pigeons abandoned sparse pickings in St Mark's Square to scavenge for crumbs in other parts of the city.

Meanwhile the other Venice, the one inhabited by Venetians, was as busy as ever – the neighbourhood shops, the vegetable stands, the fish markets, the wine bars. For these few weeks, Venetians could stride through their city without having to squeeze past dense clusters of slow-moving tourists. The city breathed, its pulse quickened. Venetians had Venice all to themselves.

But the atmosphere was subdued. People spoke in hushed, dazed tones of the sort one hears when there has been a sudden death in the family. The subject was on everyone's lips. Within days I had heard about it in such detail I felt as if I had been there myself.

It happened on Monday evening, 29 January 1996.

Shortly before nine o'clock, Archimede Seguso sat down at the dinner table and unfolded his napkin. Before joining him, his wife went into the living room to lower the curtains, which was her long-standing evening ritual. Signora Seguso knew very well that no one could see in through the windows, but it was her way of enfolding her family in a domestic embrace. The Segusos lived on the third floor of Ca' Capello, a sixteenth-century house in the heart of Venice. A narrow canal wrapped around two sides of the building before flowing into the Grand Canal a short distance away.

Signor Seguso waited patiently at the table. He was eighty-six – tall, thin, his posture still erect. A fringe of wispy white hair and flaring eyebrows gave him the look of a kindly sorcerer, full of wonder and surprise. He had an animated face and sparkling eyes that captivated everyone who met him. If you happened to be in his presence for any length of time, however, your eye would eventually be drawn to his hands.

They were large, muscular hands, the hands of an artisan whose work demanded physical strength. For seventy-five years, Signor Seguso had stood in front of a blazing hot glassworks furnace – ten, twelve, eighteen hours a day – holding a heavy steel pipe in his hands, turning it to prevent the dollop of molten glass at the other end from drooping to one side or the other, pausing to blow into it to inflate the glass, then laying it across his workbench, still turning it with his left hand while, with a pair of tongs in his right hand, pulling, pinching, and coaxing the glass into the shape of graceful vases, bowls, and goblets.

After all those years of turning the steel pipe hour after hour, Signor

Seguso's left hand had moulded itself around the pipe until it became permanently cupped, as if the pipe were always in it. His cupped hand was the proud mark of his craft, and this was why the artist who painted his portrait some years ago had taken particular care to show the curve in his left hand.

Men in the Seguso family had been glassmakers since the fourteenth century. Archimede was the twenty-first generation and one of the greatest of them all. He could sculpt heavy pieces out of solid glass and blow vases so thin and fragile they could barely be touched. He was the first glassmaker ever to see his work honoured with an exhibition in the Doge's Palace in St Mark's Square. Tiffany sold his pieces in its Fifth Avenue store.

Archimede Seguso had been making glass since the age of eleven, and by the time he was twenty, he had earned the nickname 'Mago del Fuoco' (Wizard of Fire). He no longer had the stamina to stand in front of a hot and howling furnace eighteen hours a day, but he worked every day nonetheless, and with undiminished pleasure. On this particular day, in fact, he had risen at his usual hour of 4.30 a.m., convinced as always that the pieces he was about to make would be more beautiful than any he had ever made before.

In the living-room, Signora Seguso paused to look out of the window before lowering the curtain. She noticed that the air had become hazy, and she mused aloud that a winter fog had set in. In response, Signor Seguso remarked from the other room that it must have come in very quickly, because he had seen the quarter moon in a clear sky only a few minutes before.

The living-room window looked across a small canal at the back of the Fenice Opera House, thirty feet away. Rising above it in the distance, some one hundred yards away, the theatre's grand entrance wing appeared to be shrouded in mist. Just as she started to lower the curtain, Signora Seguso saw a flash. She thought it was lightning. Then she saw another flash, and this time she knew it was fire.

'Papa!' she cried out. 'The Fenice is on fire!'

Signor Seguso came quickly to the window. More flames flickered at the front of the theatre, illuminating what Signora Seguso had thought was mist but had in fact been smoke. She rushed to the telephone and dialled 115 for the fire brigade. Signor Seguso went into his bedroom and stood at the corner window, which was even closer to the Fenice than the living-room window.

Between the fire and the Segusos' house lay a jumble of buildings that constituted the Fenice. The part on fire was farthest away, the chaste neoclassical entrance wing with its formal reception rooms, known collectively as the Apollonian rooms. Then came the main body of the theatre with its elaborately rococo auditorium, and finally the vast backstage area. Flaring out from both sides of the auditorium and the backstage were clusters of smaller, interconnected buildings like the one that housed the scenery workshop immediately across the narrow canal from Signor Seguso.

Signora Seguso could not get through to the fire brigade, so she dialled 112 for the police.

The enormity of what was happening outside his window stunned Signor Seguso. The Gran Teatro La Fenice was one of the splendours of Venice; it was arguably the most beautiful opera house in the world, and one of the most significant. The Fenice had commissioned dozens of operas that had premièred on its stage – Verdi's *La Traviata* and *Rigoletto*, Igor Stravinsky's *The Rake's Progress*, Benjamin Britten's *The Turn of the Screw*. For two hundred years, audiences had delighted in the sumptuous clarity of the Fenice's acoustics, the magnificence of its five tiers of gilt-encrusted boxes, and the baroque fantasy of it all. Signor and Signora Seguso had always taken a box for the season, and over the years they had been given increasingly desirable locations until they finally found themselves next to the royal box.

Signora Seguso had no luck getting through to the police either, and now she was becoming frantic. She called upstairs to the apartment where her son Gino lived with his wife and their son, Antonio. Gino was still out at the Seguso glass factory in Murano. Antonio was visiting a friend near the Rialto.

Signor Seguso stood silently at his bedroom window, watching as the flames raced across the entire top floor of the entrance wing. He knew that, for all its storeyed loveliness, the Fenice was at this moment an enormous pile of exquisite kindling. Inside a thick shell of Istrian stone lined with brick, the structure was made entirely of wood – wooden beams, wooden floors, wooden walls – richly embellished with wood carvings, sculpted stucco, and papier-mâché, all of it covered with layer upon layer of lacquer and gilt. Signor Seguso was aware, too, that the scenery workshop just across the canal from his house was stocked with solvents and, most worrying of all, cylinders of propane gas that were used for welding and soldering.

Signora Seguso came back into the room to say she had finally spoken to the police.

'They already knew about the fire,' she said. 'They told me we should leave the house at once.' She looked over her husband's shoulder and stifled a scream; the flames had moved closer in the short time she had been away from the window. They were now advancing through the four smaller reception halls towards the main body of the theatre, in their direction.

Archimede Seguso stared into the fire with an appraising eye. He opened the window, and a gust of bitter-cold air rushed in. The wind was blowing to the south-west. The Segusos were due west of the theatre, however, and Signor Seguso calculated that if the wind did not change direction or pick up strength, the fire would advance towards the other side of the Fenice rather than in their direction.

'Now, Nandina,' he said softly, 'stay calm. We're not in any danger.'

The Segusos' house was only one of many buildings close to the Fenice. Except for Campo San Fantin, a small plaza at the front of the theatre, the Fenice was hemmed in by old and equally flammable buildings, many of them attached to it or separated from it by only four or five feet. This was not at all unusual in Venice, where building space had always been at a premium. Seen from above, Venice resembled a jigsaw puzzle of terracotta rooftops. Passages between some of the buildings were so narrow one could not walk through them with an open umbrella. It had become a speciality of Venetian burglars to escape from the scene of a crime by leaping from roof to roof. If the fire in the Fenice were able to make the same sort of leap, it would almost certainly destroy a sizeable swath of Venice.

The Fenice itself was dark. It had been closed five months for renovations and was due to reopen in a month. The canal along its rear façade was also closed – empty – having been sealed off and drained so work crews could dredge the silt and sludge from it and repair its walls for the first time in forty years. The canal between the Segusos' building and the back of the Fenice was now a deep, muddy gulch with a tangle of exposed pipes and a few pieces of heavy machinery sitting in puddles at the bottom. The empty canal would make it impossible for fireboats to reach the Fenice, and, worse than that, it would deprive them of a source of water. Venetian firemen depended on water pumped directly from the canals to put out fires. The city had no system of fire hydrants.

The Fenice was now ringed by a tumult of shouts and running footsteps. Tenants, routed from their houses by the police, crossed paths with patrons coming out of the Ristorante Antico Martini. A dozen bewildered guests rolled suitcases out of the Hotel La Fenice, asking directions to the Hotel Saturnia, where they had been told to go. Into their midst, a wild-eyed woman wearing only a nightgown came stumbling from her house into Campo San Fantin screaming hysterically. She threw herself to the ground in front of the theatre, flailing her arms and rolling on the pavement. Several waiters came out of the Antico Martini and led her inside.

Two fireboats managed to navigate to a water-filled canal a short distance from the Fenice. The hoses were not long enough to reach round the intervening buildings, however, so the firemen dragged them through the kitchen window at the back of the Antico Martini and out through the dining room into Campo San Fantin. They aimed their nozzles at flames burning furiously in a top-floor window of the theatre, but the water pressure was too low. The arc of water barely reached the windowsill. The fire went on leaping and taunting and sucking up great turbulent currents of air that set the flames snapping like brilliant red sails in a violent wind.

Several policemen struggled with the massive front door of the Fenice, but to no avail. One of them drew his pistol and fired three shots at the lock. The door opened. Two firemen rushed in and disappeared into a dense white wall of smoke. Moments later they came running out. 'It's too late,' said one. 'It's burning like straw.'

The wail of sirens now filled the air as police and firemen raced up and down the Grand Canal in motorboats, spanking up huge butterfly wings of spray as they bounced through the wakes of other boats. About an hour after the first alarm, the city's big fire launch pulled up at the landing stage behind Haig's Bar. Its high-powered rigs would at last be able to pump water the two hundred yards from the Grand Canal to the Fenice. Dozens of firemen ran hoses from the fire launch into Campo Santa Maria del Giglio, feverishly coupling sections together, but it was immediately apparent that the hoses were of different gauges. Leaks sprayed from the couplings, but the firemen carried the linked hoses, such as they were, up to the rooftops around the Fenice anyway. They directed half of the water on to the theatre in an attempt to contain the fire and the rest of it on to adjacent buildings. Fire Commandant Alfio Pini had already made a momentous strategic decision: the Fenice was lost; save the city.

When the lights went out, Count Girolamo Marcello was mid-sentence in a conversation over dinner with his son on the top floor of his palace less than a minute's walk from the front of the Fenice. Earlier in the day, Count Marcello had learned that the exiled Russian poet and Nobel laureate Joseph Brodsky had died suddenly of a heart attack, at fifty-five, in New York. Brodsky had been a passionate lover of Venice and a friend and house guest of Marcello's. It was while he was staying in Marcello's palace, in fact, that Brodsky had written his last book, *Watermark*, a lyrical reflection on Venice. That afternoon Marcello had spoken by phone to Brodsky's widow, Maria, and they had discussed the possibility of burying Brodsky in Venice. Marcello knew that this would not be easily arranged. Every available plot on the burial island of San Michele had been spoken for years ago. It was generally understood that any new arrival, even a native Venetian, would be dug up in ten years and moved to a common burial site farther out in the lagoon. But for a non-Venetian Jewish atheist, gaining approval for even a temporary burial would be a quest fraught with obstacles. Still, there had been notable exceptions. Igor Stravinsky had been buried on San Michele, and so had Sergei Diaghilev and Ezra Pound. They had all been buried in the Anglican and Greek Orthodox section, and all would be allowed to remain there in perpetuity. So there was reason to hope that Brodsky could be buried there, too, and this was on Marcello's mind when the lights went out.

Father and son sat in darkness for a while, expecting the lights to come back on. Then they heard the sirens, lots of them, many more than usual.

'Let's go up and see what's happened,' said Marcello. They headed upstairs to the wooden deck on the roof, the *altana*, and as soon as they opened the door, they saw the raging fire.

Marcello decided they should leave the house at once. They descended the stairs, feeling their way in the darkness, Marcello wondering if the six-hundred-year-old palace was doomed. If it was, the most impressive private library in Venice would disappear with it. Marcello's library occupied most of the second floor. It was an architectural delight, a high-ceilinged space complete with a wrap-around wooden gallery that could be reached only by climbing a secret stairway hidden behind a panel in the wall. The floor-to-ceiling shelves held forty thousand volumes of private and state papers, some of them more than a thousand years old. The collection amounted to a treasure trove of Venetian history, and Marcello regularly made it available to scholars. He himself spent long hours sitting in a thronelike black leather armchair perusing the archive, especially the papers of the Marcello family, which was one of the oldest in Venice. Marcello's ancestors included a fifteenth-century doge, or head of state. The Marcellos had, in fact, been among the families that built the Fenice and owned it until just before the Second World War, when the municipality of Venice took it over.

Marcello walked to the edge of Campo San Fantin and found himself standing in the midst of a crowd that included the entire city council, which had rushed in a body from Ca' Farsetti, the town hall, where it had been in an evening session. Marcello was a familiar figure around town, with his bald head and close-cropped grey beard. The press frequently sought him out for comment, knowing they could count on a frank, often provocative quote or two. He had once described himself to an interviewer as 'inquisitive, restless, eclectic, impulsive and capricious'. It was the last two of these behavioural quirks that asserted themselves as he stood in Campo San Fantin looking at the burning opera house.

'What a shame,' he said. 'It's gone. I suppose I will never see it again. The reconstruction will take so long, I'm sure I won't be alive when it's finished.' This remark was nominally directed to the person next to him, but it was really intended for the ears of a handsome man with a dark beard in his mid-fifties who was standing a few feet away: the mayor of Venice, Massimo Cacciari. Mayor Cacciari was a former Communist, a professor of philosophy and architecture at the University of Venice, and Italy's most highly regarded contemporary philosopher. Being mayor automatically made him president of the Fenice, which meant he had been responsible for the security of the theatre and would now be in charge of rebuilding it. Marcello's remark clearly implied that, in his opinion, neither Cacciari nor his left-wing government had the competence to do it. Mayor Cacciari gazed at the fire with a look of deep despair, unfazed one way or the other by Marcello's obliquely worded taunt.

'But I would suggest,' Marcello went on, 'that if they want to rebuild the place as it was in its prime – and by that I mean as a social place, a meeting place – they should make it into a great discotheque for young people.'

An old man standing in front of Marcello turned around, aghast, tears rolling down his cheeks. 'Girolamo!' he said. 'How can you say such a thing? Anyway, who knows what the hell young people will want five years from now?'

A deafening crash resounded in the depths of the Fenice. The great crystal chandelier had fallen to the floor.

'You have a point,' Marcello replied, 'but, as everybody knows, going to the opera has always been a social thing. You can even see it in the architecture. Only a third of the seats are positioned so they have a good view of the stage. The rest, particularly the boxes, are really best for looking at the audience. The arrangement is purely social.'

Marcello spoke with a gentle bemusement and without any trace of cynicism. It seemed to tickle him that anyone could think that generations of opera-goers, like the Marcellos, had been drawn to the opera by anything as lofty as music or culture – Benedetto Marcello, the eighteenth-century composer and one of Girolamo Marcello's forebears, notwithstanding. Throughout its existence, the Fenice had been hallowed ground in the social landscape of Venice, and Girolamo Marcello had a broad knowledge of Venetian social history. He was, in fact, regarded as something of an authority on the subject.

'In the old days,' he said, 'the private boxes had curtains you could close, even during the performance. My grandfather loved going to the opera, but he didn't give a damn about music. He would open the curtains only for highlights on the stage. He would say, "Silence! Now we have the aria!" and he would pull open the curtains and applaud . . . "Good! Lovely! Well done!" Then he would close the curtains again, and a servant would come from the house with a basket of chicken and some wine. Opera was just a form of relaxation, and anyway it was cheaper to take a box at the opera than heat a whole palace for an evening.'

Suddenly another enormous boom shook the ground. The floors in the entrance wing had collapsed, one on to another. People standing at the edge of the *campo* leaped backward just as the roof of the entrance wing fell, sending flames and burning debris high into the air. Marcello went back upstairs to his rooftop *altana*, this time fortified with a bottle of grappa, a video camera, and a bucket of water in case any of the airborne embers should happen to land on his roof.

Within minutes – as Girolamo Marcello's video camera whirred and clicked, as Archimede Seguso stared in silence from his bedroom window, as hundreds of Venetians watched from rooftops, and as thousands more all over Italy followed live television coverage of the fire – the roof of the auditorium collapsed with a thunderous boom and a volcanic eruption that shot flaming debris 150 feet into the air. A powerful updraught sent chunks of burning embers, some as big as shoeboxes, arcing over Venice like comets.

Shortly after eleven, a helicopter appeared above St Mark's, swung low over the mouth of the Grand Canal, and scooped up a tankful of water. Then it soared aloft again, banked over the Fenice and, to cheers from rooftops, dropped its water. A hissing plume of steam and smoke coiled up from the Fenice, but the fire kept burning undiminished. The helicopter turned and flew back to the Grand Canal to load up again.

It suddenly occurred to Girolamo Marcello that his wife, Lesa, who was out of town, might hear about the fire before he had a chance to tell her that her family and her house were safe. He came down from the roof to telephone her.

Countess Marcello worked for Save Venice, the American non-profit organization devoted to raising money for restoring Venetian art and architecture. Save Venice was headquartered in New York. Lesa Marcello was the director of its Venice office. Over the past thirty years, Save Venice had restored scores of paintings, frescos, mosaics, statues, ceilings, and building façades. Recently, Save Venice had restored the Fenice's painted curtain, at a cost of $100,000.

Save Venice had become a hugely popular charity in America, largely because it was set up to be, in a sense, a participatory charity. Save Venice would organize event-filled, four-day galas in Venice in late summer during which, for three thousand dollars a person, subscribers could attend elegant lunches, dinners, and balls in private villas and palaces not open to the public.

In winter Save Venice kept the spirit alive by mounting a fund-raising ball in New York. Lesa Marcello had flown to New York earlier in the week to attend the winter ball. This year it was to be a masked ball, based on the theme of Carnival, and it would be held in the Rainbow Room on the sixty-fifth floor of the Rockefeller Center. As he picked up the telephone to call his wife, Girolamo Marcello suddenly remembered that the ball was scheduled for this very night.

The towers of Manhattan glittered in the late-afternoon sun as Lesa Marcello made her way to the telephone through a confusion of people rushing to finish decorating the Rainbow Room. The interior designer John Saladino was fuming. The unions had allowed him only three hours to install his decorations, so he had been forced to deploy the entire domestic staff of his twenty-three-room house in Connecticut, plus twelve people from his office. He intended to transform the Rainbow Room's art-deco ballroom into his version of the Venetian Lagoon by nightfall.

'The Rainbow Room is dominated by a cabal of union-clad people,' he said, loud enough to be overheard by some of those very people. 'Their role in life is to make everyone around them miserable.' He glared at a foursome of slow-moving electricians. 'I'm decorating eighty-eight tables so that each one will represent an island in the lagoon. Over each table we're suspending a cluster of silver, helium-filled balloons that will reflect candlelight from the table below, creating the effect of a glowing *baldacchino*.' Mr Saladino looked around imperiously. 'I wonder if anyone within the sound of my voice knows what a *baldacchino* is?' He was clearly not expecting an answer from any of the people inflating balloons or making centrepieces, or from the technicians loudly testing sound levels on Peter Duchin's bandstand, or from the two jugglers rehearsing their act, clomping around on stilts, tossing balls in the air and spinning plates on the ends of their fingers.

'A *baldacchino*!' said a barrel-chested man, standing in front of an easel by the bandstand. He had long white hair, an aquiline nose, and a silk scarf hanging loosely around his neck. 'A *baldacchino* is our word for "canopy",' he said. Then he shrugged and went back to setting up his easel.

This was Ludovico De Luigi, one of the best-known contemporary Venetian artists. He had been brought to New York by Save Venice to help raise money at the ball tonight. In the course of the evening, he would execute a watercolour that would later be auctioned off for the benefit of Save Venice.

Ludovico De Luigi was a man of supreme self-confidence and dramatic flair. His futuristic, Daliesque paintings tended towards the metaphysical-surreal. Typically they were spectral landscapes of familiar Venetian buildings in stunning juxtapositions – the domed Santa Maria della Salute Church as an oil rig in the middle of an ocean, or St Mark's Square as a body of water with a huge Polaris submarine surfacing and ploughing ominously towards the basilica. Though verging on kitsch, De Luigi's works were technically brilliant and always eye-catching.

In Venice he was known as much for his public antics as for his art. On one occasion, he had been granted permission to display his sculpture of a horse in St Mark's Square and, without telling the authorities, he invited a notorious member of the Italian parliament to attend: Ilona Staller, a Radical deputy from Rome, better known to fans of her porn movies as 'Cicciolina'. She arrived at St Mark's by gondola, topless, and climbed up on to the horse, proclaiming herself a living work of art surmounting an inanimate one. Parliamentary immunity protected Cicciolina from prosecution for obscene acts in public, so De Luigi was charged instead. He told the presiding judge, who happened to be a woman, that he had not expected Cicciolina to take her clothes off.

'But, knowing Miss Staller's history, Signor De Luigi,' the judge said, 'couldn't you *imagine* she would take her clothes off?'

'Your Honour, I am an artist. I have a lively imagination. I can imagine *you* taking your clothes off right here in court. But I don't expect you to do it.'

'Signor De Luigi,' said the judge, 'I, too, have an imagination, and I can imagine sending you to jail for five years for contempt of court.' In the end, she gave him a sentence of five months in jail, which was quashed in a general amnesty a short time later. In any case, tonight in the Rainbow Room, Ludovico De Luigi was going to paint a picture of the Miracoli Church as a tribute to Save Venice's current, and most ambitious, restoration project. As he went back to mixing colours on his palette, Lesa Marcello picked up the telephone and turned towards the windows and the view of Manhattan.

Countess Marcello was a dark-haired woman with a quiet manner and an expression of infinite patience. She pressed her free hand against her ear to shut out the noise and heard Girolamo Marcello say that the Fenice had caught fire and was burning out of control. 'It's gone,' he said. 'There is nothing anybody can do. But at least we are all safe, and so far the fire has not spread.'

Lesa sank into a chair by the window, dazed. Tears welled in her eyes as she tried to absorb the news. For generations, her family had played a prominent role in the affairs of Venice. Her grandfather had been mayor between the wars. She gazed blankly out of the window. The setting sun cast shimmering red-and-orange reflections on the glass skyscrapers of Wall Street, creating an effect that made it look, to her eyes, as though the city were on fire. She turned away.

'God, no!' Bea Guthrie gasped when Lesa told her about the Fenice. Mrs Guthrie was the executive director of Save Venice. She put down the centrepiece she had been working on as a look of panic crossed her face. In an instant, the masked ball had been reduced to a horribly inappropriate frivolity, and it was too late to cancel it. Six hundred costumed merrymakers would be arriving at the Rainbow Room in a matter of hours, dressed as gondoliers, popes, doges, courtesans, Marco Polos, Shylocks, Casanovas, and Tadzios, and there was nothing anybody could do to head them off. The guest of honour, Signora Lamberto Dini, the wife of Italy's prime minister, would certainly have to bow out, and that would only emphasize the inappropriateness of the ball. Clearly the party would turn into a wake. Something had to be done. But what?

Bea Guthrie called her husband, Bob Guthrie, who was president of Save Venice and chief of reconstructive and plastic surgery at New York Downtown Hospital. Dr Guthrie was in the operating theatre. She then called Larry Lovett, the chairman of Save Venice. Lovett had been chairman of both the Metropolitan Opera Guild and the Chamber Music Society of Lincoln Center. In recent years, he had bought a palace on the Grand Canal and made it his principal residence. He reacted to the news with as much anger as sadness. Whatever the cause had been, he was certain that negligence had been a contributing factor, knowing the way things worked in Venice. Dr Guthrie heard the news as he was coming out of the operating theatre. His shock was tempered by a dash of pragmatism. 'Well,' he said, 'there goes the curtain we just restored for a hundred thousand dollars.'

Neither Larry Lovett nor Bob Guthrie could suggest any quick fix for the party. It would simply have to go on as planned. For one fleeting moment, they all wondered whether it might be possible to say nothing about the fire, assuming that only a few people would have heard about it before coming to the ball. But that, they decided, might only make matters worse.

Bea Guthrie returned her attention to her unfinished centrepiece as a smiling, ruddy-faced man with dark, curly hair came walking into the Rainbow Room and waved to her. He was Emilio Paties, a Venetian restaurateur who had also been flown to New York by Save Venice to cook dinner for six hundred people tonight. He was just now pacing off the distance from the stoves on the sixty-fourth floor to the tables here on the sixty-fifth. As he walked, he kept looking at his watch. His main concern was the white truffle and porcini mushroom risotto.

'The final two minutes of cooking happen after you take the risotto off the heat,' he was saying to the headwaiter walking beside him. 'When it comes off the stove, it is absorbing water very quickly, and in exactly two minutes it will be done. It must be served on the plate immediately, or it will turn to mush! We have two minutes to get it from the stoves downstairs to the plates up here. Two minutes. No more!' When Signor Paties reached the far side of the room, he looked at his watch and then looked back at Bea Guthrie, beaming. 'One minute and forty-five seconds! *Va bene!* Good!'

Later in the afternoon, when the decorations were finished, Bea Guthrie went home to change, depressed, dreading the next several hours. But then the guest of honour, Signora Dini, called with an idea. 'I think I know what we can do,' she said, 'if it meets with your approval. I will come to the ball tonight. After the guests have arrived and the announcement is made about the fire, I will say, speaking for all

Italians, that we are very grateful that this afternoon the board of directors of Save Venice agreed that all the money raised tonight will be dedicated to rebuilding the Fenice.'

That would put a positive spin on the evening. The Save Venice board could be canvassed quickly, and they would surely agree. Suddenly feeling much better, Mrs Guthrie went upstairs and laid out her harlequin costume in preparation for the ball.

Signora Seguso nearly wept for joy when her son, Gino, and her grandson, Antonio, returned home. The moment the electricity had gone off, the flickering light from the fire had invaded the house, its reflection dancing and leaping over the walls and furniture, making it seem as if the house itself had caught fire. The Segusos' telephone had been ringing constantly, friends wanting to know if they were all right. Some had even come to the door with fire extinguishers. Gino and Antonio were downstairs talking with the firemen, who were urging the Segusos to evacuate, as others in the area had already done. The officers spoke in lowered voices and with considerably more deference than usual, because they were aware that the old man at the window upstairs was the great Archimede Seguso.

And Archimede Seguso would not leave the house.

Nor would any of the Segusos consider leaving while he was still in it. So Gino and Antonio busied themselves moving furniture away from the windows, taking down curtains, rolling up rugs, and moving flower boxes indoors. Antonio went upstairs to the terrace, ripped the awning off its rod, and sprayed water on the roof tiles, which had become so hot that steam rose up from them. Signora Seguso and her daughter-in-law meanwhile put things into suitcases in order to be ready to flee the moment Archimede changed his mind. Gino, noticing his wife's suitcase in the hall, lifted the lid to see what valuables she had put in it. It was filled with family photographs still in their frames.

'We can replace everything else,' she said, 'but not the memories.' Gino kissed her.

Suddenly, there was another earth-shaking boom. The roof over the backstage had fallen in.

A fire captain came up the stairs and told the Segusos, almost apologetically, that his men would have to run a hose through their living-room to a window facing the Fenice, just in case the fire breached the wall across the canal. But first the firemen cleared a path for the hose. With care verging on reverence, they moved Archimede Seguso's works of art in glass – the abstract, modernist pieces he had made in the 1920s and 1930s when most other Venetian glassmakers were still turning out flowery, eighteenth-century designs. When they laid down the fire hose, it was flanked by an honour guard of glass objects touched by Seguso's genius – bowls and vases embedded with fine threads of coloured glass resembling lace, or with undulating ribbons of colour, or with tiny bubbles suspended in rows and spirals. There were remarkable solid sculptures of people and animals made from single masses of molten glass, a seemingly impossible feat that he alone had mastered.

Gino came to his father's bedroom door accompanied by the fire captain. The captain, rather than presuming to address the old man directly, turned to Gino and said, 'We are very concerned for the maestro's safety.'

Signor Seguso continued to stare out the window in silence.

'Papa,' said Gino in a gently pleading voice, 'the fire is getting closer. I think we should leave.'

Gino's father kept his eye on the Fenice, watching as bursts of green, purple, umber, and blue flames punctuated the fire. He could see the flames through the slits in the louvred shutters at the back of the Fenice, and he saw their reflections on the rippling puddles at the bottom of the canal. He saw great, long tongues of fire licking out through windows and geysers of glowing ash soaring through holes in the roof. The winter air outside the bedroom window had turned blazing hot. The Fenice had become a furnace.

'I'm staying here,' Archimede Seguso said quietly.

In conversations at Haig's Bar, certain words kept coming up again and again, words that seemed to have nothing to do with the Fenice or with each other: Bari . . . Petruzzelli . . . San Giovanni in Laterno . . . Uffizi . . . Milano . . . Palermo. But there was another word, also frequently overheard, that tied them all together: Mafia.

The mob had recently been engaged in arson and bombings. The most unsettling incident, in view of what was happening tonight at the Fenice, was the 1991 fire that destroyed the Petruzzelli Opera House in Bari. It was subsequently discovered that the Mafia boss in Bari had ordered the fire after bribing the manager to award him lucrative contracts for the reconstruction. More than a few people watching the Fenice fire believed that this was a replay. The Mafia was also suspected in the deadly car-bomb attacks that had destroyed parts of the Church of San Giovanni in Laterno in Rome, the Uffizi Gallery in Florence, and the Gallery of Modern Art in Milan. The bombings had been interpreted as a warning to Pope John Paul II for his frequent anti-Mafia statements and to the Italian government for its aggressive judicial crackdown on the mob. Even now, in Mestre on the mainland shore of the Venetian lagoon, a Sicilian don was being tried for the car-bomb murder of a tough anti-Mafia judge, his wife, and bodyguards in Palermo. The fire at the Fenice could be a heavy-handed warning to stop the trial.

'The Mafia!' Girolamo Marcello exclaimed, speaking to friends who had joined him on his *altana*. 'If they did set the fire, they could have saved themselves the trouble. The Fenice would have burned without any help from them. It's been chaos over there for months.'

'Just after the renovation work started,' Marcello went on, 'the superintendent of the Fenice asked me to come and see him. Save

Venice had just restored the Fenice's curtain, and now he wanted me, as a member of the Save Venice board, to ask Save Venice to restore the frescos of Dante's *Divine Comedy* in the bar. The superintendent invited me to come and look at the frescos, and I couldn't believe what I saw. The place was madness. Everywhere you looked, there were flammable materials. I don't know how many cans of varnish, turpentine, and solvents there were – open, closed, spilled on the floor – lengths of wooden parquet in stacks, rolls of plastic carpeting piled high, heaps of rubbish everywhere. In the midst of all this, men were working with blowtorches! Can you imagine? Soldering irons! And surveillance? Zero, as usual. Responsibility? Zero. I thought, "They're mad!" So if the Mafia wanted the Fenice to burn, all they had to do was wait.'

By 2.00 a.m., even though the fire was still officially out of control, Archimede Seguso could see that an equilibrium had been reached between the flames and the firemen. He appeared in the doorway of his bedroom, the first time he had come away from the window in four hours.

'We're out of danger now,' he said. He kissed his wife. 'I told you not to worry, Nandina.' Then he embraced his son, his daughter-in-law, and his grandson. With that, and without saying another word, he went to bed.

As Signor Seguso fell asleep, a parade of Prussian generals, court jesters, and fairy princesses began stepping out of elevators into the candlelit Rainbow Room in New York. A bishop in full regalia handed a drink to a belly dancer. A hooded executioner chatted with Marie Antoinette. A cluster of people had gathered around the painter Ludovico De Luigi, who had sketched the outlines of the Miracoli Church and was beginning to apply colours to its inlaid-marble façade. The hired entertainers – stilt-walking jugglers, acrobats, fire-eaters, and mimes in *commedia dell'arte* costumes – strolled among the guests, most of whom had no idea the Fenice was on fire. The only coverage of it on American television so far had been an eleven-second mention, without pictures, on the *CBS Evening News*.

Peter Duchin sat at the piano, perched like an exotic bird with black-and-white feathers rising from the brow of his black mask. When he saw Bob Guthrie come to the microphone, he cut off the music with a wave of his hand.

Guthrie, his large frame wrapped in a red-and-white caftan, welcomed the guests and then told them he hated to be the bearer of bad news. 'The Fenice is burning,' he said. 'It cannot be saved.' A collective gasp and cries of 'No!' resounded throughout the ballroom. Then the room fell silent. Guthrie introduced the guest of honour, Signora Dini, who stepped up to the microphone with tears rolling down her cheeks. In a tremulous voice, she thanked the board of Save Venice, which, she said, had voted late that afternoon to dedicate the evening to raising money to rebuild the Fenice. The silence was broken by scattered applause; the applause swelled to an ovation, and the ovation crested on a burst of cheers and whistles.

Ludovico De Luigi, his face ashen, took the Miracoli painting off the easel and put a blank canvas in its place. In pencil he quickly sketched the Fenice. He put it in the middle of the Venetian lagoon, for ironic effect, and engulfed it in flames.

Several people headed for the elevators to go home and change into traditional evening clothes, saying they were no longer in the mood to be in costume. Signora Dini turned away from the microphone and dabbed her eyes with a handkerchief. Bob Guthrie stood nearby, speaking to a cluster of people a few feet from the still-open microphone, which picked up part of his conversation. 'We'll probably raise close to a million dollars for the Fenice tonight,' he said, citing the thousand-dollar price of admission, the auction of Ludovico De Luigi's painting, and spontaneous donations. In answer to a question about the money, Guthrie could be heard to say, 'No, no! Certainly not. We won't hand the money over to Venice until the restoration starts. Are you kidding? We're not that stupid. We'll keep it in escrow till then. Otherwise, there's no telling whose pocket it might end up in.'

By 3.00 a.m., the fire was finally declared under control. There had been no secondary fires, despite the flying debris, and no one had been seriously hurt. The Fenice's thick walls had contained the blaze, preventing the fire from spreading, while incinerating everything inside. Instead of destroying Venice, the Fenice had, in a sense, committed suicide.

At 4.00 a.m., the helicopter made its last overhead pass. The Fenice's sad fate was written in the leaky hoses snaking through Campo Santa Maria del Giglio from the Grand Canal to the Fenice.

Mayor Massimo Cacciari was still standing in Campo San Fantin in front of the Fenice, looking glumly at what was left of the opera house. A perfectly preserved poster, enclosed in a glass case mounted on a wall by the entrance, announced that a Woody Allen jazz concert would reopen the renovated opera house at the end of the month.

At 5.00 a.m., Archimede Seguso opened his eyes and sat up in bed, refreshed despite having slept only three hours. He went to the window and opened the shutters. The firemen had set up floodlights and trained their hoses on the gutted interior. Billowing smoke rose from the Fenice's shell.

Signor Seguso dressed by the light reflected from the Fenice's floodlit walls. The air was thick with the smell of charred wood, but he could smell the coffee his wife was brewing for him. As always, she was standing by the door waiting for him with a steaming cup, and, as always, he stood there with her and drank it. Then he kissed her on both cheeks, put his grey fedora on his head, and went downstairs. He paused for a moment in front of the house, looking up at the Fenice. The windows were gaping holes framing a view of the dark, pre-dawn sky. A strong wind whipped around the dismal shell. It was a cold wind from the north, a bora. If it had been blowing eight hours earlier, the fire would certainly have spread.

A young fireman was leaning against the wall, exhausted. He nodded as Signor Seguso approached.

'We lost it,' the fireman said.

'You did all you could,' Signor Seguso replied gently. 'It was hopeless.'

The fireman shook his head and looked up at the Fenice. 'Every time a piece of that ceiling fell, a piece of my heart fell with it.'

'Mine, too,' said Signor Seguso, 'but you must not blame yourself.'

'It will always haunt me that we couldn't save it.'

'Look around you,' Signor Seguso said. 'You saved Venice.'

With that the old man turned and set off slowly down Calle Caotorta on his way to Fondamente Nuove, where he would take the *vaporetto*, or water bus, to his glassworks factory in Murano. When he was younger, the mile-long walk to the *vaporetto* had taken him twelve minutes. Now it took an hour.

In Campo Sant'Angelo, he turned and looked back. A wide, spiralling column of smoke, floodlit from beneath, rose like a lurid spectre against the sky.

At the far side of the *campo*, he entered the shopping street, Calle de la Mandola, where he encountered a man in a blue workman's jumper washing the windows of the pastry shop. Window-cleaners were the only people who were at work at that early hour, and they always greeted him as he walked by.

'Ah, Maestro!' said the man in blue. 'We were worried about you last night, living so close to the Fenice.'

'You're very kind,' said Signor Seguso, bowing slightly and touching the brim of his hat, 'but we were never really in any danger, thank goodness. We've lost our theatre, though . . .'

Signor Seguso neither stopped nor slowed his pace. Shortly after six, he arrived at the glassworks and walked into the cavernous furnace room. Six large furnaces clad in ceramic blocks were ranged about the room, set well apart, all of them firing and filling the space with a constant, rumbling roar. He conferred with an assistant about the colours he wanted to prepare for the day. Some would be transparent, some opaque. There would be yellow, orange, red, purple, umber, cobalt, gold leaf, white, and black – more colours than he normally used, but the assistant did not ask why, and the master did not offer to explain.

When the glass was ready, he stood in front of the open furnace, steel pipe in hand, looking calmly, deeply into the fire. Then, with a smooth, graceful motion, he dipped the end of the pipe into the reservoir of molten glass in the furnace and turned it slowly, over and over, pulling it out when the glowing, pear-shaped lump at the end was just the right size to begin making the vase he had in mind.

The first vase, of what would eventually be more than a hundred, was unlike anything he had ever made before. Against an opaque background as black as night, he had set swirling ribbons of sinuous diamond shapes in red, green, white, and gold, leaping, overlapping, and spiralling upward around the vase. He never explained what he was doing, but by the second vase, everyone knew. It was a record of the fire in glass – the flames, the sparks, the embers, and the smoke – just as he had seen it from his window, glinting through the louvres, reflected in the rippling water at the bottom of the canal, and rising far into the night.

In the coming days, the municipality of Venice would conduct an inquiry to discover what had happened on the evening of 29 January 1996. But on the morning of the thirtieth, while the Fenice's embers still smouldered, one pre-eminent Venetian had already started to compose his own testimony in glass, while at the same time creating a work of terrible beauty.

2

Dust & Ashes

I HAD BEEN TO VENICE a dozen times or more, having fallen under its spell when I first caught sight of it twenty years before – a city of domes and bell towers, floating hazily in the distance, topped here and there by a marble saint or a gilded angel.

On this latest trip, as always, I made my approach by water taxi. The boat slowed as we drew near; then it slipped into the shaded closeness of a small canal. Moving at an almost stately pace, we glided past overhanging balconies and weatherworn stone figures set into crumbling brick and stucco. I looked up through open windows and caught glimpses of painted ceilings and glass chandeliers. I heard fleeting bits of music and conversation, but no honking of horns, no squealing of brakes, and no motors other than the muffled churning of our own. People walked over footbridges as we passed underneath, and the backwash from our boat splashed on moss-covered steps leading down into the canal. That twenty-minute boat ride had become a much-anticipated rite of passage, transporting me three miles across the lagoon and five hundred to a thousand years backwards in time.

To me Venice was not merely beautiful: it was beautiful everywhere. On one occasion I set about testing this notion by concocting a game called 'photo roulette', the object of which was to walk around the city taking photographs at unplanned moments – whenever a church bell rang or at every sighting of a dog or cat – to see how often, standing at an arbitrary spot, one would be confronted by a view of exceptional beauty. The answer: almost always.

But irritatingly often, before taking a picture I had to wait for a straggle of tourists to step out of the frame, even in the outlying quarters where tourists supposedly never went. This is why I decided to come to Venice in midwinter: I would see it without the obscuring overlay of other tourists. For once I would have a clear view of Venice as a functioning city. The people I saw in the street would be people who actually lived there, going about their business purposefully, casting familiar glances at sights that still had the power to stop me in my tracks. But as I came across the lagoon that morning in early February 1996 and caught the first faint whiff of charcoal, I realized I had arrived in Venice at an extraordinary moment.

A stunning, full-colour, aerial photograph of Venice dominated the front page of the morning's *Il Gazzettino*. It was a panoramic view of the city taken the day after the fire, with the burned-out Fenice at the centre of it, a faint plume of smoke rising from its blackened crater as if from a spent volcano. 'Never again! No more pictures like this,' the newspaper promised its readers.

There had been an outpouring of sympathy for Venice. The opera singer Luciano Pavarotti had announced he would give a concert to help raise funds to rebuild the Fenice. Plácido Domingo, not to be outdone, said he would also give a concert, but *his* concert would be in St Mark's Basilica. Pavarotti shot back that he, too, would sing in St Mark's, and that he would sing there *alone*. Woody Allen, whose jazz band was to have reopened the newly renovated Fenice with a concert at the end of the month, quipped to a reporter that the fire must have been set by 'a lover of good music', adding, 'If they didn't want me to play, all they had to do was say so.'

The destruction of the Fenice was an especially brutal loss for Venice. It had been one of the few cultural attractions that had not been ceded to outsiders. Venetians always outnumbered tourists at the Fenice, so all Venetians felt a special affection for it, even those who had never set foot inside the place. The city's prostitutes took up a collection and presented Mayor Cacciari with a cheque for $1,500.

The *Gazzettino* reported on a series of revelations about the fire that had come out in the last two days. Even for people not normally susceptible to suggestions of conspiracy, there were a number of suspicious coincidences.

It was discovered, for example, that someone had unplugged both the smoke alarm and the heat sensor two days before the fire. This had supposedly been done because fumes and heat from the renovation work had been setting off the alarms repeatedly, annoying the workers.

The Fenice's sprinkler system had been dismantled before a newly installed system could be activated.

The lone caretaker of the Fenice had not made an appearance at the fire until 9.20 p.m., at least twenty minutes after the first alarm had been called in. He claimed he had been wandering around inside the building, trying to find the source of the smoke.

It had also come to light that a small fire had broken out two weeks earlier, caused by a blowtorch, possibly on purpose, but the incident had been hushed up.

Conspiracy or no, there was ample evidence of negligence, starting with the empty canal. Mayor Cacciari had initiated a commendable and long-overdue plan to dredge and clean the city's smaller canals. However, a year before the fire, the city's prefect, or chief adminis-trator, had sent the mayor a letter warning that no canal should be drained until the city had first secured an alternative source of water in case of fire. His letter had gone unanswered. Six months later, the prefect sent a second letter. The answer to that one was the fire itself.

The dry canal was only part of the story of malfeasance and negligence. People who had been involved in the renovation of the Fenice described the work site as chaotic. Security doors had been left unlocked or even wide open; people came and went as they pleased, authorized or not; copies of the keys to the front door had been handed out haphazardly, and several were unaccounted for.

There was also the curious tale of the Fenice's café. Officials had ordered the café shut down during renovation, but the café manager, Signora Annamaria Rosato, had begged her bosses to let her keep it open as a canteen for the workers. They had relented, telling her, 'Just be careful.' So Signora Rosato set up her electric coffee-maker and her electric hotplate for making pasta. She moved this makeshift kitchen from room to room, staying out of the way of the renovation work as best she could. But since the fire had started in the Apollonian rooms, very close to the site of her operations of the moment, Signora Rosato and her coffee-maker became a media sensation. The police called her in for questioning as a suspect. They cleared her, but not before her unexpected notoriety had made her so resentful that she began suggesting names of other people she thought might be worth looking into as suspects – the workers who had used her stove on the afternoon of the fire, for example, and the conservators who had left powerful heat lamps aimed at wet patches of stucco overnight in order to dry them. All the people she fingered were brought in for questioning and later released.

The prosecutors, despite having interviewed dozens of witnesses, admitted to the *Gazzettino* that at this point they did not know how the fire had started. Prosecutor Felice Casson appointed a panel of four experts to investigate the fire and told them to begin work immediately.

One thing was already painfully clear, however: neither of the two major evils confronting Venice could be blamed for the fire – not the rising sea level, which threatened to inundate the city at some unspecified time in the future, nor the overabundance of tourists, which was choking the life out of the city. There had been no high water and hardly any tourists in Venice on the night the Fenice burned. This time Venice had only itself to blame.

According to the *Gazzettino*, there was to be a town meeting to discuss the Fenice later in the day. It would be held at the Ateneo Veneto, a monumental sixteenth-century palace on the opposite side of Campo San Fantin from the Fenice. The Ateneo Veneto had originally been the home of a black-hooded fraternal order dedicated to escorting condemned prisoners to the gallows and providing them with a decent burial. For the last two hundred years, however, it had served as the Academy of Letters and Sciences, the cultural Parnassus of Venice. Lectures and convocations of the highest literary and artistic significance were held in the ornate Great Hall on the ground floor. For an event merely to be scheduled at the Ateneo Veneto meant that the cultural élite of Venice considered it important.

I went to Campo San Fantin half an hour before the meeting and found a sombre gathering of Venetians filing past the Fenice in silent mourning. Two *carabinieri*, or policemen, stood guard in front, smartly dressed in dark blue suits with rakish red stripes along the trouser seams. They were smoking cigarettes. At first glance, the Fenice looked just as it always had – the formal portico, the Corinthian columns, the ornamental iron gates, the windows and balustrades – all completely intact. But of course this was just the façade, and façade was all there was. The Fenice had become a mask of itself. Behind the mask, the interior had been reduced to a pile of rubble.

The crowd in front of the Fenice drifted across the *campo* to the Ateneo Veneto for the town meeting. The Great Hall was already filled to overflowing. People stood at the rear and along the sides of the room, while the speakers milled around nervously in front. The audience buzzed with conversation and conjecture.

A woman standing near the door turned to another woman. 'There are no accidents,' she said. 'Just wait. You'll see.' The other woman nodded in agreement. Two men discussed the middling quality of the Fenice's resident company in recent years, especially the orchestra. 'It's a shame the Fenice had to burn,' one said to the other. 'A pity it wasn't the orchestra.' A young woman, arriving at the hall out of breath, made her way towards a young man who had saved a seat for her. 'I haven't told you where I was the night of the fire,' she said as she slipped into her seat. 'I was at the cinema. The Accademia was showing *Senso*. Can you believe it? The only movie that has a scene shot inside the Fenice. Visconti made it look like the 1860s, so it was lit by gas lamps. Gas lamps! Little fires inside the Fenice! Then afterwards I came out and saw people running and shouting, "The Fenice! The Fenice!" I followed them to the Accademia Bridge, and then I saw the fire. I thought I was dreaming.'

Several of the Fenice's immediate neighbours had come to the meeting and were adjusting in various ways to living in the shadow of a ghost. Gino Seguso said that since the fire, his father had been spending most of his time at the glassworks, turning out vases and bowls to commemorate that awful night. 'He's made more than twenty so far,' he said, 'and he continues to prepare more quantities of molten glass. My father said only, "I have to make them," and we have no idea when his passion will run its course. But the pieces are beautiful, every one of them.'

Emilio Baldi, the owner of the Antico Martini restaurant, gloomily estimated the losses he would suffer for the months, if not years, during which the view from his restaurant would be a noisy construction site instead of a lovely square. 'There has been one hopeful sign,' he said, managing a weak smile. 'We had eight tables of diners when the fire broke out, and naturally everybody took their coats and left in a hurry. Since then seven of the eight have come back and insisted on paying their bill. Perhaps that means things will turn out all right eventually.'

I took a seat beside an elderly English lady who was showing the couple in front of her a little square of painted canvas the size of a postage stamp. It was charred around the edges.

'It's a piece of scenery,' the lady said. 'Isn't it sad?'

'We found it on our *altana*,' her husband chimed in. 'We live at Palazzo Cini and were having dinner at the Monaco. Suddenly the waiters seemed distracted and went away from the dining room. We asked if there was anything wrong, and they told us there seemed to be a fire near the Fenice. We went up to the roof of the Saturnia Hotel, which has a splendid view of the Fenice. The fire was right in front of us, so close that Marguerite's fur coat was singed. A little while later, as we walked home, clouds of sparks blew overhead.'

'Terrifying,' said his wife. 'The next morning our *altana* was covered in ash. Christopher found this little square of burnt canvas. It had blown all the way across the Grand Canal.' She wrapped the charred relic in a handkerchief and put it back in her handbag. 'I don't suppose we shall ever know what opera it came from.'

The meeting was opened by the general manager of the Fenice, Gianfranco Pontel, who wept and swore he would not sleep soundly again until the Fenice was rebuilt and back in operation. Pontel, a political appointee with no musical background, said he saw no reason to resign, as several people had publicly demanded he do.

Following Pontel, one official after another came forward to bewail the fate of the Fenice, pray for its resurrection, and absolve himself of any blame. As they spoke, high above them on the coffered ceiling, legions of tormented souls languished in Palma Giovane's *Cycles of Purgatory*, in silent mockery of their every word.

Mayor Cacciari, his black hair tousled, came to the microphone. The day after the fire, he had announced that the city would rebuild the Fenice within two years and that it would be rebuilt just as it was before, rather than as a modern theatre. He revived the old slogan *Com'era, dov'era* (As it was, where it was), first invoked in the campaign to build an exact replica of the Bell Tower in St Mark's Square, the Campanile, after it collapsed in 1902. The city council quickly ratified Cacciari's decision.

Today the mayor repeated his promise. He was forthright about the rationalizations that kept running through his mind. 'Afterwards you invent ten thousand excuses,' he said. 'You tell yourself, "You can't simultaneously be the custodian of the Fenice, the police, the public utilities, the fire department. You cannot be expected to keep watch over the city house by house, church by church, museum by museum." You can say all these things to yourself, but you keep thinking, "No, it's not possible, this cannot happen. No, it didn't happen. The Fenice cannot burn . . ."'

Though the audience was clearly unhappy, the august setting of the Ateneo Veneto served to enforce a measure of civility, if not quite the usual pin-drop silence. The assemblage gave voice to its general disgruntlement by maintaining a constant murmur that rose and fell in response to the remarks of the speaker. There came a point, however, when actual words leaped out of the undertone, distinctly audible words, angry words, sharply spoken and coming from among those standing on the left side of the hall.

'When we elected you,' the voice called out to Cacciari, 'we gave you the most beautiful theatre in the world, *intact!* And you have given it back to us in ashes!' The voice belonged to the painter Ludovico De Luigi, freshly returned from New York, where his spontaneous painting of the Fenice on fire had been auctioned off by Save Venice to benefit the Fenice. De Luigi, his face flushed, his white hair flowing, pointed an accusing finger at the mayor. 'It's a disgrace!' he shouted. 'Somebody has to take responsibility! If not you, then who?' The murmuring swelled to a buzz, and the buzz was punctuated by the syllables of De Luigi's name: 'Ludovico, -vico, -vico, -vico.'

Members of the audience craned their necks in half-embarrassed expectation. Would this outburst turn into one of Ludovico's happenings? Were his nude models waiting in the wings? Would he haul out another version of his bronze viola sculpture, the one with a large phallus protruding from it? Would he let rats out of a cage as he had once done in St Mark's Square? Apparently not. De Luigi had not had time to bring anything to this meeting but himself.

Mayor Cacciari looked wearily at him. 'Venice is unique,' he said.

'It's like no other place on earth. One cannot expect me or any other elected official to assume responsibilities beyond what's reasonable and normal.'

'But that's why we elected you,' said De Luigi. 'We put you in charge, whether you accept that or not! And *you!*' he bellowed, now pointing his finger at the startled general manager, Pontel. 'For God's sake, stop that snivelling! You're like a baby whose toys have been taken away. Do the honourable thing. Resign!'

Satisfied that he had made his point, De Luigi subsided, and a superintendent stepped forward to say that the task of rebuilding the Fenice would help revive old crafts that no longer existed in Venice. There would be a need for artisans who could reproduce, by hand, the wood and stone carvings, the sculpted stucco and papier mâché, the parquet floors, the paintings, the frescos, the gilding, and the richly intricate fabrics for curtains, tapestries, and upholstery. The loss of the Fenice was a tragedy, he said, but the rebuilding of it would create a renaissance of all the old crafts. The cost of the reconstruction would be upwards of $60 million, but money would not be a problem, because Rome recognized the value of the Fenice as a national treasure. The money would come.

The woman by the door nudged her friend. 'What did I tell you? There are no accidents.'

The last to speak was a vice mayor. 'Venice is a city of wood and velvet,' he said. 'The damage could have been much worse . . .'

The audience filed back out into the sunlight of Campo San Fantin, where the two cigarette-smoking policemen were now engaged in banter with a trio of pretty young girls. They were explaining that they would love to take the girls into the theatre for a peek at the wreckage, but it had been sealed by the police, and nobody could go in. Ludovico De Luigi's voice rang out as he headed away in the company of friends. 'I *meant* to insult them! Let them be angry.' He gestured at the Fenice as he passed it. 'Venice once had twelve opera houses. Now we have none.

One more nail in the coffin. Look at it! An empty shell. Just like Venice.'

The death of Venice had been predicted, pronounced, and lamented for two hundred years, ever since 1797, when Napoleon brought the once-mighty Venetian Republic to its knees. At the height of its glory, Venice had been the world's supreme maritime power. Its reach had extended from the Alps to Constantinople, and its wealth had been unequalled. The architectural variety of her palaces – Byzantine, Gothic, Renaissance, baroque, neoclassical – chronicled an evolving aesthetic shaped by a millennium of conquests and their accumulated spoils.

But by the eighteenth century, Venice had given itself over to hedonism and dissipation – masked balls, gaming tables, prostitution, and corruption. The ruling class abandoned its responsibilities, and the state became enfeebled, powerless to resist Napoleon's approaching army. The Great Council of the Venetian Republic voted itself out of existence on 12 May 1797, and the last in the line of 120 doges resigned. From that day forward, there had been no doges in the Doge's Palace, no Council of Ten in the Great Council Chamber, no shipbuilders turning out warships in the Arsenal, no prisoners shuffling across the Bridge of Sighs on the way to the dungeons.

'I will be an Attila for the Venetian state!' Napoleon had thundered – in Italian so as not to be misunderstood. He proved good to his word. His men looted the Venetian treasury, demolished scores of buildings, pulled precious stones from their settings, melted down objects of gold and silver, and carted off major paintings for installation in the Louvre and the Brera Museum in Milan.

Venice emerged from its defeat an impoverished provincial village, unable to do much more than settle into a languid and picturesque decline. It is this Venice that we have come to know – not the triumphant and arrogant conqueror but the humbled and crumbling ruin.

The fallen Venice became a symbol of faded grandeur, a place of melancholy, nostalgia, romance, mystery, and beauty. As such, it was irresistible to painters and writers. Lord Byron, who lived in a palace on the Grand Canal for two years, seemed almost to prefer the decaying Venice – 'Perchance even dearer in her day of woe,/Than when she was a boast, a marvel, and a show.' Henry James saw Venice as a much-used tourist attraction, 'a battered peep-show and bazaar'. John Ruskin, focusing on the city's architectural riches, hailed Venice as 'the paradise of cities'. To Charles Dickens, Venice was a 'ghostly city', and for Thomas Mann it was a darkly seductive curiosity – 'half fairy tale, half snare'.

I understood why so many stories set in Venice were mysteries. Sinister moods could be easily conjured by shadowy back canals and labyrinthine passageways, where even the initiated sometimes lost their way. Reflections, mirrors, and masks suggested that things were not what they seemed. Hidden gardens, shuttered windows, and unseen voices spoke of secrets and possibly the occult. Moorish-style arches were reminders that, after all, the unfathomable mind of the East had had a hand in all this.

In the soul-searching aftermath of the Fenice fire, Venetians seemed to be asking themselves the very questions that I, too, had been wondering about – namely, what it meant to live in so rarefied and unnatural a setting. Was there anything left of the Venice that Virginia Woolf described as 'the playground of all that was gay, mysterious and irresponsible'?

This much I knew: the population of Venice had been declining steadily for the past forty-five years – from 174,000 in 1951 to 70,000 at the time of the Fenice fire. The rising cost of living and the scarcity of jobs had caused a migration to the mainland. Venice was no longer impoverished, however. On the contrary, northern Italy now had one of the highest per capita incomes in Europe.

Because of its two centuries of poverty, the city's architectural heritage was still remarkably free of modern intrusions. The nineteenth and twentieth centuries had left barely any mark on it at all. Walking through Venice now, one still encountered a succession of vistas that looked much as they had when Canaletto painted them in the eighteenth century.

Within days of my arrival, I began to consider the idea of extending my stay and living in Venice for a while. I had learned basic Italian grammar at the age of sixteen, when I spent the summer in Torino as an exchange student living with an Italian family, and it had stayed with me. I could read the newspaper with ease, understand the spoken word passably, and speak well enough to make myself understood.

I decided I would live in an apartment, not a hotel. I would walk around the city with a notebook and, on occasion, a small tape recorder. I would have no fixed agenda, but I would look more at the people who lived in Venice than at the eleven million tourists who filed through it every year.

In preparation for this undertaking, I reread the classic texts. They were not at all encouraging. Mary McCarthy put it bluntly in *Venice Observed*: 'Nothing can be said [about Venice] (including this statement) that has not been said before.' McCarthy's parenthetical comment, 'including this statement', was an allusion to Henry James, who had written in 'Venice', an 1882 essay, 'There is notoriously nothing more to be said on the subject . . . It would be a sad day indeed when there should be something new to say . . . I am not sure there is not a certain impudence in pretending to add anything to it.'

These declarations were not as forbidding as they seemed. Mary McCarthy was referring mainly to clichéd observations about Venice that people mistakenly think they have originated – for example, that St Mark's Square is like an open-air drawing room, that Venice at night resembles a stage set, and that gondolas are all painted a funereal black and look like hearses. Henry James was reacting to the overabundance of travelogues and personal reminiscences of Venice, which was an ultra-fashionable travel destination in his day.

My interest, in any case, was not Venice *per se* but people who live in Venice, which is not the same thing. Nor, apparently, had it been a common approach in books about Venice. The best-known novels and movies set in Venice tended to be about people who were just passing through: *Death in Venice, The Wings of the Dove, The Aspern Papers, Don't Look Now, Summertime, Across the River and Into the Trees, The Comfort of Strangers.* The main characters of all these stories, and many more besides, were neither Venetians nor resident expatriates. They were transients. My view of Venice would focus on people who, for the most part, lived there.

Why Venice?

Because, to my mind, Venice was uniquely beautiful, isolated, inward-looking, and a powerful stimulant to the senses, the intellect, and the imagination.

Because, despite its miles of tangled streets and canals, Venice was a lot smaller and more manageable than it seemed at first. At eighteen hundred acres, in fact, Venice was barely twice the size of Central Park.

Because I had always found the sound of church bells pealing every fifteen minutes – close at hand and distant, solo and in concert, each with its own persona – a tonic to the ears and nerves.

Because I could not imagine a more enticing beat to assign myself for an indefinite period of time.

And because, if the worst-case scenario for the rising sea level were to be believed, Venice might not be there very long.

3

At Water Level

I TOOK AN APARTMENT IN CANNAREGIO, a residential quarter
sufficiently removed from the main tourist thoroughfare that it
still retained its old local atmosphere: housewives shopping at the
open-air food market, children playing in the squares, the Venetian
dialect making a lilting singsong of the spoken word. Footsteps and
voices were, in fact, the dominant sounds in Venice, since there were no
cars to drown them out and very little vegetation to absorb them.
Voices carried with startling clarity through the stone-paved squares
and alleys. A few fleeting words spoken in the house across the *calle*
sounded surprisingly close, as if they had been uttered by someone in
the same room. In the early evenings, people gathered in clusters to
gossip in Strada Nuova, the main street of Cannaregio, and the sound
of their mingled conversations rose in the air like the buzz of a cocktail
party in a large room.

My apartment occupied part of the ground floor of Palazzo da Silva,
which had been the British embassy in the seventeenth century. It was
just outside the Ghetto, the five-hundred-year-old Jewish quarter,
which, as the world's first ghetto, gave its name to all future ghettos.
My new home had three rooms with marble floors, beamed ceilings,
and a view of the Misericordia Canal, which flowed along the side of
the building like a moat, lapping at the stones ten feet below my
window.

On the far side of the canal, the foot traffic along the walk in front
of a row of small shops was as peaceful as that of a country lane. The
canal itself was a narrow, lightly travelled backwater. Boats passed just

often enough to keep the water churning and splashing appealingly. At high tide, traffic was visible above the windowsill, and the boatmen's voices rang clear and close at hand. As the tide lowered, the men and their boats slipped out of sight, like window-cleaners on a descending scaffold. Their voices receded and acquired an echo as the canal became a deepening trench. Then the tide came in again and lifted the men and boats back into view.

My landlords, Peter and Rose Lauritzen, lived two floors above, on the main floor of the palace, the *piano nobile*. Peter was American, Rose was English; they had lived in Venice for nearly thirty years. I called them at the suggestion of friends who said they were agreeable people, extraordinarily knowledgeable about Venice, and might have a small guest apartment available in their building.

Peter Lauritzen had written four well-regarded books about Venice, concerning its history, its art, its architecture, and efforts at preservation. His history of Venice, published in 1978, was one of the few to have been written in English since the first, by Horatio Brown, in 1893. Once his books had established him as a cultural historian, Peter began to make his living as a lecturer for upper-echelon tours of Italy and Eastern Europe. His roster of upmarket clients included museum trustees, groups of academic specialists, and wealthy individuals in search of an expert guide. Peter was a man of somewhat formal demeanour, I was told, but dynamic.

It was Rose who had answered the telephone when I called about the apartment months before. She spoke in a swooping, full-throated English drawl that subsided every so often into an incomprehensible mumble before regaining clarity and taking flight again. This remarkable voice materialized, upon my arrival, in the form of a strikingly beautiful woman in her late forties with large, wide-set, smoky-blue eyes, a broad smile, and a billowing mane of shoulder-length brown hair. She was tall, dressed in black, and precariously thin, but fashionably so. As she showed me around the apartment, I discovered she had a wacky charm that expressed itself in emphatic, slightly absurd, often self-mocking remarks. 'In Venice,' she said, 'no matter what you say, everyone will assume you're lying. Venetians always embellish, and they take it for granted you will, too. So you might as well. Because, funnily enough, if they discover you're someone who tells the truth all the time, they'll simply write you off as a bore.'

Rose explained that the apartment had originally been a storage room with an earthen floor, a *magazzino*. 'We were terribly pleased with ourselves for renovating it,' she said, 'until the Comune of Venice, the city government, sent us a letter declaring it illegal! I mean, completely . . . totally . . . illegal! Because we hadn't got permission. Mind you, the space hadn't been anything but a rubbish bin for four hundred years, I mean, literally. There was nothing of any architectural value in it. No woodwork, no carvings, no frescos, no gilt, no anything! I suppose we should have known we had to get permission, but if we *had* known, we'd probably have dropped the whole idea, because it would have meant having to deal with the Venetian bureaucracy, which is an absolute nightmare, *night*mare, *niiiight*mare!'

In the kitchen, Rose demonstrated how to operate the washing-machine without causing a flood, and how to light the oven without igniting a fireball.

'At any rate,' she went on, 'when the notice from the Comune arrived, Peter had a megawobbly, and I was frantic, because it meant *I* would have to go to the Comune and sort it out. Nightmare! But all our friends said, "Don't be silly. Nobody ever bothers to get approval. You simply make whatever renovations you like. Then you go to the city officials and confess! You pay a fine. And they give you a piece of paper called a *condono*, which makes it all perfectly legal."'

Rose showed me into the living-room, which was comfortably furnished with arm-chairs, reading lamps, a dining-room table, and floor-to-ceiling bookshelves crammed with histories, biographies, art books, travel books, and novels ranging from literary classics to pulp fiction. It was the overflow from the Lauritzens' library upstairs.

'So I went round to the Comune,' she said, 'heart in my mouth, and I said, "I'm dreadfully sorry. We had no idea! *Non lo sapevamo!*" The man didn't believe a word I was saying, of course, but he took pity on me – how could he not, seeing my face creased with worry, hair a tangle, voice a pathetic whine? Anyway, he gave me a *condono*, thank God, because he could have made us tear out all the improvements and turn the apartment back into a storage room again. I mean, torture! Torture, torture, *torture!*'

Rose was now standing at the window. She pointed out the various shops on the other side of the canal – the butcher's shop, the hardware shop, the local headquarters of the Communist Party, a photo shop with faded wedding pictures in the window. A picturesque trattoria, the Antica Mola, stood at centre stage; it had tables set up in front despite the chilly weather. 'After you've eaten at the Antica Mola a few times,' said Rose, 'Giorgio will know you're not a tourist, and he'll give you a discount. And that is one of the great secrets of Venice: the discount – *lo sconto!* Tourists would be furious if they ever found out Venetians pay thirty to forty per cent less than they do.'

And not only at restaurants, apparently. It would be worth my while, Rose pointed out, to make myself known to various shopkeepers, especially the fruit-and-vegetable vendors. 'You're at their mercy,' she said. '*They* select the tomatoes or whatever for you. There's no self-service. And if they know you – and like you – they won't slip anything damaged or overripe into your bag.

'And you should remember: everything is negotiable in Venice. I mean everything: prices, rents, doctors' fees, lawyers' fees, taxes, fines, even jail terms. Everything! You should even get to know a taxi driver, too, because otherwise the rates can be horribly expensive. That white water taxi parked over there belongs to my pet driver, Pino Panatta, who's very nice. The taxi is always immaculate, and he's terribly convenient, because he lives on the other side of the canal, just above the Communists.'

Having shown me all there was to see, Rose invited me to join her and Peter upstairs for a drink. I accepted, and as I turned away from the window, I asked why, in addition to having iron bars, the windows had been fitted with wide-mesh wire screens. The screens would keep bees and butterflies out, I said, but mosquitoes and gnats could fly right through.

'Oh, the screens!' she said, as we left the apartment. 'They're not for mosquitoes. They're for . . . *i ratti!*' Never had I heard the nearness of rats alluded to in such a lighthearted way. Rose's laughter echoed in the double-height entrance hall as she led the way up a long, broad flight of stone steps.

The spacious, high-ceilinged central hall, or *portego*, served as the Lauritzens' living-room. At one end, a bay of tall, arched windows opened through french windows on to a balcony that overlooked the same stretch of Misericordia Canal I could see from water level two floors below. A clear northern light poured into the room, setting the creamy yellow walls aglow. Doors led to rooms on either side of the living-room in the classic symmetrical layout of Venetian palaces, as described in Peter Lauritzen's book *The Palaces of Venice*.

Lauritzen himself emerged from his study issuing hearty greetings and carrying a bottle of chilled prosecco, the sparkling white wine of the Veneto region. He was wearing a quilted black velvet smoking jacket over a white shirt and patterned tie, and his hair was combed straight back. A neatly trimmed moustache and Vandyke beard framed his words, which, although he was from the American Midwest, he spoke in a crisp, headmaster's English accent. His manner was, if anything, even more spirited than his wife's.

'Well!' he said. 'You've certainly chosen a dramatic moment to arrive in Venice!'

'Pure coincidence,' I said. 'What have you been hearing about the Fenice?'

'The usual rumours,' he said. 'The most common, as always, involve the Mafia.' He handed me a glass of prosecco. 'But no matter what the investigation turns up, the general expectation is that we'll never really know what happened. Nor, finally, does it matter that much. What does matter is the tragedy of losing the Fenice. And I should think the key question would be "Will it ever be rebuilt?" rather than "Who did it?" Now, that may surprise you, because of all the talk about rebuilding it. In Venice, if you want to fix a crack in a wall, you must get twenty-seven signatures from twenty-four offices, and then it takes six years to fill the crack. I'm not exaggerating. How can anyone build an opera house with that sort of foolishness going on? No, no, Venice's real Achilles' heel is not fire and it's not high water. It's bureaucracy! I'll grant you, bureaucracy has prevented a lot of disasters happening in Venice, like the scheme to demolish all the buildings along the Grand Canal near Piazza San Marco in order to make way for a crystal palace. Still, the bureaucracy is an infuriating irritant.'

'Maddening,' said Rose, 'absolutely maddening.'

'And now we have this sloganeering,' said Peter, 'this *Com'era, dov'era*, meaning "As it was, where it was." It's impossible to rebuild the Fenice exactly as it was, because the old structure was made of wood, which was essential for the acoustics, and the new one will have to be made of concrete. Can you imagine how a Stradivarius would sound if it were made of concrete?'

'Hideous,' said Rose. 'I mean really hideous!'

'And what does "as it was" really mean?' Peter went on. 'Does it mean "as it was" in 1792, when Giannantonio Selva's original Fenice opened?

'Or "as it was" in 1808, when Selva redesigned the interior and built an imperial box for Napoleon?

'Or "as it was" in 1837, after fire destroyed the Fenice the first time and it was rebuilt by the Meduna brothers significantly changed, because the original Selva plans had been lost?

'Or "as it was" in 1854 . . . or in 1937 . . . ?'

With each new name and date, Peter's voice increased in urgency, in the manner of a prosecuting attorney enumerating a series of ever more serious charges. He stood in the centre of the room clutching a lapel with one hand and gesticulating vigorously with the other. His Vandyke jutted out as he spoke, as if to reinforce the assertiveness of his pronouncements.

'There've been at least five Fenices in two hundred years,' he said, 'not counting dozens of minor alterations in between.'

As Peter spoke, Rose went right on interjecting her own brand of commentary. 'Faulty wiring,' she said. 'That's probably what it was. In Venice electricity travels through cables that lie in the muck at the bottom of the canals – worn out, threadbare, corroded. Then they snake up into old buildings, where they were never meant to go, and come right back down into the water in the form of grounding wires. So if your toaster has a short circuit, you've probably electrocuted your neighbour.'

But Peter steered the main conversation. 'You must keep in mind,' he said, 'that Venice is a very Byzantine city. That explains a lot of things. For example: if you are a property owner, you are responsible for making certain repairs to your property. But before you make those repairs, you must get a permit, and permits are very difficult to come by. You find yourself having to bribe city officials to give you a permit so you can make repairs that those very officials would fine you for not making, or for making without a permit.'

'Bribery is a way of life in Venice,' said Rose. 'But you can't really call it bribery. It's accepted as a legitimate part of the economy.'

'The Anglo-Saxon mentality simply does not exist in Venice,' said Peter. 'The Venetian concept of law, for example, is certainly not Anglo-Saxon. A few years ago, two hundred and forty-seven people were indicted for various crimes in the lagoon. What happened? All two hundred and forty-seven were absolved. The penal code is still the one set up by Mussolini. There have been fifty or sixty governments in Italy since the Second World War, and none has been in power long enough to effect a change.'

'There are laws that have been on the books for centuries,' said Rose. 'If you added up all the taxes and fees you supposedly owe, you'd have to pay something like one hundred and forty per cent of your income.'

Peter noticed that my glass was nearly empty and moved quickly to refill it. 'I trust,' he said, pausing to allow the bubbles to settle, 'that we're not giving you the wrong impression – i.e., that we don't love Venice.'

'We adore it,' said Rose.

'We wouldn't live anywhere else,' said Peter. 'Apart from the obvious attractions, we live in Venice because it has the cleanest air of any city in the world. Not only does Venice have no cars – and you'd be surprised how many people don't realize that – there's no burning of fossil fuels at all, because Venice outlawed the use of heating oil in 1973 and switched to methane gas, which burns clean.'

I could not let that remark pass without comment.

'But what about the industrial smokestacks belching smoke just across the lagoon in Marghera and Mestre?'

'What about them?' said Peter, his smile broadening in anticipation of scoring a point. 'The prevailing winds blow inland,' he said, 'just as they do in all port cities. So the pollution you see coming out of those smokestacks on the mainland blows away from us, not towards us.'

It made sense to me that people who lived in Venice would talk a lot about Venice, the business of Venice being, after all, Venice itself. But I doubted that many Venetians were as vociferous on the subject as the Lauritzens were. Peter held forth in a manner more in the nature of oratory than conversation – informed, didactic, fiery, confrontational –

his discourse punctuated by the occasional 'whilst' or 'schedule'. Rose, speaking in verbal italics, evoked a Venice of wild extremes – horrific and blissful, ghastly and exquisite, hideous and enchanting. Whether they realized it or not, both Lauritzens presented themselves as beleaguered, like the city itself – but gamely, almost proudly belea- guered, in love with Venice despite its shortcomings. In their eagerness to explain Venice to me, they occasionally overlapped each other, both speaking at the same time without seeming to notice. At such moments, I found myself looking from one to the other, my head nodding and swivelling, as I tried to avoid making the social gaffe of listening to one and ignoring the other.

Peter, for example, was saying, 'Venice is not for everybody. To live in Venice, you must, first of all, like living on an island, and you must like living near water . . .' And Rose, at the same time, was saying, 'It's exactly like an Irish village where everybody knows everybody else . . .' Ob- livious, Peter went right on, 'And to live in Venice, you must be able to do without much greenery, and you must not mind walking a great deal.' I heard this over Rose's, 'You're always running into people you know, because the only way to get around in Venice, whether you're a countess or a shopkeeper, is to walk or take the *vaporetto*. You can't move about unseen in a private car, and in that respect Venice is terribly democratic.'

Keeping up with the Lauritzens at these moments was like listening to stereo with each of the speakers playing a different tune. In one ear, I heard Peter say, 'Now, those are very unusual circumstances, and a lot of people who say they love Venice eventually discover they do not.' With the other ear, if I understood correctly, I heard Rose saying, '. . . When I've come back from having gone out shopping, Peter doesn't ask me what I bought. He asks who I saw.'

'The key word is "claustrophobic",' said Peter. 'I listen for it. Because whenever I hear "claustrophobic" mentioned in connection with Venice, I know that the person who said it would never be happy living here.'

'Funnily enough, I *like* it that Venice is a village,' said Rose simultaneously.

The Lauritzens displayed the fervour of converts. Venice had been their chosen home. They had not simply been born in it and stayed. Their spirited defence of the city was, it seemed to me, partly a defence of their decision to live there, in self-imposed exile.

Peter had been born in Oak Park, Illinois. His arrival in Venice had been by way of the Lawrenceville School, Princeton, and a Fulbright Scholarship to Florence, where he studied the Provençal language in the poetry of Dante. His father had wanted him to become a baseball player and enter the business world, but Peter never moved back to the United States. Instead he became an acolyte of the Anglican priest who presided over the American Church in Florence, and when the priest was reassigned to Venice to establish an English church there, Peter came with him, met Rose, fell in love, and married her.

By the time he arrived in Venice, Peter bore little resemblance to the boy from Oak Park, Illinois. He had re-created himself, and he was disarmingly candid about it. 'My father never understood why anybody would pick up and move to Italy. Italy of all places. He enjoyed visiting us here, but he could never take my living in Italy seriously. To him it seemed like a nice joke. When our son, Frederick, was born, my father offered to pay for his college tuition, but only on the condition that he go to an American college. He was afraid we were going to make Frederick into an Englishman. He got this notion, no doubt, because of the way I speak and because I married an English girl. However, I'm pleased to say that every bit of Frederick's education, to date, has been in Venice – he's a Venetian, not an Englishman. He'll soon go off to college – but to Oxford, not to America. And as for my living in Italy, it was the best decision I've ever made. I luxuriate in this world I've invented for myself.'

As for Rose, living in Venice came naturally. She was a member of the British aristocracy. For centuries her family had lived in great manor houses and passed along such titles as Baron Ashford, Lord Bury, and the Earl of Albemarle among the males. Her ancestral line did have its quirky elements: Rose's great-great-aunt, Alice Keppel, was the publicly acknowledged mistress of Edward VII. Mrs Keppel's daughter, Violet Trefusis – 'Aunt Violet' to Rose – had become famous as the eccentric and irrepressible lover of Vita Sackville-West. When Rose was a teenager, she visited her ageing, expatriated Aunt Violet in Florence. Violet advised her in matters of style and society, contributing significantly to Rose's worldliness and dramatic poise. Although Rose was entitled to be addressed as 'Lady Rose', her family background seemed a matter of indifference to her. She had settled in Venice in part to get away from it. And because she had lived for most of her childhood at Mount Stewart, a family estate in Northern Ireland, she often replied to questions about her origins by saying simply, 'I'm bog Irish.'

Rose had been coming to Venice since the age of sixteen, usually in the company of her mother, who bought an old gondolier's cottage as a retreat for summer vacations. Ezra Pound lived next door in an identical cottage, which he had shared with his mistress, Olga Rudge, since the 1920s.

'Pound had just been released from St Elizabeth's Hospital for the Criminally Insane,' Rose recalled, 'and by the time I saw him in the early 1960s, he was old and hermitlike. He had taken his famous vow of silence.

'We'd see the two of them, Olga and Ezra, quietly strolling in the area and having coffee at one of the cafés along the Zattere. She was diminutive and very beautiful. He was tall and dignified and always elegantly dressed: a broad-brimmed felt hat, a wool coat, tweed jacket, a flowing tie. His face was craggy, and his eyes were immensely sad. When people stopped to greet them, he would stand patiently, in silence, while Olga made pleasantries. We never saw him speak in public, but at home we could hear him reading his poetry aloud in a strong, rhythmic voice. My mother was a fan of Pound's, so she rang the doorbell and asked if she might have an audience with him. Olga very politely told her to go away: it was no use, he wouldn't talk to anyone. We finally realized we'd been hearing recordings of Pound reading his poems. He'd been sitting on the other side of our common wall, listening quietly, just as we had. Pound died ages ago, but Olga lives on. She's over a hundred now.'

The Lauritzens' circle of friends included both Venetians and expatriates, among them the art collector Peggy Guggenheim. Peter frequently accompanied Peggy on late-afternoon rides in her gondola, which was the last private gondola in Venice. 'She knew every foot of every back canal,' he said. 'She would sit in her little chair with her Lhasa apsos lounging underneath and her gondolier standing behind her on the stern deck, rowing. She'd give him directions with hand signals, as if she were driving a car, without so much as saying a word or looking back at him. Peggy was notoriously stingy. She hired the city's corpse collector as her gondolier, because he was available at a better price. She didn't seem to mind that he serenaded her with funeral dirges and that he was very often drunk.

'I went to see Peggy during her final illness,' Peter went on. 'She was rereading Henry James. She told me she had given instructions that she was to be buried with her dogs in the garden of her palazzo on the Grand Canal. She made me promise to see that her wishes were carried out, and I did. In fact, by the time she died, fourteen of her dogs were already in the garden waiting for her. Peggy was still alive when the last of them was laid to rest. During the burial ceremony, while the butler was poking around in the dirt with a spade looking for an empty spot, he unearthed a Lhasa apso skull that rolled to a stop at Peggy's feet. Peggy was sobbing into her handkerchief and didn't notice.'

In his study, Peter showed me the 1922 edition of the works of Henry James that Peggy had bequeathed to him. Each volume was signed with the first of her three married names: 'Peggy Vail'.

Peggy Guggenheim was never accepted by members of Venetian society, who professed to be appalled by her sexual promiscuity. But the Lauritzens had been taken up by Venetians and frequently attended Venetian parties. On the evening I first met them, Peter picked up an engraved invitation from his desk, studied it for a moment, and then glanced up at Rose with a look that seemed to ask, 'Should I?' Rose nodded her assent. Twelve Venetian families were giving a formal Carnival costume ball in two weeks. The Lauritzens had been invited to come and to bring a guest of their own. When Peter extended the invitation to me, I readily accepted. 'You'll see what I mean when I say Venice is really just a small village,' said Rose.

Before leaving, I signed the Lauritzens' guest book, and as I did, a question that had occurred to me earlier in the evening came to mind again.

'By the way,' I said to Rose, 'how did the Comune ever find out you had renovated the apartment downstairs?'

Rose smiled conspiratorially. 'Someone informed on us, apparently. We don't know who. It might have been a neighbour.'

'Ah,' I said, 'so if Venice is a village, it's a village . . . with an edge?'

'Oh, absolutely,' she said with a broad smile. 'It definitely has an edge.'

4
Sleepwalking

QUITE APART FROM THE TWICE-DAILY tidal rise and fall of the Misericordia Canal, life outside my window had a special rhythm of its own. Typically the day began in the pre-dawn stillness when a fruit-and-vegetable dealer stepped into his boat, moored opposite my window, gently started his motor, and chugged slowly and quietly down the canal – the equivalent, for a motorboat, of tiptoeing. Then everything fell silent again, except for the lapping of water against the stones.

At about eight o'clock, life along the canal officially awoke, as shopkeepers on the other side started opening their doors and rolling up their metal gates. Giorgio set his tables and chairs out in front of the trattoria. The butcher took delivery of meat from a passing barge.

Pedestrians began moving across my field of vision like actors crossing a stage: a labourer shambling unhurriedly, a man in a business suit walking at a more purposeful pace. Customers stopped in at the trattoria for coffee and a glance at the morning's *Gazzettino*. Next door, at the local Communists' shopfront headquarters, with posters bearing the hammer-and-sickle insignia on the walls, there were generally one or two people sitting at a desk, talking on the phone or reading a newspaper. The small shop next to that one had been the workshop of Renato Bonà, one of the last Venetian craftsmen who specialized in making oars and oar posts for gondolas. Bonà's genius as a sculptor – particularly his mastery of the curving, twisting oar posts – had made him a demigod among gondoliers. Since his death two years earlier, his shop had become something of a shrine, commemorated by a plaque next to the door. The Misericordia Canal was not on any of the usual gondola routes, but every so often a gondola would glide by in silent tribute to Bonà. One gondola, however, had its regular mooring spot in front of the house. It was a wedding gondola, so it had elaborate carving and ornamentation, but it was still black like all the others. At some point during the day, the gondolier would ready it for a wedding by putting gold-and-white slipcovers over the chairs and cushions.

At one o'clock, the rolling of metal gates sounded again as the shops closed for midday. Only the trattoria stayed open, serving local seafood specialities to a predominantly local clientele. The pace of life slowed until late afternoon, when the shops reopened and people walked at a quickened step: students released from class, housewives hurriedly shopping for dinner.

As darkness fell, the metal gates rolled down again, and the lights of the trattoria came up at centre stage. People moved now at a leisurely stroll, and convivial voices floated in the night-time air. Towards midnight, the sounds of boats and backwash died down. The voices drifted away. Giorgio dragged the chairs and tables back inside and turned off the lights. By that time, the fruit-and-vegetable dealer had long since tethered his boat to its mooring poles, and Pino, the owner of the white water taxi, had pulled a canvas sheet over the open part of his deck and retired to his apartment above the Communists.

Venice could be a disorienting place, even for people who lived there and thought they knew it well. The narrow, winding streets, together with the serpentine course of the Grand Canal and the absence of any landmarks visible from a distance, made it difficult to keep one's bearings. Ernest Hemingway described Venice as 'a strange, tricky town' and walking in it as 'better than working crossword puzzles'. To me it occasionally felt like walking through a funhouse, especially at times when, twenty minutes after having set out on a course that I had thought was a straight line, I discovered I was right back where I started. But the streets and squares of Cannaregio became familiar to me sooner than I expected, and so did some of its characters. I had been in residence barely a week when I met the Plant Man.

He appeared at first to be a shrub that moved. He was an oasis of rubber plants, ficus trees, heather, and ivy that floated along Strada Nuova, calling out in a voice that carried in all directions, 'O-la! O-la! Have you got a house? Have you got somewhere to go?' As he drew closer, I made him out to be a short, solid man with wiry grey hair who loped along half hidden at the centre of a mass of greenery protruding out of sacks hanging from his shoulders and clutched in both hands. He stopped to talk to a stout woman with short, battleship grey hair.

'This one costs eighty thousand lire,' he said, 'but I'll give it to you for twenty thousand. It'll last for years!'

'Don't lie to me,' the woman said.

The man set his sacks on the ground and emerged from his personal forest. He was barely five feet tall and wore a bright red jacket, a yellow shirt, a tie that was far too short, and high-top sneakers.

'It will last!' he crowed. 'I've known you for a lifetime, sister. O-la! And you love plants, really love 'em. All the better, all the better. The man who marries you will be a lucky one!'

'She's already married,' a man standing nearby said.

The woman handed the Plant Man ten thousand lire and took the plant, somewhat dubiously.

'Thank you, sister,' he said. 'May God let you live to be a hundred! Give it a little chamomile tea for the vitamins, but no water from the tap unless you filter out the chlorine first! Chlorine is poison.'

A teenager coming the other way called out, 'Hey, man! You got a house? You got somewhere to go?'

The Plant Man looked at me. 'See? They know me. Hey, kid! You've known me all your life, right?'

'Yeah, you're always singing,' the boy said.

'See?' he said. 'I invented this song when I was at the Zamperini Stadium, where the Venice soccer team plays. I sing it to the losing team – "You got a house?" It means, "What are you hanging around here for? What's the use? You got a house? You might as well go home!" And now all the kids sing it. They've even made it into banners that they wave at the games. Yeah, I invented it.'

'Where do these plants come from?' I asked.

'We have our own farm half an hour outside Venice – my wife and me. We work it ourselves. It's near Padua. I've been coming to Venice every day for twenty-eight years. Only to Venice, nowhere else, because Venice is the only city I truly have in my heart. Venetians are the best people, kind people, courteous. Monday I did a terrace for a doctor near the Rialto fish market. I brought him veronica. I go to all the parishes and the churches. I do them all, from Sant'Elena to San Giobbe. I'm the only one who does it. I have chickens, too.' He reached deep into one of his sacks and pulled out a chicken. It had been beheaded, gutted, plucked, but it still had feet.

'I just gave one to the pharmacist in Campo San Pantalon, and I now have to deliver this one to Luigi Candiani, the notary.'

'Will it still be fresh by the time you get it there?' I asked.

'Fresh? O-la! Yes, my good man, it will be fresh! It won't smell! This is not commercial stuff. We raise these chickens on grains, grass, and vegetables, all from our fields. You can eat it now, or in two days, or if you put it in the freezer, three months . . . Hey, brother,' he called to an old man walking past, 'you got a house?'

'Nah, I don't have a house,' the man said with a smile.

'You want to buy a live chicken?'

'Nah.'

'You want half a live chicken? No? Well, it was worth asking.' Then, turning back to me, 'And you? You want anything?'

I pointed to a small pot of heather.

'Perfect choice!' he said. 'It sprouts nice pink flowers, and when you get tired of watering it, you can just let it dry out. That way you'll have it for ever.'

He patted my shoulder. 'My name is Adriano Delon. I come to Venice every day except Sunday. That's when I go ballroom dancing with my wife. It's on television. You can see us on channel nine! We waltz, we tango, and we samba.' Adriano raised his arms in the air and swivelled his hips. 'O-la! Ballroom dancing will never go out of style. Well, I'd better go and deliver Candiani's chicken.'

With that, Adriano Delon hoisted his sacks into position. Then, once again surrounded by his portable thicket and singing at the top of his lungs, he set off down Strada Nuova, this time with a sweeping stride that, to my inexpert eyes, resembled something between a waltz and a tango.

One morning I rose very early with the intention of taking a walk when the streets would be virtually empty. I headed in the direction of the Church of Santa Maria della Salute, and as I came into Campo San Vio, I noticed four men in work clothes standing by the side of the English Church. Two of them were crouching at the base of the church wall, about thirty feet apart, at opposite ends of a net that lay loosely gathered on the ground between them. Each man drove a single nail through a corner of the net, anchoring one side of it to the pavement. Then each held a free corner in his hand and, still crouching, watched a third man, who was carrying a canvas sack. The man walked to the centre of the *campo*, reached into his sack, and started tossing bread-crumbs on to the ground. Within minutes, pigeons began to alight and peck at the crumbs – forty pigeons, fifty pigeons. The man now threw the breadcrumbs slightly closer to the men with the net. And then closer still. The pigeons followed the moving feast, jostling each other as they pecked and hopped. When they were within a few feet of the net, the two men flung the free end over the pigeons and trapped them. A furious fluttering and tumbling swelled the net as the men skilfully pulled it around and under the pigeons until they were fully enclosed. Only a few escaped. The fourth workman now rushed over and threw a large black cloth over the pigeons. They were instantly becalmed. The men then picked up the net, now heavy with pigeons, and carried it to a boat waiting in the canal.

It was no secret that most Venetians hated pigeons. Mayor Cacciari had called them 'flying rats', but his proposals to reduce their number had been noisily opposed by animal-rights activists. Apparently a pigeon-control programme was proceeding anyway, quietly, under the cover of early-morning hours.

The men climbed into the boat and had started transferring pigeons from the net into empty cages when I approached. One of them waved me away.

'No Greens! No Greens!' he said. 'Are you with the Green Party?'

'No,' I said, 'I'm just curious.'

'Well, you can see we handle the birds very gently,' the man said. 'We're taking them to the veterinarian. He will inspect them and release the healthy ones. The sick ones will be put to sleep.'

I asked how many pigeons they expected to catch this way, but my voice was drowned out by the motor revving up. The men clearly had no interest in talking to me, but as they pulled away, the driver shouted out the name of their boss: Dr Scattolin. 'He knows about all this stuff.'

To my surprise, when I called Dr Mario Scattolin, he invited me to come and see him that very afternoon. Dr Scattolin's proper title was Director of Animal Affairs, and he worked in a fifteenth-century palace on the Grand Canal that served as a municipal building. I arrived at his office through a series of cramped, winding hallways.

'Ordinarily I wouldn't discuss our netting operation,' Dr Scattolin said affably as he ushered me in. 'I prefer to deny we do it. But since you saw it with your own eyes . . . *beh!*' He shrugged.

Dr Scattolin had wavy salt-and-pepper hair and wore a light grey suit. He had a large office, and his desk and shelves were piled high with papers and reports. Tall windows looked out on a narrow, gloomy interior courtyard.

'Look,' he said, 'Venice has a hundred and twenty thousand pigeons. That's far too many. When pigeons are overcrowded, they get stressed, their immune system weaken, and they become susceptible to parasites that can cause pneumonia, chlamydia, toxoplasmosis, and salmonella when they are passed to human beings.' As he spoke, Dr Scattolin sketched the outline of a pigeon on a pad of paper. He drew little droppings coming from under the pigeon's tail feathers and an arrow to indicate parasites under the wings.

'All the tourists want to be photographed feeding the pigeons in St Mark's Square,' he said. 'They buy a bag of corn for four thousand lire, they toss a few kernels on the ground, and immediately they are surrounded by a swarm of grateful pigeons.' He imitated a pigeon walking, his head bobbing forward in syncopation with the movement of his shoulders, then dipping to peck at a kernel of corn. Bob and dip, bob and dip. He had the pigeon strut down perfectly.

'If you can get a pigeon to stand in your palm, that's good,' he said. 'Even better if there are two or three more on your arm and one or two on your shoulder. Why not? I've seen people completely covered with pigeons.

'You can't tell from the photographs, but pigeons smell horrible. It's the same with penguins. People love to see movies of penguins.' Now Dr Scattolin imitated the stiff-shouldered penguin waddle. 'But if you were to stand in the midst of penguins, you'd discover they stink. That's because penguins and pigeons have one very unpleasant behavioural oddity in common: they both build their nests with their own excrement.' He made a face.

'Pigeons colonize dark places, especially narrow passages where the sun doesn't penetrate. That's what happened in the little *calle* that leads into Campo San Vio, where you saw the netting going on this morning. The pigeons had made that *calle* impassable. It was disgusting. We had a great many complaints, so I sent the men there to clean it out. The two men you saw handling the net are a father-and-son team. They've been doing it for twenty years. They've developed a very rare expertise: they know just the right moment to swing the net. If one pigeon becomes frightened, he flees. That sends an instantaneous signal to the others, and in a fraction of a second, they are all gone.'

'Are you really going to release the healthy ones?' I asked.

'No, we will examine some of them, but they will all be chloroformed. The men were probably just trying to mollify you in case you were a member of the Green Party or an *animalista*. They take a lot of abuse from those people. They scream things like, "Nazi murderers! Gas chambers!"

'In Venice there is so much food available for the pigeons, they reproduce all year – seven or eight times, two eggs each time. That's not a natural cycle. In London pigeons reproduce only once a year. So Venice has to work at pigeon-control all year round.

'We want to reduce the pigeon population by twenty thousand a year until we reach a total of forty thousand. We've tried everything. We've mixed food with birth-control chemicals, but the pigeon population only increased. We're now testing chemicals containing hormones that simulate pregnancy, which we hope will eliminate the mating urge in females. Years ago we even imported peregrine falcons to prey on the pigeons, but each falcon killed only one pigeon a day and dumped faeces that were much worse than a pigeon's. The *animalisti* have offered their own proposals. They said we should catch male pigeons and castrate them. Imagine! It would cost a hundred thousand lire a pigeon.'

'I have an idea,' I said.

Dr Scattolin raised his eyebrows.

'I've noticed there are eight corn-vending stands in St Mark's Square. Why not just get rid of them?'

'Ah!' he said. 'Because that would be the sensible thing to do.'

'But really, why not?'

'Two reasons. One: because Venice wants to keep the tourists amused, and the tourists are amused by pigeons, and two: because, believe it or not, selling corn at four thousand lire a bag is such a lucrative business that each vendor can afford to pay the city three hundred million lire for a licence. However, we do place a strict limit on where the pigeons can be fed. It is legal only in St Mark's Square, nowhere else in Venice. If you are caught feeding pigeons even ten feet outside St Mark's, you will be fined a hundred thousand lire.'

'That's absurd,' I said.

'It's worse than absurd,' said Dr Scattolin. 'It's contradictory, hypocritical, irresponsible, dangerous, dishonest, corrupt, unfair, and completely mad.' He leaned back in his chair. 'Welcome to Venice.'

It has been observed that on a map Venice looks something like a fish swimming east to west. The tail fins are the outlying districts of Castello and Sant'Elena. The body is the busy heart of Venice: St Mark's and the Rialto. The head is the railway station and the parking area, Piazzale Roma, which are connected by a long bridge to the mainland. The bridge itself could be the line that the fish has taken in its mouth. One could even go so far as to designate the Grand Canal, which travels an S-shaped course through town, as the fish's alimentary canal.

To the south of Venice, immediately underneath the fish, is a long, slender island that could be seen as a platter for the fish to be served on: the Giudecca.

Whatever else it might be, the Giudecca is a now-bucolic spit of land, three hundred yards across the Giudecca Canal from the heart of Venice. It has one important church, no major tourist attractions, and no tourist shops. It was the site of the last real factories in Venice and has thus been associated with a somewhat different, rougher working class than elsewhere in the city. People who live on the Giudecca consider themselves a breed apart, which, in one way or another, is how residents of all the islands in the lagoon feel about themselves.

For a long time, I had hoped to get a look at a mysterious walled garden on the Giudecca that I had read about but never seen. Designed and built in the late nineteenth century by Frederic Eden, the great-uncle of the British prime minister Anthony Eden, it was called, naturally enough, the Garden of Eden. At four acres, it was the largest private garden in Venice. No one I knew had ever been inside the walls.

It was only a three-minute ride to the Giudecca on the *vaporetto*, that clanging, groaning water bus with a flat roof over an open foredeck that bears an odd resemblance to Humphrey Bogart's riverboat in *The African Queen*. On this occasion, our *vaporetto* was met at the landing platform by a uniformed conductor who guided it to the dock with an extravagant waving of arms and excited instructions to the pilot: 'Come forward a bit! Now back up! A little more! Closer, closer! Now wind the rope round. That's right!' The man reminded me of the policemen in Milan who used to direct traffic with a comical ballet of swinging arms and pirouettes. The conductor – tall, thin, about fifty-five – had a look of angelic ebullience and seemed overjoyed to see the passengers arrive.

As we disembarked, he stood at attention and saluted. I heard someone address him as 'Capitano Mario'. I was charmed, but all of this struck me as highly unusual, if not bizarre. I had never seen a conductor guide a *vaporetto* to a landing. Pilots managed it well enough by themselves. Docking a *vaporetto* was no more complicated than pulling up to a bus stop.

In any case, that afternoon I had no luck getting into the Garden of Eden and came away with nothing more than a tantalizing view of the tops of magnolias, cypresses, and pollarded willows protruding above its twenty-foot walls. When I enquired at one of the wine bars on the quay, I was told the garden now belonged to an Austrian painter named Hundertwasser, who did not live there and who had purposely allowed it to revert to its wild state. However, the garden's former caretaker invariably came to the bar at predictable hours, and if I returned on Friday afternoon, I might be able to talk to him. When I came back on Friday, I met the ex-caretaker, but he said he was no longer in touch with the owner and that, as far as he knew, nobody had been allowed into the garden for years.

I was on the point of leaving when I noticed a *carabiniere* standing at the bar having a drink. He was in full uniform – white shirt, blue tie, and dark blue suit with wide, bright red stripes down the sides of the trouser legs. I had been mildly surprised by the sight of the two uniformed *carabinieri* casually smoking cigarettes while standing guard at the Fenice some days before. But drinking in a bar? Even for the famously non-military Italians, this seemed beyond the pale. That is, until I realized that the *carabiniere* was the same man who had been the *vaporetto* conductor earlier in the week.

Looking at him more carefully now, I saw that his shirt was a bit rumpled, his tie soiled and askew, and his suit in need of a few repairs and a good dry-cleaning. The scuffed black shoes were, if I was not mistaken, the same ones he had worn as a *vaporetto* conductor. It was all becoming a little clearer, and a week later it became clearer still, when I was on my way to an appointment on the Giudecca and saw him sitting at a table outside a quayside wine bar. This time he was decked out in naval dress whites and the same black shoes. I was about half an hour early for my appointment, so I took a seat at the table next to him and ordered a beer. When the man turned my way, I nodded and said, '*Buon giorno, Capitano.*'

He saluted and then put out his hand. 'Capitano Mario Moro!'

'Nice to meet you,' I said. 'Wasn't that you I saw at the *vaporetto* stop the other day?'

'At Palanca? Yes, it was! Sometimes I'm over at the Redentore stop, or Zitelle.' He gestured with his beer bottle at the location of the other two stops farther down the quay.

'And then again on Friday,' I said, 'if I'm not mistaken, I did see you here at the wine bar in a *carabiniere* uniform, didn't I?'

He snapped to attention in his chair again and saluted.

'Today,' I said, 'I take it you're a naval man.'

'Yes!' he said. 'But tomorrow . . . *tomorrow* . . . !'

'What's tomorrow?'

He leaned towards me, his eyes wide. '*Guardia di Finanza!*' The financial police.

'Splendid!' I said. 'And what colour is that one?'

He drew back, surprised at my ignorance. 'Grey, of course,' he said.

'Yes, of course. And where does it go from there? I mean, what others have you got?'

'Very many,' he said. 'Many, many.'

'Soldier?'

'But of course!'

'Airman?'

'Yes. That, too.'

'And what about fireman?'

Suddenly he jumped up, turned on his heel, and strutted off, disappearing into a passageway between two buildings. A man sitting at another table had watched the whole exchange.

'Maybe I shouldn't have been so inquisitive,' I said. 'I hope I didn't offend him.'

'I don't think you did,' the man said. 'Mario doesn't take offence that easily.'

'What made him leave so quickly?'

The man cast a glance in the direction Mario had gone. 'I don't know,' he said. 'Mario's in his own world. He's an electrician, you know, and a very good one. He does little jobs for people here on the Giudecca. And if you saw him at work, especially before ten in the morning, before he's had a beer, you wouldn't notice much unusual about him – although one time when he came to my house to repair some wiring, he was dressed as a prison guard. He's been wearing those uniforms as long as I can remember.'

'Where does he get them?'

'People are always giving him things. Sometimes a full uniform, sometimes just parts – like a hat, a jacket, and no trousers. He's got uniforms from the army, the navy, the marines, the fire brigade, and the *Guardia di Finanza*, as he just told you. Lately I've seen him wearing a bright orange jumpsuit that someone at the gas company must have given him.'

'Not exactly a common hobby,' I ventured.

'No,' the man said, 'his head is in the clouds. He's in a dream state. Just as we all are at times.'

'Only more so.'

'True, but as I said, he's not the only one. Our waiter here, for example. He dreams of being a soccer star. He's obsessed by it. He can't talk about anything else. At home the walls of his room are covered with soccer posters and banners and photographs of his heroes. Once in a while, you'll see him give the air a sharp kick, as if he's about to score a goal, and then he'll pump his fist. If he were Mario, right now he'd be wearing knee socks, shorts, and a regulation jersey. That's the only difference.'

I glanced inside the restaurant. A television set over the bar was tuned to a soccer game. The waiter looked at it as he passed.

'It's the same with the families who've lived in palaces for generations,' the man went on. 'They think it's still three hundred years ago, when being nobility really meant something. Every artist you see setting up an easel around here – in their heads they see themselves as the next Tintoretto or de Chirico. And believe me, fishermen who float in the lagoon all day do not think only about fish. It's the same with Mario.'

The man lowered his voice, as if to impart a confidence. 'And, like some people, Mario sometimes forgets he's only dreaming.'

As we were finishing our beers, Mario reappeared at our table with a click of his heels and a crisp salute. He had changed into fireman's gear – black hat, black boots, and a long black coat emblazoned with eye-catching yellow reflective stripes.

'Bravo, Mario!' said the man at the other table.

Mario spun around to show us the words VIGILI DEL FUOCO, 'Firefighters', spelled out in reflective letters across his back. 'When there's a fire,' he said proudly, 'they call me.'

'And you go and help put out the fire?' I asked.

'Sometimes.'

'Tell me, what did you do on the night the Fenice burned? Did you help?'

'I was in Do Mori when I heard about it,' he said, gesturing towards the restaurant. 'We all came outdoors, and we could see the flames from here.' He swept his outstretched hand along the panorama on the other side of the Giudecca Canal: the littoral of the Zattere, Santa Maria della Salute, the St Mark's Bell Tower, and the island of San Giorgio Maggiore.

'The sky was red,' he said. 'Burning pieces of wood were flying overhead, all the way from the Fenice. I went home right away and changed into my uniform.'

'And then you went to the Fenice?'

'No. That night my . . . my colleagues were there instead. I had to be here to direct the helicopter.'

Mario reached into a voluminous pocket and pulled out a pair of bright orange plastic earphones. He put them on his head. In one hand he held a megaphone, in the other a pair of binoculars. Then, looking up at the sky above St Mark's, he fanned his arms in imitation of a ground-crew technician on the Tarmac signalling to an aeroplane pilot. His motions were so exaggerated that he could just as easily have been taken for a man marooned on a desert island desperately trying to catch the attention of a passing plane.

'When the helicopter flew over the Grand Canal to pick up water,' he said, 'I gave them the go-ahead!'

Mario went on waving his arms and staring up at the sky with a beatific smile on his face.

People walking along the quayside paused to look up, too, wondering what the commotion was about. All they could see was a peaceful daytime sky. How could they know that Capitano Mario Moro was reliving his imagined heroics of the night the Fenice burned – sending signals to a helicopter pilot who acknowledged his command with a crisp salute, then banked into a steep descent, skimmed the surface of the Grand Canal, and scooped up another tankful of water.

My chance encounter with Mario Moro happened while I was on my way to see a man who had piqued my curiosity earlier in the week by giving a newspaper interview in which he lambasted the management of the Venice Film Festival as 'corrupt petty officials, who chose lousy little flavour-of-the-month films to compete for awards over bigger, quality movies'.

The man could not be dismissed as a mere crank, because he was Count Giovanni Volpi, the son of the festival's founder – Count Giuseppe Volpi – and every year he provided the Volpi Cups that were presented to the best actor and best actress. As it happened, the film festival was only one of many targets of Giovanni Volpi's rage. He was angry with all of Venice.

Chief among Volpi's grievances was the posthumous condemnation of his father, which Giovanni considered flagrantly unjust. Despite what people thought about the late Giuseppe Volpi, it was generally conceded that he was the most significant Venetian of the twentieth century, and the film festival was among the least of his achievements.

Giuseppe Volpi brought electric power to Venice, north-east Italy, and most of the Balkans in 1903. He conceived of and built the mainland port city of Marghera. He widened the railway bridge to the mainland, making it possible for cars and trucks to reach Piazzale Roma in Venice. He restored a shabby old palace on the Grand Canal and turned it into the world-famous Gritti Hotel; then he bought five-star hotels throughout Italy, creating a monopoly and founding the luxury hotel chain CIGA. He was instrumental in creating the Correr

Museum in St Mark's Square. He negotiated the Turkish-Italian peace treaty of 1912, which gave Libya and the island of Rhodes to Italy, and he later served as Libya's governor. He mediated the payment of Italy's debt to the United States and Great Britain after the First World War, on extremely favourable terms for Italy. He attended the Versailles Peace Conference in 1919 as a member of the Italian delegation, and he later became Mussolini's finance minister.

For most of his career, Giuseppe Volpi was popularly known, in person and in the press, by the nickname 'the Last Doge of Venice'. But now, fifty years later, he was primarily remembered as being a high-ranking member of the Fascist regime. He was regarded in Venice with ambivalence at best, and this was what most infuriated his son.

Giovanni Volpi's comments about the film festival made him a topic of conversation for a few days, and I learned the outline of his story.

He had been born out of wedlock in 1938 to Giuseppe Volpi and his mistress, Nathalie La Cloche, a French Algerian, a *pied-noir* – blonde, brilliant, and beautiful. Giuseppe, who was married and the father of two adult daughters, legitimized Giovanni's birth by arranging to have the government pass a law that was wiped off the books as soon as it had served its purpose. Four years later, in 1942, Count Volpi's wife died, and he married Nathalie La Cloche. They lived most of the time in Volpi's huge palace in Rome and spent summers in a villa on the Giudecca.

Toward the end of the war, the Germans captured Volpi and injected him with powerful chemicals to try to make him talk but succeeded only in destroying his health. He died in Rome in 1947 at the age of seventy, leaving the nine-year-old Giovanni a vast estate that included the seventy-five-room Palazzo Volpi on the Grand Canal, a three-hundred-room palace in Rome, a four-thousand-acre ranch in Libya, and other properties and holdings sufficient to keep Giovanni living in style in the well-appointed, fully staffed villa on the Giudecca. He had a flotilla of three motorboats, including the oldest one in

Venice – his father's 1928 handcrafted Celli, which turned heads everywhere he went in it. Giovanni Volpi never moved into his palace on the Grand Canal, and in fact, after the death of his mother, no one lived there. Nevertheless, he kept it furnished and spotlessly maintained.

'Ah, Giovanni,' said a Venetian woman who knew him well. 'He can be so witty and full of fun, but most of the time he's deeply discontented. He has an almost princely status in Venice, but he rejects it. If you invite him to a party, he won't say yes, he won't say no, and he won't show up. He hates Venetians!'

For some reason, however, Volpi got on well with Americans. When I heard this, I decided to give him a call, thinking it might be worthwhile to hear a contrarian's view of Venice. 'No problem,' he said as soon as I asked. 'Come on over.'

Volpi's house on the Giudecca, the Villa Ca' Leone, lay behind a high brick wall that ran along a quiet canal directly across from the mysterious Garden of Eden, which hid behind its own brick wall. A housekeeper answered the door and led me through an *allée* of fragrant gardenias into the living-room. French windows looked out on a broad view of the lagoon, southward – in other words, away from Venice. The décor of the room was not especially identifiable as Venetian, which may have been its point. I could hear Volpi in the next room winding up a telephone conversation in French. He joined me as soon as he was through and, after offering me a drink, sat down opposite me. He was wearing a dark wool shirt, corduroy slacks, and heavy all-weather shoes. He had a brooding expression, which broke into a brief, fleeting grin.

'Okay, go ahead!' he said. 'What would you like to know?'

'Forgive me for being blunt,' I said, 'but what's the problem between you and Venice?'

He laughed, but as soon as he started talking, I could tell it was no joking matter. He spoke fluent English in an earnest, low-pitched voice.

'I am the son of a self-made man who single-handedly propelled Venice into the twentieth century and maintained it in perfect working order until the war. He died in 1947, and ever since then it's been downhill.'

'In what way?'

'It's hard to know where to begin. Well, okay, the industrial port of Marghera. That's the Big Polluter, the Destroyer of the Ecology in the lagoon! Right? And my father is supposedly a villain for building it. When my father designed Marghera in 1917, Venetians were starving. They were wearing rags, living five in a room. Ten thousand jobs were needed. So he built the port, filled in some marshes, developed the site for the government, and sold parcels of land to various industries – shipyards and manufacturing. It was only after the war, after he was dead, that the people in charge, the idiots, filled in two more big sections of the lagoon. He never intended to do that, and now of course everyone knows it was an ecological mistake.

'But worst of all, also after he was dead, they built oil refineries in Marghera and brought big tankers into the lagoon. Oil tankers draw more water than any other ship in the world, so an extremely deep channel had to be dug for them. The average depth of the lagoon is four or five feet, but the tanker channel is fifty feet deep. Water used to flow gently into and out of the lagoon with the tides. Now it whooshes in and out, and the bottom gets all stirred up. That's what's really destroying the ecology. My father would never have allowed that to happen. And yet he's blamed for it.

'If you watch the tankers cruising through the lagoon, they don't seem to be making waves, but they're displacing eighty thousand tons of water as they move, and the water has to rush in behind them to fill the vacuum. Today the tankers give Venice a wide berth, but in the first few years they came so close they sucked water out of the little side canals as they went by. I used to see it happen outside my door all the time. The water level would suddenly drop – whoosh – and then come rushing back up again. That kind of turbulence destabilizes the foundations.'

Volpi was speaking with energy, but there was a note of despair in his voice. Every so often, he released a deep sigh.

'After the war, my father was investigated for profiting under the regime and brought to trial, and so were other major figures in Italy. He was winning at every turn, when an amnesty was declared and the trial was stopped. That was unfortunate for my father, because it left doubts hanging. And today people still say he got rich through Fascism, but that's just propaganda. Mussolini came to power in 1922. My father had made his fortune in electricity and the CIGA hotel chain decades earlier. He was no more or less a Fascist than Senator Agnelli, who founded Fiat.

'People also say Mussolini gave my father the title of count. Again it's an intentional lie. Wait a minute, I'll be right back.'

Volpi got up and went into the other room. He came back with a photocopy of a letter from Prime Minister Giovanni Giolitti, declaring that His Majesty the King took great pleasure in conferring the hereditary title of count upon Giuseppe Volpi. The letter was dated 23 December 1920 – pre-Mussolini.

'Because of these intentional falsehoods,' Volpi went on, 'Venetians shun the memory of my father. They rarely speak his name. And when they do, it is only because they cannot avoid it. If they give him credit for anything, they declare failure for themselves, because since he died no one in Venice has done anything as positive as he did. His real crime was being a prophet in his own time, in his own country.'

'But,' I said, 'your father is buried at the Frari Church, which is considered the Pantheon of Venice. That's a great honour, isn't it?'

'Sure it is, but Venice didn't put him there. It was Pope John XXIII who did it, and nobody dared say no to him. He knew my father, and he wrote the epitaph engraved on his tomb: 'INGENIO, LABORE ET FIDE [Intelligence, Work and Faith] Johannes XXIII p.p.' Today it would be impossible to bury him at the Frari.'

73

'How does the rest of your family feel about all this?' I asked.

'There is no "rest of the family",' he said. 'I mean, there is, but there isn't.' Volpi paused for a moment and heaved a deep sigh. Then he perked up again. 'Well, I guess now I have to tell you how, or rather why, I was born. Actually, it's a pretty good story.

'In 1937 my father was nearly sixty. He had the two married daughters, one grandson, and two granddaughters but no son of his own. So he goes to the father of his grandson, his son-in-law, who was a Cicogna, an important family name in Milan, and he says, "I'm thinking about what happens after I die. I've spent my whole life building all that I've built, but I don't have a son to leave it to. What would you say if I adopted your son? He would take the name Volpi and carry on after me." The son-in-law decides to play double or nothing, and he says indignantly, "You? A Volpi adopting a Cicogna? You want my son to give up a family name glorified through hundreds of years of history? How can you even *think* such a thing?" He expected my father to come back with an offer of a lot of money. But instead my father cuts him short and says, "Wait a moment! Stop there! Tell you what, this conversation never happened. Excuse me for even mentioning it. As far as I'm concerned, the subject never came up."

'So Cicogna doesn't get double, he gets nothing, and my father goes to my mother and says, "Do you want to make a kid?" And that's how I was born.'

'You have a lot to thank the Cicognas for,' I said.

'Mmm, sure,' said Volpi. 'Anyway, my arrival screwed up my sisters' inheritance expectations, as you can imagine. So in 1946, when my father was very ill, lawyers come to him, accompanied by the good-for-nothing sons-in-law, and they demand he pay them something like twenty million dollars in today's money.

'My father says, "Why? I give my daughters money all the time. But I never dig into capital." So the lawyers say – and this is fantastic – "This time you'll have to dig into capital. Otherwise we'll have the race laws applied, and your marriage will be annulled, because your wife was born a Jew, and to marry a Jew is forbidden, as you know. And we'll have Giovanni's legitimacy annulled as well." '

'I thought all the race laws were cancelled at the end of the war,' I said.

'Yes, but in Italy, not right away. The race laws were not being enforced, but they hadn't actually been abolished yet. So my father, who was pretty cool, sends a friend to talk with the Vatican secretary of state, who says, "As absurd as it might sound, if I were Count Volpi, I would pay, because the case could come before an anti Semitic judge who could legitimately rule against him." '

'My father knew that if he lost, the ruling would be reversed as soon as the race laws were abolished, which was only a matter of time. But by then the horse would be out of the stable, so to speak, and he would never recover all the money, or even most of it. So he takes his good, sweet time and starts paying by instalments. When he's paid three-quarters of it, the race laws are abolished and he stops paying. My half-sisters have always sworn they never blackmailed their father, but there's the record of the money he paid them. So then they say, well, it was their husbands who did it.'

'Where are your half-sisters now?'

'They were thirty years older than me. One's dead, the other lives near the Salute.'

'Is she as resentful as you are about the lack of respect for your father's memory?'

'Resentful? On the contrary,' said Volpi, 'she denounced him herself! She gave interviews on American television in the 1960s and 1970s, saying her father had "unfortunately" created Marghera. When you hear that from one of his daughters, you naturally have to assume that Giuseppe Volpi must really have been a criminal.'

'Have you ever talked to her about it?'

'I haven't spoken to her since 1947.'

'That's heavy.'

'Well, but it's so unjust! Venice was my father's passion. He had nothing but the best interests of Venice at heart. Somebody – I won't tell you who – somebody wrote a really wonderful description of him. I'll read it to you.'

Volpi took a book from the shelf and read a passage from it:

'"Count Giuseppe Volpi is perhaps the only Venetian who truly loves his hometown. For him, Venice is the universal city. If the world became one big Venice, the site of the foremost of human sentiments, he would deem himself to be a happy man. His melancholy hinges on the knowledge that this dream can never be realized."'

Volpi closed the book.

'Okay,' I said. 'Who wrote it?'

'Mussolini.'

'Could you ever love Venice?' I asked.

'I do love Venice. It's the Venetians I'm pissed off with. They're consumed by jealousy and envy – of everyone and everything. They're clowns.'

'What would it take for you, finally, to let go of your anger?' I asked.

Volpi thought for a moment, then sighed one of his deep sighs. 'The accounts between this city and my father are not settled yet. If Venice names a street or a square after him – and not a minor one – then, and only then, I might feel they've given him the recognition he deserves.'

5

Slow Burn

O N THE SAME AFTERNOON THAT Mario Moro was reliving the night of the Fenice fire, waving signals to his imaginary water-bearing helicopter, the panel of experts investigating the fire handed the chief magistrate their preliminary report: arson had not been the cause.

The experts had reached this conclusion, they said, because it had been established that the last workmen had left the theatre at 7.30 p.m., and the fire had not broken out until at least an hour later. According to their theory, fires caused by arson generally involve the use of a highly flammable substance and are raging within minutes of being set. Accidental fires tend to smoulder awhile, and from all appearances the fire at the Fenice had smouldered for at least two hours. Heavy wooden beams supporting the floor of the foyer on the third level, the *ridotto del loggione*, where the blaze had presumably started, had burned through completely, indicating a slow, penetrating start to the fire. Most likely, according to the preliminary report, the fire started when resins used to refinish the wooden flooring had been accidentally ignited by a spark, or a short circuit, or the stub of a cigarette, or the heat from an overloaded electrical cable. More than a thousand kilos of the resins had been stored in the *ridotto*, and some of the containers had been left open. The experts also noted that eight people who had been in the vicinity of the Fenice that evening had come forward after the fire to say they had smelt something burning as early as six o'clock. This, too, would have been consistent with a smouldering fire.

Given what they knew, the experts estimated that the fire had smouldered for two or three hours, meaning that it had started around 6.00 p.m.

In their initial report, the experts cited the chaotic conditions at the Fenice that had made an accidental fire a near inevitability. The prosecutor, Felice Casson, compiled a list of people he deemed responsible for those conditions, then summoned them to the chief magistrate's office and informed them they were under investigation for criminal negligence. It was understood that if the investigations resulted in formal charges, he would seek jail terms.

Mayor Massimo Cacciari headed the list of possible defendants. As mayor, Cacciari was automatically president of the Fenice, so the safety of the theatre was his responsibility. The others under investigation included the general manager of the Fenice, the secretary-general, the financial chief, the custodian, the director of the restoration work, and the chief engineer of Venice.

Most of the accused were men of influence, and they immediately hired the most politically powerful lawyers available. Despite elements of the case in their favour, however, there was one significant factor working against them: Felice Casson, an unusually courageous and relentless prosecutor.

The forty-two-year-old Casson did not look the part. Bespectacled and slight of stature, he had lank brown hair, a pallid complexion, and a youthful face, the most prominent feature of which, paradoxically, was a receding chin. Casson had been born in Chioggia, a tiny fishing village at the southern tip of the Lido, and he was utterly without social pretence or ambition. His one sartorial quirk was a preference for collarless sport shirts, which he wore virtually all the time, even under his black judicial robes. He played on a soccer team with other magistrates, but his real passion was American basketball. On trips to the United States, even business trips, he always made arrangements to see at least one NBA game, and he still talked about a memorable contest between the Chicago Bulls and the New York Knicks in which

Michael Jordan managed to brush off two defensive players assigned to guard him throughout the game. But, all in all, Felice Casson was the sort of person who could pass through a roomful of people unnoticed. His presence was so light that you could almost imagine him walking through walls. However, he had one physical characteristic that hinted at the presence of an inner turbulence, of banked fires waiting to burst into flame. It was the tendency, when he was angered, for his face to turn pink, then red, then scarlet, from the top of his forehead to the neckband of his collarless shirt. Neither his expression nor his voice betrayed the slightest emotion, but there was no disguising the litmus of his face. He was known for it. Defendants due to be cross-examined by Casson were cautioned to watch for the crimson blush and to be guided accordingly.

Casson had established himself as a hard-driving investigating prosecutor early in his career when, in 1982, he reopened an unresolved 1972 bombing case in which three policemen had been murdered near Trieste. The policemen, responding to a telephone tip about a suspicious car, had opened the bonnet of the car and set off a bomb that killed them instantly. The deaths were blamed on the militant Red Brigades, and hundreds of leftists were brought in for questioning, but no one was ever charged. Ten years later, Casson, then a twenty-eight-year-old prosecutor, was given the task of reviewing the case in the expectation that he would tie up a few loose ends and close the file for good.

Instead, despite receiving intentionally misleading information from the police and the secret service, Casson managed to turn the case on its head. He discovered, first of all, that the police had never investigated the incident. When he traced the explosives, he found that the trail led to a *right*-wing group. He quickly arrested the culprit and obtained a confession that included the startling revelation that within three weeks of the bombing, the true story had been known to the police, the Ministry of the Interior, the Customs and Excise police, and the civilian and military secret services. All of these agencies had conspired to cover it up for political reasons. Casson put the guilty party behind bars, but he did not stop there.

He demanded and was granted permission to search the archives of the Italian secret service. There he found documents revealing the existence of a covert, high-level paramilitary army, code-named Gladio, that had been set up and financed by the American CIA in 1956 for the purpose of waging guerrilla warfare in case the Soviet Union ever invaded Italy. Gladio was furnished with a secret training camp in Sardinia and had 139 arms and weapons depots hidden across northern Italy. Gladio's 622 operatives were trained in intelligence-gathering, sabotage, radio communications, and creating escape networks.

While the establishment of a 'stay-behind' resistance militia could be justified in the Cold War environment, Casson found disturbing references to 'internal subversion' in the Gladio documents. Casson then discovered that the organization's largely far-right-wing network of operatives had used Gladio's supplies and infrastructure to stage terrorist attacks within Italy, with the intention of implicating domestic political parties on the left.

Quietly pursuing his investigation through the 1980s, Casson uncovered evidence linking Gladio to a wave of deadly bombings in Italy during the 1970s and 1980s, all of which had been blamed on the left. The chain of evidence also suggested that Gladio had taken part in no fewer than three abortive attempts to overthrow the legitimate government of Italy – in 1964, 1969, and 1973.

Casson finally went public in 1990, when he insisted on interviewing Italy's prime minister, Giulio Andreotti. He forced Andreotti to go before Parliament and deliver a detailed report about Gladio, which for thirty years he had denied existed. At the same time, Casson subpoenaed President Francesco Cossiga and compelled him to admit under oath that he had helped organize Gladio when he worked in the Ministry of Defence in the 1960s. Andreotti soon ordered Gladio dismantled.

As a direct result of Casson's revelations, information came pouring out about the existence of similar Gladio-type secret armies set up by the CIA in France, Spain, Belgium, the Netherlands, Greece, Germany, Switzerland, Austria, Denmark, Sweden, Norway, Finland, and Turkey.

Casson's pursuit of Gladio was unflinching, despite the obvious danger. As he later admitted, 'It was a terrible feeling to realize that I was the only person who knew about the existence of Gladio, except for the members of Gladio themselves, and to think they could kill me at any moment.'

Compared to the harrowing ordeal of stalking a murderous clandestine militia all by himself, the prospect of taking on a group of genteel white-collar functionaries for malfeasance at the Fenice Opera House must have seemed to Casson like gliding in a gondola.

Knowing that any attempt at deal-making would be futile, lawyers for the accused instead attacked the credibility of Casson's panel of experts. Francesco d'Elia, the attorney for the Fenice's custodian, heaped scorn on the selection of two of the experts: Alfio Pini, the head of the fire brigade, and Leonardo Corbo, the national director of civil protection.

'They name the fire chief as an expert?' d'Elia exclaimed to a television reporter. 'He should be a defendant! He was five minutes away from the Fenice when the fire started, but he didn't get there until half an hour later. What took him so long? Even I was there before he was. And his boss in Rome, Corbo, he should be held responsible too, because the fire brigade mishandled the fire in every way. Did they use the proper procedures? Did they have the proper equipment? The fire chief and his boss say yes, but what do you expect them to say? If they had told the truth, it would have amounted to an admission of guilt.

'The firemen didn't know in advance that the canal at the Fenice was empty and closed, and they should have. They had to turn back and go down another canal, wasting precious minutes.

'All they had with them were old canvas hoses, three of which broke and had to be fixed.

'They had old wooden ladders, which were too short to reach the windows.

'They didn't have fire-resistant uniforms.

'They didn't have canisters that release oxygen-absorbing chemicals that literally suffocate a fire. This is standard equipment for fighting fires in empty buildings today. The firemen were inadequately equipped, and that's the fault of Pini and Corbo, the so-called experts.'

In response to these charges, Casson explained that the fire chief, Alfio Pini, was included in the panel in order to provide safe access to the Fenice and help the panel obtain anything it felt it needed in the way of evidence. Leonardo Corbo, the director of Italy's civil protection, had a lengthy list of credentials as an expert in fires and firefighting, with special expertise relating to fires in theatres. Though Casson coolly dismissed d'Elia's objections, it was noted that the telltale flush in Casson's face had reached a dangerous shade of pink.

Casson had been the magistrate on call the night the Fenice caught fire, which meant that he was the first city official the police and fire departments were supposed to contact in case of an emergency. In the excitement, they forgot. However, Casson lived with a woman who was a television journalist for RAI; they were at home in Cannaregio when she received a call from RAI about the fire. They went up to their *altana* and saw the flames. Five minutes later, Casson was in a police launch on the way to the Fenice. He arrived on the scene in time to witness a territorial dispute between the local police and the national police, the *carabinieri*. Both were claiming they had arrived at the fire first. A police officer was saying to an officer of the *carabinieri*, 'In any case, we have jurisdiction in the city, and you don't,' and the *carabiniere* countered with, 'But we are better equipped to handle this kind of investigation than you are.' Casson performed his first official act of the night by intervening and telling both sides that the office of the public prosecutor was responsible, so he, Casson, would decide who was in charge of what.

Shortly before midnight, Casson went to police headquarters, the Questura, and signed an order sealing the theatre and making it a crime for anyone to enter it without authorization. His intention was to protect the integrity of the evidence, and to do that he was willing to keep the theatre sealed for months if necessary. He would not permit salvage crews to move any of the debris until the investigators had finished their work. He even rebuffed the superintendent, who was struggling to arrange a benefit concert for the Fenice and wanted to retrieve files on major donors from his office, which was in a part of the building that was not completely destroyed.

Casson gave the panel of experts sixty days to complete their technical analysis of the evidence and issue a final report. He wanted answers to eleven questions: the time and place the fire started; whether the cause was arson or negligence; the time of the 'flashover', when the fire spread to other parts of the theatre; the condition of the theatre before the fire; the extent of fire-prevention systems inside and outside the theatre; the situation regarding the canals around the Fenice; the condition of smoke and fire detectors prior to the fire; the nature of substances present in the theatre at the time of the fire; analysis of the ashes from the *ridotto*; a description of the wiring in the theatre; and, finally, an estimate of damages and identification of those responsible for any dangerous conditions.

It was generally assumed that the panel's ultimate conclusions would confirm its preliminary finding, which, as the *Gazzettino* reported, ruled out arson 'with near-mathematical certainty'.

Leonardo Corbo, the civil protection chief from Rome, had been named chairman of the panel. He announced that they would study the rubble of the theatre with forensic precision, as if the Fenice were a corpse laid out on an autopsy table.

'Every fire has its DNA,' he said, 'its black box. Fires leave certain indelible traces. Some are obvious and can be identified at a glance. Others cannot be seen with the naked eye but can be analysed with the help of sophisticated technologies and instruments, which, fortunately, we have.'

Two weeks after the fire, courtesans and Casanovas began appearing in the streets of Venice, the former in low-cut bodices and silk stockings, the latter in knee breeches, all in powdered wigs. People in masks, capes, gowns, frock coats, buckled shoes, and all manner of silly hats swarmed through the streets from early morning till late at night in celebration of Carnival. A mime, his hands, face, and hair painted silver to match his silver clothes, stood stock-still at the foot of the Accademia Bridge, a statue in monochrome. A circle of onlookers stood around him, watching for the slightest blink or tremble to assure themselves they were looking at a live person. Another mime, this one solid gold, struck poses in St Mark's Square; a third, pure white, stood immobile for thirty minutes in Campo San Bartolomeo, near the Rialto.

The colourful celebration swirling through the streets was actually a recent revival of the centuries-old Venetian festival. Napoleon had put an end to it when he defeated the Venetian Republic. By then Carnival had reached the height of decadence, having grown from a two-week period of merrymaking to six months of parties, dances, spectacles, games, and walking around Venice behind masks, incognito. It was not until the late 1970s that a serious revival took place; it was prompted in part by Federico Fellini's exotic and surreal 1976 film *Casanova*. The reincarnation of Carnival started in a small way, on the island of Burano and in working-class districts, with plays and costume parties in the local squares. Before long the revels became citywide, then tourists started joining in, and finally an industry grew up around them, the most noticeable feature being the mask shops opening all over Venice. They were little nooks of colour and fantasy, their stage-lit windows lighting up darkened side-streets all year long. Soon masks were a favourite tourist icon. But with the appearance of each new mask shop, there always seemed to be one fewer greengrocer, one fewer bakery, one fewer butcher's shop, to the consternation of Venetians, who found themselves having to walk twice as far to buy a tomato or a loaf of bread. Mask shops became a detested symbol of the city's capitulation to tourism at the expense of its liveability.

One mask shop, however, was spared any such opprobrium. It was Mondonovo, the studio of Guerrino Lovato, a sculptor and set designer, who had been instrumental in resurrecting Carnival back in the days when it was attended only by Venetians. Lovato had started making masks in his sculpture studio, almost as a public service. They were a beloved novelty, and his studio became the first mask shop in Venice.

Mondonovo was a few steps beyond the Ponte dei Pugni, the 'Bridge of Fists'. The front of the shop was cluttered with sculpted objects piled on shelves, hanging on walls, suspended from the ceiling, leaning, standing, and stacked on the floor. There was hardly any room for customers to move. In addition to masks, Signor Lovato and his assistants also made figurines, busts, cherubs, escutcheons, and various pieces of architectural ornamentation in the baroque rococo style. But masks predominated.

Signor Lovato was a muscular man with a dense, dark beard turning white. The day I met him, he was wearing a bulky grey sweater and a knitted cap. While a young assistant sat at a worktable applying gold paint to a papier-mâché mask, Signor Lovato showed me the classic Carnival masks, starting with the earliest, which were based on the *commedia dell'arte* characters – Pulcinello, Pedrolino, Harlequin, the Plague Doctor, and Brighella. The mask for each character was distinguished by a salient feature: a hooked nose, a long nose, a wart on the forehead.

'By the eighteenth century,' Lovato said, 'people were wearing masks in public most of the time, and for one reason only – to be anonymous. So the most popular masks then were plain ones that covered the whole face and represented no characters at all. They, too, have become classics.' He showed me two: a plain black mask for women, called a *morello*, and a white mask for men, called a *bauta*, which had a jutting, prowlike nose and a jaw that came all the way down to the chin. The *bauta* was usually worn with a tricorne hat.

While the *bauta* had no expression at all, its ghostly pallor and sharp features gave it a malevolent look. So I decided to buy a conservative, dark purple mask of the Lone Ranger variety to wear at the Carnival ball the Lauritzens had invited me to attend.

As I was paying the young assistant, I peered over her shoulder into Signor Lovato's workroom. Large photo art books were strewn about the place, propped up and open to photographs of the Fenice – the golden tiers of balconies, close-up shots of sculpted figures and gilded ornamentation.

'I see you're studying the Fenice,' I said.

'A disaster!' said Lovato.

'Do you expect to have a hand in the reconstruction?'

'Who knows? There aren't many of us left who do this kind of work.' He motioned for me to come into his workroom.

'There's a tremendous amount of sculptural detail that will have to be remade,' he said. 'But, unfortunately, nothing survived the fire, and the original drawings have been lost. About the only documents that remain are old engravings and photographs. The trouble is, they are only two-dimensional. A thousand photographs of the same figure will all look different, depending on the lighting, the lens, the camera, the angle of the shot, and the colour reproduction.'

He picked up one of the books. It was open to a photograph of a creamy white mermaid rising from a swirl of gold-leaf waves and curlicues. 'There were twenty-two of these beautiful nymphs around the periphery of the ceiling. They were almost three-quarters life size. If just one of them had survived, even partly, it could answer a lot of questions, but they're all gone.' He turned to a photograph of a cherub. 'Putti,' he said. 'Four of them were playing little wind instruments in the royal box, and there were hundreds of other figures intertwined in the gold-leaf foliage all around the theatre, some of them half hidden. It will take detective work to find them all and then a lot of patience to duplicate them. That is . . . if the Fenice is ever rebuilt.'

'Why wouldn't it be rebuilt?' I asked.

'Everybody wants it to be rebuilt. But this is Italy. The opera house in Genoa, which was bombed during the Second World War, didn't reopen until 1992, forty-eight years later. The Teatro Regio in Turin burned in 1937, and that one took thirty-seven years to be rebuilt.'

'But isn't the Fenice even more important symbolically to Venice than those were to Genoa and Turin?'

'Yes,' said Lovato, 'because of its role in the history of opera. And the design of it makes it even more deeply symbolic of Venice than most people realize. I'll show you what I mean.'

He thumbed through one of the books until he came to a diagram of the Fenice.

'The audience comes in here, through the Apollonian entrance wing, which is neoclassical in style. Apollo is the god of the sun, the god of order and reason. The rooms are formal and symmetrical, and although the decoration is opulent, it is very restrained. Then, as the members of the audience pass from the Apollonian wing into the auditorium, they suddenly find themselves in the midst of a fantastic forest glade, flamboyantly decorated with flowers, vines, faces, masks, satyrs, nymphs, cherubs, griffins, and other mythical creatures. This is the exuberant realm of Dionysus and Bacchus, the ancient gods of wine and revelry.

'The dichotomy between the two cults – Apollonian restraint and Dionysian abandon – is very important to the Italian theatre, and particularly to Venice. Do you know the difference between Apollonian music and Dionysian music? Apollonian music is the music of the city, and that includes opera. It has a codified form and follows accepted structural norms.

'The music of Dionysus is the music of the countryside. It is improvised music, spontaneous, without structure, formless. Nowadays we would call it pop music. It evokes a sense of pure pleasure. It is the music of oblivion, of alcohol, of wine and drunkenness . . . of Dionysus and Bacchus.

'The architect Giovanni Battista Meduna understood that, for Italians, opera is more than just what happens on the stage. The whole experience of going to the opera is a gradually unfolding ritual that begins with the anticipation, getting dressed for the evening, then coming to the theatre, and then entering the place where the main event is going to happen. As with any ritual, whether it takes place in a temple, an arena, or a theatre, the setting is part of the experience.

'Meduna planned the décor of the auditorium so there would be a crescendo of ornamentation. This was the plan: from the orchestra, your eye would be carried upward through the foliage of the magic garden to the wonder of the sky, represented by the shades of blue in the ceiling and the light of the central chandelier, which is Apollo – Apollo being, as I said, the god of the sun. All the other figures in the auditorium belonged to the cult of Dionysus and Bacchus and the woodland spirit of Arcadia, because that's really what the place was meant to represent. There was even a satyr above the stage. The theatre was like a clearing in the forest, an enormous outdoor gazebo with the sky above. The audience was immersed in nature, relaxed, preparing itself for the performance, waiting for the music of Apollo – opera – so they could observe and learn. This was the iconography of the Fenice, and this is how the theatre should be read.'

'I would guess,' I said, 'that you're opposed to the idea of building a modern interior inside the existing shell of the Fenice.'

'Yes, of course, and it really isn't a question of aesthetics. It's a question of preserving the Dionysian experience that Meduna created for the spectator in the auditorium. The lights in the theatre were never completely turned off, even during the performance. They were dimmed to a soft glow, so the spectators could still see the images. The images kept them company. You might have gone to the theatre alone, but you still had company. This is a relationship that modern theatre does not care about. The focus today is completely on the stage. The show is sacred. Everyone must be quiet and watch. Modern theatres are sterile places that have great acoustics and great visibility – but no decoration. You no longer have any company.

'A new Fenice should have state-of-the-art air-conditioning and modern equipment backstage to move scenery, but it really must retain the Dionysian theatre hall.'

'Because Venice is a Dionysian city?'

Lovato laughed. 'Look around you! Look at this shop. Look at the people passing in the street. Carnival is a celebration of the magic, the mystery, and the decadence of Venice. Who would want to lose that?'

The brief lull was over for Venice. Carnival had begun. Narrow streets that had been easily passable for the last few weeks were now solid with tourists, shuffling along in masks and fanciful hats with bells. Venetians no longer had Venice all to themselves, but at least there was the saving grace of a buoyant, lighthearted spirit. The partygoing masquerade rolled through every quarter of the city. It spilled into shops, museums, and restaurants, and floated along the canals on gondolas, water taxis, and *vaporetti*. Even the taste buds rejoiced with the reappearance of the Carnival pastry, *frittelle* – small, sweet fritters studded with raisins and pine nuts and, if one chose, filled with zabaglione or vanilla cream.

Into this madhouse vision of eighteenth-century Venice slipped an unassuming figure who was joined by Mayor Cacciari and a mob of reporters and photographers. Woody Allen had come to Venice to pay his respects to the city he loved and where he and his jazz band were to have given a concert two weeks hence to reopen a renovated Fenice Opera House. Instead, he said, he would now give a concert at the Goldoni Theatre as a benefit for the Fenice. Mayor Cacciari took Woody Allen into the ruin of the Fenice. Allen stared at the bare, horseshoe-shaped brick shell. The only traces of the golden tiers were five rows of evenly spaced holes in the wall where beams supporting the balconies had once been inserted.

'Terrible,' he said. 'Terrifying. It's total devastation. It's unreal.'

The sense of unreality deepened as they emerged from the theatre into the midst of the gaily costumed Carnival throng. Neither man had any idea how much more unreal it would soon become, until Felice Casson issued a warrant charging Woody Allen with trespassing.

6

The Rat Man of Treviso

T WO TIERS OF TALL GOTHIC windows were ablaze with candle-light as the Lauritzens and I approached the landing platform of Palazzo Pisani-Moretta. The Carnival ball was already in progress. Costumed men and women stood on the balconies above us, drinks in hand, looking out over the Grand Canal and the glimmer of lights reflected on the night-blackened water.

'The façade is late-fifteenth-century Gothic,' said Peter. 'Notice the especially fine examples of quatrefoil tracery above the windows of the first *piano nobile*. They're derived, as you've no doubt already surmised, from the Doge's Palace.' Peter was wearing a long black cape and a black mask.

'Trespassing!' said Rose. 'Think of it! How horribly embarrassing for Woody Allen. But Casson was quite right to do it, you know, if he really means to find out what happened at the Fenice.' Rose's hair was combed in an upsweep, with a string of pearls laced through it. She wore a bejewelled black satin mask and an evening dress that was a column of black chiffon. 'He's one of the few honest, incorruptible prosecutors we've got left. A white *knight*! I just pray he doesn't suddenly self-destruct like all the others.'

'Then, in the eighteenth century,' said Peter, 'the strong-willed Chiara Pisani-Moretta redecorated the palazzo at enormous expense, all while laying siege to the courts, hoping to have her brother declared illegitimate so she could spend *his* share of the family patrimony on the palazzo as well.'

Rose lifted the hem of her gown in preparation for stepping on to the dock. 'But, I mean, one does feel sorry for Woody Allen,' she said. 'First his jazz concert gets burned out of the Fenice; then he's arrested for dropping by as a gesture of sympathy.' Rose became distracted by a man in a green mask who was alighting from one of the water taxis ahead of ours. 'Oh, Peter, look. That's Francesco Smeraldi.' Then, turning to me, she said, 'He's a poet nobody reads, because as soon as he finishes a poem, he locks it in a bank vault. He used to teach writing and poetry to schoolchildren until it was found out that he—'

'No, no, Rose, you're wrong,' said Peter. 'That's not Francesco Smeraldi at all. It's—'

'Well, how can anybody tell with that mask he's got on? All I can see is a mouth and chin. Anyway, whether that's him or not, Francesco Smeraldi did fall out of favour when it was discovered he'd taken a group of children on a tour of loos to read the graffiti!'

At the water entrance, we stepped on to a carpeted platform flanked by two flaming torches and walked into a cavernous entry hall with large, gilt-framed lanterns hanging from dark beams. A monumental staircase at the far end led to the first *piano nobile* and a vast centre hall with ceilings richly frescoed in the rococo style. The room was illuminated by nine huge glass chandeliers and six sconces, all of them aglow with masses of tall white candles. Tonight every room in the palace was lit exclusively with candlelight.

The crowd numbered several hundred. The din of their voices had the excited, high-pitched sound of people enjoying the release from stiff formality that masks and costumes conferred, even though most of the people were recognizable despite their masks. There were kisses on both cheeks, overheard snatches of conversation – 'skiing in Cortina,' 'up from Rome,' *'bellissimo!'* – and waves of the hand to friends glimpsed across the room.

We stood at the centre of the room, attended by white-jacketed waiters circulating with trays of wine and pink Bellinis. The Bellinis were authentic: tonight's party was being catered by Harry's Bar, the establishment that invented the drink, a combination of prosecco and the juice of fresh white peaches.

'This palazzo was vacant for over a century,' said Peter. 'It was without central heating, plumbing, gaslight, or electricity until 1974, when it was lovingly restored. The remarkable thing is that the detailing is not only original but intact – the frescos, the mantelpieces, the stucco ornamentation. It took three months just to clean the floor, and what has emerged from the grime is a brilliant example of eighteenth-century terrazzo in perfect condition. As I always say: nothing preserves like neglect.'

'Alvise!' Rose called out, to a shortish, florid-faced, bald-headed man who was walking in our direction at a regal pace. He lifted Rose's hand and nodded towards it, then shook hands with Peter.

'Now, Alvise Loredan is someone you must meet!' Peter said as he introduced me. 'Count Loredan is a quintessential Venetian and a member of one of the oldest patrician families.'

Alvise Loredan fixed his gaze on me and beamed. He had an aristocratic hooked nose, jowls, a fringe of hair, and a solid jaw that in profile I could imagine adorning a coin.

'There have been three doges in my family,' he said in English, holding up three fingers. 'Three!'

'Indeed,' said Peter, 'and Alvise is too modest to tell you, so I will: one of the Loredan doges was Leonardo Loredan, the sixteenth-century doge whose magnificent portrait by Giovanni Bellini is arguably the finest Venetian portrait ever painted. The pity is, it hangs in the National Gallery in London rather than here in Venice.'

Loredan nodded. 'My family goes back to the tenth century in Venice. Loredans won every war they ever fought in, and they fought in all of them. This is very important! If the Loredans hadn't defeated the Turks, first in 1400 and then in Albania, the Turks would have crossed the Adriatic, occupied the Vatican, and wiped out Christianity!'

Count Loredan was alternating between English and Italian now.

'In the state archives,' he said, 'there are letters between popes and the Loredan doges using the familiar *tu* form of address. They were on the same level, both princes. I have copies. I can show you. I have a copy of a letter from Henry VIII to Leonardo Loredan, calling him "our dearest friend". It's all there. This is very important!'

'And,' said Peter, 'as for Loredan palaces . . .'

'There are several in Venice,' the count said proudly. 'Palazzo Loredan in Campo Santo Stefano, where Napoleon established the Venetian Institute of Science, Letters and Arts. Palazzo Corner-Loredan, which is part of the Venice town hall. Palazzo Loredan degli Ambasciatori, which the Holy Roman Empire rented from my family for many years as its embassy to the Republic of Venice. Palazzo Loredan-Cini in Campo San Vio; it was the home of Don Carlos, the pretender to the throne of Spain. And . . . did I say Palazzo Loredan in Campo Santo Stefano? Yes, I said that one . . . Napoleon . . . the institute . . . very important. The most famous one is the Palazzo Loredan-Vendramin-Calergi, where Richard Wagner composed *Parsifal* and died. It is now the Municipal Casino.'

'And it's a masterpiece of Renaissance architecture,' said Peter. 'You can tour it and, while you're there, try your luck at gambling. But we can't go with you, legally. An old statute still on the books forbids residents of Venice to enter the Municipal Casino. But we can ride by it on the *vaporetto* and see the Loredan family motto carved in stone on the waterside façade: NON NOBIS DOMINE NON NOBIS — "Praise us not, O Lord." It's a declaration of humility by a very powerful family.'

'The sign of the Loredan,' said the count, 'was inscribed in many places around Venice. It's at the Rialto and even carved into the façade of St Mark's. This is very important! The basilica is a most prestigious place. But because of the corrosion from pigeon droppings, you can't see the Loredan insignia! It's a paradox. Squalid pigeons are the symbolic heroes of democracy! They are the heroic warriors in democracy's crusade to obliterate any vestige of historic nobility and grandeur.'

Loredan raised an index finger. 'I have written a book about democracy. It's called *Democracy: A Fraud?*. Democracy disgusts me. It makes me sick!' He delivered this sentiment forcefully but without any lapse of affability. As he warmed to his topic, he abandoned English and was now speaking entirely in Italian.

'Do you know what democracy is based on? Numbers! But as everybody knows, when quantity increases, quality decreases. Democracies have a degrading base, because the quality only gets worse and worse. That is why democracies have inept leaders, elected at random. A far better course is to put government in the hands of an élite aristocracy – people who have inherited an aptitude for justice and good government from their noble ancestors. This is true. The best governments have always taken the form of monarchies and élite aristocracies. This has been confirmed historically, genetically, and biologically!'

'I take it,' I said, 'you are referring to such élite governments as that of the old Venetian Republic.'

'*Ecco!* Exactly! The ruling patriarchy. There are very few of us left. The Barbarigo family is extinct. So are the Mocenigos. The Pisanis, who built this palace, have died out, too. So have the Grittis, the Dandolos, the Faliers, the Sagredos, and the Contarinis – eight of the hundred and twenty doges were Contarinis.

'What doges' families are left?'

'The Gradenigo family is still around – they are an old family, but not very important. And, let me see . . . the Verniers. And the Marcellos. You would find my book *Nobility and Government* interesting. I am now writing a book proving the existence of reality! It is already two thousand pages long.'

A book on the subject of reality written by a Venetian had curious possibilities. Loredan seemed on the verge of explaining, but his wife was tugging at his sleeve.

'Well . . . another time,' he said. 'But I will send you a copy of my book explaining why democracy is a fraud.' As he shuffled away, his wife tugging and smiling apologetically, he raised his hand as if to wave goodbye. Instead he held up three fingers. 'Three!' he said. 'Three doges!'

We started walking towards the tall windows on the Grand Canal. Rose pointed out a couple looking in our direction. The man was corpulent and had a head of untamed, wispy red hair and a broad, gap-toothed grin. The woman was dark-haired, lithe, and younger.

'That's Alistair and Romilly McAlpine,' she said. 'Alistair is very tight with Margaret Thatcher. He was treasurer of the Conservative Party when she was prime minister. He collects things. Serious things like paintings by Jackson Pollock and Mark Rothko, and less serious things like shepherds' crooks, rag dolls, and police truncheons – he's got about nine hundred truncheons by now, I think. Romilly has exquisite taste and a huge collection of Vivienne Westwood dresses. Anyway, the McAlpines aren't so much living in Venice as hiding out here, because their house in London was fire-bombed by the IRA, and they've had to – Romilly! Alistair!'

The McAlpines exchanged jolly greetings with the Lauritzens and pronounced themselves pleased to meet me.

'How's the collecting going?' Peter asked.

'I've sold everything!' Lord McAlpine trumpeted.

'That must be a wrenching thing to do,' said Peter.

'Not at all. I have the soul of a nomad and set little store by possessions: I am anxious in their pursuit and casual in their disposal. But I'll admit I'm rather wistful about my collection of garden implements, especially the horse-drawn lawn mower with leather shoes for the horse's hoofs – to protect the lawn. I put all of it under the hammer.'

'Why all?' asked Peter.

'To rid myself of the chore of making a choice!'

'You haven't given up collecting altogether, have you?' Rose asked.

'No, no. I'm always on to something new. I've become interested in neckties, in a small way. I've picked up a few good ones.'

'Oh, Alistair, why not just tell them?' said his wife. 'He's got about four thousand neckties at this point.'

I was fascinated by the McAlpines, but I could not help imagining the sounds of bombs and sirens going off in counterpoint to their small-talk. The fact that they were wearing masks — his being a harlequin style, hers a mass of pink sequins — lent a touch of farce to the notion that they were on the run from the IRA. As soon as they moved on, I asked Rose what she had meant by 'hiding out' from the IRA.

'That's why they're here. After the IRA bombed their house in London, they decided to move to Australia, but the London CID told them, "Don't be silly. All the worst killers in the IRA hide out in Australia." So naturally they asked where it would be safe to go, and funnily enough the police told them Venice! And it's true. In Venice you're very likely to be swindled or have your pocket picked, but you almost certainly won't be kidnapped or murdered.'

'What's to stop someone just shooting you?' I asked. 'Or blowing up your house?'

'Nothing. That would be easy. Escaping would be the hard part, because the police can seal off all the escape routes within minutes. They can close the bridge to the mainland and alert the water taxis. And of course it would be sheer madness for anybody to try making a getaway in a boat by himself. The lagoon may look like a tranquil pond, but it's really very treacherous. One has to know all about the currents, the channels, the sandbars, the tides, the speed limit, and the meaning of all the buoys and signal lights. Anyway, the boat would probably be noticed by all the boatmen in the lagoon — they all know every boat.

'And anyone who wanted to kidnap you would somehow have to drag you out of the house, down the *calle* or whatever, and into a boat without being seen. And that would be impossible, because everywhere in Venice the eyes are watching. And unless the kidnapper was an experienced Venetian boatman himself, he'd have to hire one as an accomplice, and that would complicate matters endlessly, so nobody bothers. Anyway, the murder rate in Venice is practically nil, and that's why rich Italians took apartments here when the Red Brigades were marauding in the 1980s.'

'Rose has been reading too many mystery stories,' said Peter.

Just then, Count Girolamo Marcello walked past, engrossed in conversation with another man. 'A disgrace,' he was saying with a curious smile, 'a disaster! But, actually, it has not been all bad. Before the Fenice burned, my television·reception was very poor. Now I get all the channels with perfect clarity.' Marcello had gained approval for the burial of his friend, the Russian poet Joseph Brodsky, in the cemetery on San Michele, and that, too, had cheered him.

Within half an hour, the crowd began drifting towards the stairs and up to the second *piano nobile*, where waiters in white tunics stood behind two long buffet tables laden with food: platters of thinly sliced prosciutto and air-dried beef, tureens of vegetable-and-shrimp risotto, baked courgettes, and serving dishes heaped with an array of Venetian specialities, including calf's liver and onions, squid and polenta, and a creamy *bacalà mantecato*.

We found seats at a large round table for ten, the Lauritzens directly across from me. To my left, a man and a woman were talking about the Fenice. The man was saying, 'It's the only opera company in the world that kept the original scores of the operas it commissioned, signed by the composer. There were hundreds of them. *La Traviata, Rigoletto, Tancredi*. Today those handwritten scores are worth millions – if they still exist.'

'What do you think?' said the woman. 'Burned to a crisp?'

'Nothing has been said about them, so I fear the worst.'

Seated on my other side was a man whose reddish brown hair had the too-solid look of a toupee. He exuded confidence and introduced himself as Massimo Donadon.

'I'm a chef,' he said, speaking to me and the woman sitting between us. 'My cuisine is known around the world!'

'Really?' the woman said. 'Are you famous for a culinary speciality?'

'Yes,' he said. 'Rat poison.'

The woman drew back. 'You're joking.'

'No, it's true. I make the world's best-selling rat poison. It's called Bocaraton, "rat's mouth" or "mouse's mouth", like the city in Florida. I never understood why anyone would want to live in a city with such a name. But it's perfect for my speciality, which I sell all over the world — in Dubai, New York, Paris, Tokyo, Boston, South America, wherever there are rats. I have thirty per cent of the international rat-poison market.'

'What's your secret?' I asked.

'My competitors approach rat poison the wrong way,' he said. 'They study rats. I study people.' Signor Donadon pointed at my plate with his fork. 'Rats eat what people eat.'

I glanced down at my *fegato alla veneziana* and suddenly saw my dinner in a new light.

'Venetian rats would be very happy to eat what you have on your plate,' he said, 'because they're used to eating that kind of food. But German rats would not be interested at all. They prefer German cuisine — *wurstel*, *Wiener schnitzel*. So for Germany I make a rat poison that is forty-five per cent pork fat. My French rat poison has butter in it. For America I use vanilla, granola, popcorn, and a little margarine, because Americans eat very little butter. I base my New York rat poison on vegetable oils and essential oils with orange fragrance to remind the rats of hamburgers and orange juice. For Bombay I add curry. For Chile, fish meal.

'Rats are very adaptable. If their hosts go on fad diets, the rats go on the diets, too. I maintain thirty research stations around the world so I can update the tastes and flavours of my poisons in order to make them consistent with the latest trends in human dining.'

'What's in your Italian rat poison?' I asked.

'Olive oil, pasta, honey, espresso, green-apple juice, and Nutella. Especially Nutella. I buy tons of it. Rats love it. I told the Nutella company I would be happy to endorse it on television, and they said, "Oh, God, no! We beg you. Please tell no one!"'

The woman sitting on the far side of Signor Donadon put both of her hands flat on the table as if to steady herself. 'I simply will not listen to a discussion of rats while I'm having dinner!' she said, and then, as much in the spirit of melodrama as of anger, she turned her back.

Signor Donadon continued unperturbed. 'Everyone is fascinated by rats. Even people who say they're not. What they really mean to say is, "Oh, that's disgusting, I can't bear it, tell me more!"'

The couple on my left, I noticed, had stopped talking about the Fenice and were giving Donadon their full attention.

'But if a rat is hungry,' I said, 'won't it eat just about anything?'

'Absolutely,' said Signor Donadon, 'but rats are better fed than ever, because there's more rubbish than ever. So they've become very choosy about what they eat. In the 1950s, people used to throw only one-half of one per cent of their food into the rubbish, and rats had to eat whatever they could find. Today seven per cent of our food ends up in the rubbish, and it's a never-ending banquet for rats. The challenge, for me, is to make my rat poison more appetizing than rubbish. Rubbish is the real competition.

'Rats are smarter than men and better organized. They have instinctive rituals designed to ensure the survival of their species. For instance, whenever rats find something that looks like food, the oldest rats always eat it first. Other brands of rat poison cause immediate pain, a burning sensation, or dizziness. If the older rats display any ill effects, the younger ones won't touch it. But Bocaraton outwits them. It causes no pain at all when it's eaten. It takes four days to have an effect, and by then the younger rats have eaten it, too.'

'Tell me,' said the woman to my left, 'how does a person decide to devote his life to the killing of rats?'

'Ah, Signora!' said Donadon. 'When I stood at my grandmother's deathbed, she made me promise to make a contribution to humanity. Since I was a boy, I had always been interested in chemistry and medicine. I decided I would find a cure for cancer. I knew that DDT caused cancer, so I went into several butcher shops and told them I was representing an American company named Max Don Brasileria – I made up the name – and that we made insecticides without using DDT. I said, "I will get rid of your flies."

'The first butcher said, "If you can do that, I'll pay any price." Flies were depositing their eggs all over his meat. It was a disaster. I picked a number out of the air, and I said, "It will cost you thirty thousand lire," and he said, "Do it." By the end of the day, I'd picked up order worth one hundred and fifty thousand lire, which was a lot of money in those days.

'I was overjoyed. But I didn't have a product! Also, I was broke. So I stopped in at a bar in Treviso, where I live – that's eighteen miles north of Venice – and I talked two friends into going into business with me. I immediately moved into the Carlton Hotel in Treviso, and with the help of the telephone operator and the hotel porter, I led clients to believe that this was the Italian headquarters of the American insecticide company.

'How did we kill flies? We used a phosphorus compound made by Montedison. If you used it today, you would probably go to jail. It's too toxic. But it worked. Business grew. People heard about us.

'Then I got a call from Count Borletti, the sewing-machine king, and he asked me to rid his stable of flies. One day Borletti said to me, "Massimo, what are you going to do in the winter when there are no flies? Killing flies is a seasonal business. But rats are a pest all year. You should consider making rat poison."

'What a brainstorm! That very night, I started experimenting in my bathroom sink at the hotel. I kneaded ten pounds of pork fat and coumarin with my bare hands, and in the morning I changed everything – my company, its name, and its mission. That was 1970. We were an immediate success, and we've only grown since then. I admit that killing rats may not be as noble a profession as curing cancer, but at least I'm making a contribution to humanity, and my grandmother can rest in peace.'

Donadon handed each of us his card. The company's name was 'Braün Mayer Deutschland'.

'I thought you were Italian,' I said.

'I am, but if I had given my company an Italian name, people would think, "This product was made in Italy? I don't trust it." Italy has an image of being nothing but Mafia, tailors, and shoemakers. On the other hand, Germany is solid, scientific, and efficient. If anyone could be counted on to kill a rat, a German would be the one. So I chose a name that sounded very German. "Mayer" is the German equivalent of Smith. "Braün" reminds you of Wernher von Braun, the man who designed the rockets that took men to the moon, and that gives you confidence. The umlaut over the *u* shouldn't be there, but it reinforces the Germanness of the name. And "Deutschland" speaks for itself.'

'Very shrewd,' I said.

'My little company became part of the famous economic boom in northern Italy. Did you know that here in northern Italy we have the highest concentration of businesses in the world? It's true: there's one company for every eight inhabitants. They're mostly small, family-run companies. Like mine, and like Benetton, which is run by my old friend Luciano Benetton. Luciano was born and raised in Treviso, like me, and we both have our world headquarters in Treviso.'

'The Two Titans of Treviso,' I said.

'Well . . .' Signor Donadon blushed. 'Luciano has a genius for making money, and he's very good at holding on to it, too. I've known him for more than thirty years, and I love him. But as rich as he is, he's never so much as bought me lunch! He loves my cooking, though, so he comes to my house often for dinner. I cook for rats and for Luciano Benetton.'

'Have you and Benetton ever worked together?'

'No, but we've both used the same photographer for our ads – Oliviero Toscani, the guy who created the "United Colors of Benetton" ad campaign and *Colors* magazine. I got Toscani to shoot an ad for my rat poison. It was based on *The Last Supper*. All the men had rat heads, even Christ. But I got talked out of using it.'

Signor Donadon began eating his dinner, and as he did so a commotion erupted at the far end of the hall. A cluster of late arrivals had made a showy entrance involving a flowing white silk scarf and a great deal of glitter. The scarf belonged to a tall, lanky man in a dinner jacket and aviator-style horn-rimmed glasses. He was exchanging greetings with people at various tables. The glitter was his entourage: three beautiful women, one of whom was wearing a sequined body stocking.

'They're models or actresses, probably,' the woman to my left said, having noticed I was watching. 'He's Vittorio Sgarbi, an art critic and one of Italy's great seducers, self-proclaimed. He's already written his autobiography, and he's only forty-five – sees himself as a modern-day Casanova. He's very smart and extremely glib. He has a daily commentary slot on television, so he's a famous national figure.'

'Ah, the admirable Sgarbi,' said the man with her. 'I wonder if he's still barred from the Courtauld Institute in London. They caught him walking out of the door with two valuable old books not that long ago. It attracted a lot of notice in the press, not only because he was an art critic but because he was also a member of the Italian parliament. He's in the Chamber of Deputies. Chairman of the Committee on Culture, no less. He was at the Courtauld that day to speak in a symposium about painters of the Ferrara school. When they grabbed him, he claimed he had only wanted to study the books and photocopy them. In his autobiography, he said he'd been set up by another art critic who was jealous.'

Sgarbi was walking past, one hand running through his mop of brown hair, the other wrapped round the waist of one of his female friends.

The man sitting next to me, eyes on Sgarbi, continued talking. 'Then there was the business about Sgarbi and an old woman in a nursing home. Sgarbi persuaded the woman to sell a valuable painting to an art-dealer friend of his for a mere eight million lire. Three years later, the painting brought seven hundred million lire at auction. Then it turned out that the painting had been in storage in a museum in Treviso, which had an option to buy it from the woman. Sgarbi, who was working for the fine-arts superintendency at the time, had an obligation to inform the museum but didn't. When the sale was discovered, he was investigated for fraud and for private dealing while acting in an official capacity. The charges were dropped, of course.'

'I suppose the damage to his career had already been done,' I said.

'Not really. He's now being talked about as our next minister of culture.'

In my other ear, I heard the word 'rat' again – to be precise, I heard the word *pantegana*, which is 'rat' in the Venetian dialect. 'Rats cannot vomit,' Signor Donadon was saying. 'They are one of the few species on earth that are physically unable to throw up. So they cannot expel my poison once they've eaten it. But it's safe to use the poison, because if people, cats, or dogs eat even a single gram of it, they vomit immediately, before it can do any harm.'

The woman who had sworn she would not listen to talk about rats during dinner had swung back around and was now facing Signor Donadon, completely entranced.

'But if hundreds of thousands of rats die at the same time,' she said, 'won't they decompose and cause the plague?'

'My poison dehydrates them,' said Signor Donadon, patting her hand in reassurance, 'it dries them out, mummifies them. So they don't rot, and there is no plague.'

'They bite people, don't they?' she said, wrinkling her nose. 'The idea horrifies me.'

'If a rat bit you,' said Donadon, 'you might not even feel it.'

'Because I'd be in shock.'

'No. You wouldn't feel it because rat saliva contains an anaesthetic. One of the government cabinet ministers, Riccardo Misasi, was asleep in bed one night, and he felt his toe itch. The itch got stronger, and when he turned the light on, he discovered his toe had just been gnawed off by a rat!'

Signor Donadon seemed prepared to go on in this vein for quite a while, but the other guests were stirring.

'There's just one thing I wanted to ask you,' I said as I rose to leave the table. 'If your poison is as effective as you say it is, why are there any rats left in Venice at all?'

'Very simple!' he said. 'Venice doesn't use my poison. The city council always awards contracts to the lowest bidder, so I don't even bother tendering a bid. I'm prepared to make my contribution to humanity, but' – Donadon winked – 'humanity must be willing to make a contribution to me.'

The serving of coffee and tiramisu provided the occasion to change places, mill around, or head down two floors to the entrance hall, where a dance band had begun to make its presence felt. It occurred to me, as I looked at the crowd, that not a single mask remained in place. It was not just that the masks had been removed to facilitate eating. They had been pushed up on top of heads, stuffed into handbags, or otherwise made to disappear well before dinner. I noticed also that, except for the odd decorative ribbon or wild tie, almost all the men were wearing traditional formal attire rather than costumes. The women, too, had ventured no further than their accessories in fashioning their costumes: ostrich feathers, outlandish jewellery, a novel hairstyle or some other cosmetic flourish. Anyone arriving at the ball at this hour would hardly have known it was a Carnival ball, let alone a masked or a costume ball.

'What's happened to the spirit of Carnival?' I asked Peter Lauritzen as we made our way downstairs.

'Well, it will never be what it was at the height of decadence in the eighteenth century,' he said. 'Carnival was a powerful institution then. When Doge Paolo Renier died during Carnival in 1789, word of his death was suppressed until Carnival was over so as not to spoil the fun.'

As reinvented in the twentieth century, it seemed, Carnival was a tamer version of its former self. Lacking the context of pervasive decadence, even depravity, Carnival was little more than a comparatively chaste celebration of a long-gone historical phenomenon.

'Not all Carnival parties are as proper as this one,' said Rose. 'I mean, there is a more earthy side to Carnival even now.'

'And where would that be found?' I asked.

'The Erotic Poetry Festival is one place. It's usually held in Campo San Maurizio, where the eighteenth-century poet Giorgio Baffo lived. Baffo's poetry is usually described as "licentious". In fact, it's downright pornographic!'

The dance band on the ground floor was loud enough to drive all but the hardiest dancers from the palace, and we were soon standing on the landing platform waiting for our water taxi.

While we waited, a gondola approached. It was moving slowly in the direction of St Mark's and carried two passengers, both men. One was wearing a billowing, bushy black wig, a black fur jacket, black tights, and a bright red mask with a long nose.

The other man had a far stranger costume. He wore a shiny red rubber wig or headdress that formed a smooth, rounded cone from the top of his head down to the full width of his shoulders. His arms and torso were wrapped in a sheath of loosely draped pink rubber, and each of his knees was encased in a melon-size pink sphere. The meaning of his costume became abundantly clear as he slowly rose to a standing position. By the time he was fully erect, the pink rubber sheath had been stretched smooth. A white plastic drool hung from his mouth like an elongated pearl.

A woman standing next to me gasped, then giggled. A man behind me murmured, '*Fantastico!*'

Then, as the gondola glided by, the other man stood up, the man in the black fur jacket and the bushy black wig. His gaze swept the landing platform as he stared at each of us through his bright red mask, past his long red nose. Then he flung open his jacket, much in the manner of a flasher, and revealed a brilliant expanse of surprisingly lifelike pink satin labial folds.

'Now, that's what *I* call Carnival,' said Rose.

7

Glass Warfare

'MY FATHER HAS ALWAYS BEEN a man of few words,' said Gino Seguso, 'and lately he's being saying fewer words than ever — even to us.'

It was June. Archimede Seguso was deeply engrossed at his glass factory, making the series of bowls and vases that recalled the night, four months earlier, when he stood at his bedroom window and watched the Fenice burn. Gino had invited me to come to the Seguso glassworks on Murano to have a look at the 'La Fenice' collection, which by now had grown to eighty pieces. It had become Archimede Seguso's obsession.

The frenzied aftermath of the fire had abated considerably. By the end of February, prosecutor Felice Casson had dropped his trespassing charges against Woody Allen. (Months later Mayor Cacciari would officiate at the wedding of Woody Allen and Soon-Yi in a private civil ceremony at Palazzo Cavalli, the Venice city hall.) The Fenice's resident orchestra had given its first postfire concert in St Mark's Basilica with a programme of passion, hope, and optimism: Gustav Mahler's *Resurrection* symphony. As for rebuilding the Fenice, Mayor Cacciari chose to open the project to competitive bids. This course had the advantage of insulating Cacciari from accusations of favouritism or bribery, but it had drawbacks too: the process of solicitation, submission, and judging would take at least a year.

Meanwhile the opera company itself had succeeded in finding a temporary home in time to open its season on schedule and avoid having to pay refunds to thousands of ticket-holders. The opera's new venue was a giant circus tent pitched in a car park on Tronchetto Island at the foot of the bridge to the mainland. The tent was known as Palafenice, and its six white peaks became a landmark on the edge of the Venetian horizon – a visible reminder that the real Fenice lay in ruins.

At Archimede Seguso's glassworks, however, the opera house was still on fire. It flickered and shimmered, swirled and spiralled in the pieces Seguso was making. Gino walked me through the showroom on the way to the factory floor. His manner was warm, good-humoured, and correct. In his late fifties, he was stocky, balding except for a fringe of dark hair, and dressed in a business suit. We stood in front of a shelf crowded with La Fenice vases.

'People picture the flames as being bright orange and yellow,' he said, 'because that's how it looked in newspapers and magazines. They don't realize how much more than that it really was. There were greens and blues and purples. The colours kept changing all night, depending on what was burning inside the theatre. My father was as close to it as anybody, and these are his personal snapshots. They achieve an accuracy that photographs weren't able to capture.

'My father has never made anything like these before. You can see what I mean if you look around the room at the other things.'

The showroom was a museum of glass objects made by Archimede Seguso from the 1930s to the present day, including a glass table and examples of his famous series from the 1950s called Merletti (Lace) in which filaments of coloured glass were embedded in bowls and vases. As I walked around the room, I kept my hands jammed into my pockets and my arms pressed against my sides for fear I might elbow one of the larger pieces off its pedestal and send it crashing to the floor.

Gino told me a story about his father's tendency to be taciturn, probably to set me at ease in case the maestro did not engage me in conversation. Back in the 1950s, he said, a wealthy Sicilian prince brought Signor Seguso a glass bull that was supposed to have been found in an Etruscan tomb. The prince asked Seguso if he could authenticate it. Signor Seguso set the bull down on a table next to his workbench and proceeded to make an exact copy, correct to the smallest detail, including the surface patina, which he antiqued with the application of powders, minerals, smoke, and sand. When he was finished, the prince could not see any difference between the new bull and the old one. And that was Archimede Seguso's answer. He had been able to duplicate the bull so precisely that, by doing so, he proved the prince's bull could have been a fake. Scientific tests would be required to find out for certain, but Signor Seguso could respond only on his level of expertise. His answer therefore was, I don't know.

I said I would not be offended if the maestro chose to go on working rather than talk with me. But when we opened the door to the furnace room, we were bombarded by such a roar from the ovens that conversation would have been impossible anyway.

The old man, wearing dark slacks and a white shirt, was seated at his workbench in front of a blazing furnace. He was turning a steel rod at the end of which was a large cylindrical vase, its blue and white colours alternating in a supple, harlequin pattern. As he turned the rod, he shaped the mouth of the vase with a pair of tongs. Then he handed the rod to an assistant, who inserted it back into the furnace to heat the vase and soften it a bit. Gino walked over to his father and spoke into his ear. Archimede turned and looked in my direction. He smiled and indicated with his head that I should come over to him. I did, and said hello. He nodded in response. The assistant pulled the vase out of the fire and rested the rod on the edge of the workbench, still turning it. Archimede looked up at me again and pointed at the vase with his tongs. 'Dawn,' he said. 'It's dawn.' Then he went back to work, turning the rod and shaping the vase.

Those were the three words Archimede Seguso spoke to me. They were enough to let me know that the vase he was making represented the Fenice as he had seen it when he rose at five o'clock the morning after the fire: white smoke rising against a medium-blue sky just before sunrise.

We watched him work for another ten minutes and then went to Gino's office for coffee. Gino's son, Antonio, appeared at the doorway briefly. He was in his late twenties, thin and shy. He resembled his grandfather more than his father and had the deferential manner of a dutiful son and grandson. Antonio worked at the factory, Gino said, gaining experience in each of the departments. He would eventually take over the management of the business from his father. His grandfather had given him a few lessons in glassblowing.

'I've been wondering,' I said to Gino. 'Earlier generations of Segusos were glassblowers, but that required starting at such an early age that there was no time for a formal education. Neither you nor your son is a master glassblower. What happens after Archimede?'

'There will always be master glassblowers,' said Gino, 'whether or not they are Segusos. But one needs artists as well. There are masters and there are artists. An artist has an idea. A master translates that idea into glass. Very few master glassblowers are also artists. My father is a rare exception. When he dies, our glassblowers will continue to produce his classic designs, and new artists will come up with fresh ideas that the glassblowers will then execute.'

'So you and your son will carry on the family business,' I said.

'Well, yes,' said Gino. Then he hesitated, fidgeting with objects on his desk for a moment. 'But it's more complicated than that. I am not an only child. I have a brother, Giampaolo. He's four years younger. For thirty years, he worked here with my father and me, and we worked very closely. Our family was as strong as steel: my father, my mother, my brother, me – and God. Giampaolo and I were alter egos for each other. But there began to be disagreements. Then, three years ago, he left. He hasn't been in touch with us since.'

'You don't speak?'

'Only through lawyers.'

'What about the night of the Fenice fire? Did you hear anything from him then?'

'No. He didn't call and didn't come. And yet that night my son-in-law came thirty miles in his boat with a load of industrial fire extinguishers, then carried them from Campo Sant' Angelo to our house. But from my brother we heard nothing.'

'What were the disagreements about?'

'Giampaolo wanted to modernize, to change things. But more important, in my opinion, was the fact we each had four grown children. I have three daughters and one son; he has three sons and a daughter. All eight were about to start their adult lives. If they wanted to work in the company, I thought each of them should earn the right, based on merit. I didn't want the company to become a refuge for spoiled children. I insisted that we set up strict guidelines, but my brother didn't want any rules. He had faith that the children would behave properly.

'That was the first difficulty. The second was his relationship with our father. My brother often said that he and I were castrated by him, because of his strong personality. Giampaolo felt overshadowed. I never did.'

'Was there anything your brother wanted to do in the company that he was not allowed to do?'

'He was given whatever job he wanted. He worked in production, in sales, and in our stores.'

'Did he want to design glass?'

'He did some of that, too. And he could have done more if he wanted.'

'Then why did he leave?'

'Giampaolo said he wanted to lead his own life. Anyway, three years ago he announced abruptly that he was leaving, and he asked to be compensated for his share of the family business. My father had given us each thirty per cent of the company.

THE CITY OF FALLING ANGELS

'My father was indignant. He said, "I gave you a gift of part ownership of the business, and now you want me to buy you out?" Instead he gave my brother some money to help him get started. Giampaolo had said he wanted to write books on the history of glassmaking. But he had a surprise for us: he started a rival company, right here in Murano. He named it Seguso Viro. He took some of our key people with him, too – a designer, our warehouse manager, and our production manager. He even tried to get the man who assembles chandeliers. He hired some of our former employees, too. Then he opened stores close to ours – one in St Mark's, one in the Frezzeria, another in Milan.'

'Does Seguso Viro make the same designs you do?'

'Yes, many – only the most beautiful ones.'

'I'm beginning to understand why you don't speak,' I said.

'But there's more,' Gino went on. 'After he left the company, my brother filed suit, as a limited partner in the corporation, to have my father declared mentally incompetent and removed as head of the company!'

'What?'

'It's true. I can show you the documents. I would then have been appointed to run the business in his place. But Giampaolo's next step was to file a suit to kick *me* out of the company, supposedly for performing some of my father's duties, like writing letters, signing papers, and so forth. Naturally we countersued, and we won.'

'But why did he do all that?'

'We didn't know why until a few months after he left, when we discovered something even more bizarre. Without telling anybody, Giampaolo had secretly registered the name "Archimede Seguso" as a trademark – under his own name!'

'How did your father react to that?'

'He pounded his chest and said, "But it's *my* name! How is such a thing possible? How can it be legal?" We countersued to block the registration. Giampaolo claimed that he trademarked the name in order to *protect* it and to protect his thirty per cent of the company.'

'How would he be protecting the name of Archimede Seguso?'

'In my opinion, my brother had a very simple plan. If he had succeeded in removing my father and me, this company – Vetreria Artistica Archimede Seguso – would have been without a brain. It would have withered and died, and Giampaolo would have found himself in a perfect position to take over. He had already set up a copy of our company with many of our old employees. He knew all of our clients. He was familiar with every aspect of our business. He even knew my father's glassmaking secrets. Finally, he wouldn't have had to buy the name, because he would have owned it already. Without spending a penny, he would have become Archimede Seguso.'

By the time I stepped on to the *vaporetto* for the ten-minute ride back to Venice from Murano, I was burning to meet Giampaolo Seguso. My mental picture of him had grown darker with each revelation. I knew only, from the little that Gino had told me, that he was a bit overweight, grey-haired, balding, and fifty-four years old. I wondered what kind of person falsely declares his father senile and then swipes his identity – if, indeed, that was what he had done. Did this man have fangs?

I dialled Seguso Viro and was immediately put through to Giampaolo. I introduced myself and said I would like to come and talk to him.

'It would be my pleasure,' he replied. We made an appointment for the following week.

In the meantime, I did some enquiring, and the first thing I discovered was that Muranese families had a reputation for feuding. Glassblowers had been living on Murano since 1291, when Doge Pietro Gradenigo forced them to move there from Venice because of the danger of fire, and also to confine them in a kind of protective ghetto where their glassmaking secrets would remain unknown to competitors in the outside world. Seven hundred years of living in such close proximity might have had something to do with the quarrelsome nature of the Murano breed.

'The Muranese are clever people,' Anna Venini told me, 'but they are a little bit mad.' Signora Venini was speaking with special insight and a measure of detachment, having worked at the Venini glass factory on Murano for more than twenty years, having published books on the history of glass, and having been the daughter of Paolo Venini, one of the great glassmakers of the twentieth century and a rarity in that he was *not* originally from Murano; he started out as a lawyer in Milan. 'But the Muranese are generous,' she said. 'When they accept you, you are really accepted.'

Signora Venini's daughter, Laura de Santillana, an artist who lived in Venice and worked in Murano, where her modernist glass sculptures were executed, shared her mother's fond ambivalence. 'Muranese families always fight,' she said. 'Terrible people! Awful! They've barricaded themselves inside their island culture. The Muranese consider themselves completely independent from Venice. They have their own Grand Canal, their own basilica, and their own noble families.'

According to the glass historian Rosa Barovier, who is herself a member of a long-established Murano glassmaking family, the departure of Giampaolo Seguso was not the first rupture to occur in the Seguso dynasty.

'Archimede himself split off from his own brothers,' she said. 'He also fought with *his* father, who had earlier fought with *his* father. For the Segusos, business is of the greatest importance; sometimes it takes precedence over family. But the Muranese have glass in their blood. They are sustained by the excitement of it. It's been noticed that in August, when the glassworks close, they become physically ill.

'Gino and Giampaolo Seguso both have a passion for glass,' Rosa

Barovier went on, 'but they are polar opposites. Gino is a traditionalist; he feels safest with the classic designs. Giampaolo is more daring and creative. He's using his father's designs as a base and going off in new directions.'

I took the *vaporetto* back to Murano. This time, instead of walking to the left when I got off, I turned right. Giampaolo Seguso's factory, Seguso Viro, was on the opposite side of the island from Vetreria Artistica Archimede Seguso.

A receptionist led me down a corridor, through a courtyard, past several flats of crated glass objects, into a spacious, modern, well-lit furnace room. Two flights of steel steps rose from the factory floor to Seguso's office. Two long tables were covered with glass bowls, bottles, and vases, each in a different pattern or glassblowing technique.

Giampaolo Seguso was wearing a cardigan sweater and, looking at me over his half-glasses, invited me to sit down across from him at his desk by a window. He gestured to his grey hair.

'I look grey on the outside,' he said with a broad smile, 'but inside, I am the black sheep of the family.'

I took this opening remark to be a sign that he intended to be candid. Before I had a chance to ask a question, he continued, speaking slowly and choosing his words with great care.

'I am the son of Archimede Seguso, the greatest master glassmaker of the past century. The most difficult thing in my life has been to be his son. He's a great man. A man of silence. He taught us not to *say*, but to *do*, everything. He lived in a period when it was not possible for him to have a good education. I think that is one of the reasons he and I had difficulties communicating. I could not make him understand who I was, and so at a certain moment in my life, I decided to cut the umbilical cord.'

'How did that come about?' I asked.

'Over a period of time, I began to have business disagreements with my brother. Then, three years ago, I gave myself a big fiftieth-birthday party on the Lido, where I live, and invited my parents, my relatives, and my friends. I presented each person with a small glass egg, and I said, "The egg is a symbol of life, of the infinite, of rebirth. It is also a symbol of surprise." Then, addressing my parents, I said, "I gave you my first fifty years. The surprise is that the second half will belong to me. I want to start to be the owner of my life." I was not very tactful when I said that. My parents were very upset.'

'I've been told that you trademarked your father's name without telling him,' I said. 'Is that true?'

Giampaolo nodded. 'Yes,' he said. 'But . . . if I have a knife in my hand, it doesn't mean I'm a killer. I registered the name in order to keep my father's legacy intact. I felt that after his death, the only glass sold under his name should be his. I had proposed starting a new line of glass under a different name – perhaps Archimede Seguso II, or the Successors of Archimede Seguso, or something else. But my brother wanted to keep everything under the name Archimede Seguso, even glass designed and made by others after he died. That would turn the signature of a great artist into a brand name, and its meaning would be diluted. I trademarked the name in the hope of preventing that from happening.'

I could see a certain logic in that, but I was still mystified by Giampaolo's attempt to have his father declared mentally incompetent and removed as head of the company. I asked him about it.

'That was a purely legal manoeuvre,' he said. 'When I left, I wanted to be compensated for the thirty years I had put into the company. I asked my father to buy out my share, but he refused. Then I said, "Well, at least give me a couple of retail shops, so I can earn some money while I start my new life." I had intended to write books about glass, but in order to do that, I had to have a way of making a living. When we could not agree on my compensation, I realized I would have to sue the company. But that would mean suing my father, and I could never have done that. If I could persuade a judge to pronounce him mentally incapacitated, however, and appoint my brother in his place, then I would be suing my brother when I sued the company.'

I was not sure how declaring one's father mentally unfit to run his own business could be viewed as preferable to filing a financial claim against him, but I let it pass.

'Have you made any effort to get in touch with your parents since you went off on your own?'

'The first year, I sent flowers to my mother with a card for their wedding anniversary. She returned the flowers, and a couple of days later, I received a letter. My card was inside the envelope, unopened. The note to me said, "You know why."'

'Have your children also been affected by your break with your family?' I asked.

'Yes, they have. My parents refused to see them. They rejected them in different ways.'

This, then, was a dynastic rupture of sweeping proportion. Giampaolo spoke with very little emotion, but there was a heaviness in his words that betrayed a profound sense of pain.

'Where were you the night of the Fenice fire?'

'I was at home on the Lido,' he said. 'My son called from New York and asked what was happening. I didn't know. I went outside to the lagoon and saw the red sky. Then I went in and turned on the TV and began to cry. I did not call my parents. By that time, I had no connection.'

'What became of your plan to write books on the history of glass?'

'Without an income, it was not possible. I decided to go into business for myself, and I started Seguso Viro. I had to sell property in order to do it, which gives you an idea of the intensity of my passion for glass. I have three sons. They are all in the business with me. The company belongs to them. Two work here in Murano with me, and the third runs our showroom in New York.

'For a long time, I had felt that glassmaking in Murano had grown stale. In the period from 1930 through the 1950s, we had great, innovative glassmakers in Murano: Ercole Barovier, Alfredo Barbini, Napoleone Martinuzzi, Paolo Venini, my father. It was a time of planting, sowing. Then, from the 1960s to the 1990s it was a season of harvest without planting anything new. Now Murano finds itself with grey, dark fields, and they ask why. The challenge is to find new ways of using the old techniques. And that is what we are trying to do here.'

'Can you show me some examples?' I asked.

'I can show you many.' Giampaolo rose from his chair and led me over to the table covered with dozens of glass objects.

'The glass on this table represents all the techniques I learned from my father, from my uncles, and by myself. It is a re-creation of what the Seguso dynasty of Murano has done over a period of fifty years. There are a hundred and fifty designs, and for each one I've made a limited edition of ninety-nine. My idea is to find patrons who will buy full sets of a hundred and fifty pieces and give them to museums as research and to preserve and promote the myth of Murano glass.'

I was struck by the paradox. 'It's a bit ironic,' I said, 'that first you have an angry break with your father and then you painstakingly compile an homage to him.'

'But my father is a great man,' Giampaolo said. 'I'll show you three examples that illustrate how we have documented his work and at the same time made steps into the future.'

He picked up a tear-shaped vase in clear glass with a long, thin neck. Inside the vase, a slightly twisted membrane of glass divided it into two chambers. A white spiderweb made of filaments of white glass was embedded in the glass divider.

'This is an example of the filigree technique, which was invented in Murano in 1527,' Giampaolo said. 'In the 1950s, my father created new effects with it that were recognized by glass historians as the first original contribution since the Renaissance. So this vase is about our past, and yet it does have two innovations. The double-chambered effect is one, and the use of the filigree in the internal piece of glass, rather than in the outside wall of the vase, is the other. This vase was designed by my son Gianluca. He's the twenty-third generation of the Seguso dynasty.'

Giampaolo next picked up a round bowl with black filigree swirling around the bottom half and white filigree on the top. 'This is a technique called *incalmo*, which is the joining together of two hemi-spherical pieces of blown glass exactly the same diameter. It takes two glassblowers to do it, and it must be done while the glass is white-hot. Throughout the history of glassmaking, the two parts of *incalmo* glass have always been joined in a straight line. Here the connection is irregular and has a wavy effect. So this bowl has a little of the old in it and a little of the new.

'Finally this one.' He handed me a vase that had fine threads of black filigree in bands reminiscent of the lines in sheet music, running horizontally in irregular waves and swirls. The lines were mingled with gossamer streams of transparent orange. Giampaolo had designed the vase himself and named it 'Vivaldi' after the red-haired Venetian composer Antonio Vivaldi.

'This vase represents a step into our future,' he said. 'The orange filigree is made up of sixteen shades of transparent red and orange. Transparent filigree has never been seen before. The effect is original. It is very contemporary.'

The vase was exquisite. The exceptional lightness and grace of its filigree gave it a feeling of motion. A series of irregular lumps of smooth glass running up one side of the exterior created a varied texture and a sensuous play of light. Seguso was clearly very proud of it.

'Did you blow this vase yourself?' I asked.

'I am a very bad soloist,' he said with a smile, 'but a good director. I have an understanding with my sons. If they want their father to work with them, they have to give him one day a week at the furnace, to give him a chance to play. So five days a week, I wear a manager's hat, and one day a week, I stand at the furnace – beside the master glassblower – and I direct.'

He walked back to his desk and stood looking out of the window. Then he turned to me with what seemed to be a satisfied expression.

'I have four goals,' he said. 'First, I would like people to see our glass and recognize it immediately as Venetian. Second, I would like them to say, "Oh, this is glass made by Seguso." My third goal is that they will say, "This is glass made by Seguso Viro." My fourth goal is that perhaps one day people will say, "This is glass made by Giampaolo Seguso."'

I had a feeling that the fourth goal was the one he dreamed of most often.

'Is it your ambition to become a famous designer?' I asked.

'My view is that I belong to a great relay race of Murano glass-makers. In my opinion, the last runner does not exist. The only race you can run is part of a larger effort. The challenge is to be recognized as someone who has added something to the tradition along the way.'

Giampaolo sat down at his desk again. 'And that,' he said, 'is one of the major differences between my father and me. My father thinks of himself as the last runner in the race.'

8

Expatriates: The First Family

S EVERAL TIMES A WEEK, I had occasion to walk across the
Accademia Bridge, and whenever I did, I turned and looked down
the Grand Canal towards the great domes of Santa Maria della Salute,
easily one of the most familiar picture-postcard images of Venice.

Late one afternoon, as I was crossing the bridge and looking in this
direction, I happened to notice an elegant motor launch idling quietly
in front of a Gothic palace about sixty yards away, the second palace
from the bridge on the St Mark's side. The boat was a venerable Riva,
the doge of luxury motorboats. It was about forty years old, twenty feet
long, and made of a rich mahogany trimmed in chrome. A tall man with
grey hair stood at the wheel, holding his hand out to a woman who was
stepping from the dock into the boat. She was dressed completely in
white, from headband to shoes. Even her glasses had white frames, and
her hair was white as well. After the woman had taken her seat, the man
eased the boat out into the Grand Canal, stern first, as casually as if he
were backing a car out of a garage. Then he turned and headed in the
direction of the Salute Church and St Mark's.

I was struck by the idea that a ride on the Grand Canal in this
motorboat, which would have been a thrill for me, was most likely a
daily routine for this couple. They might have been going shopping, to
dinner, or to visit friends. They moved around Venice not only in style
but low to the water, the way Venetians had done for centuries, much
closer to water level, at any rate, than if they had been standing on the
deck of a lumbering *vaporetto*.

A week or so later, I saw the couple in their boat again. They were returning to the palace from the direction of the Rialto. As before, the woman was dressed completely in white, but this time she had on slacks instead of a skirt and a sweater instead of a blazer.

'That had to be Patricia Curtis,' Rose Lauritzen said later on. 'She always wears white.'

'Always?' I asked. 'Why?'

'I really don't know. She's worn white as long as I've known her. Peter, why does Patricia wear white?'

'I haven't any idea,' said Peter.

'White may just be her colour,' said Rose. 'It's probably as simple as that.'

'But now that you mention it,' said Peter, directing his comment to me, 'I must tell you that Patricia Curtis is an interesting woman for many reasons, the very least of which is that she always wears white.'

'The man you saw her with is her husband, Carlo Viganò,' said Rose. 'He's terribly nice. They both are. I mean, really . . . nice . . . people.'

'Patricia Curtis,' said Peter, 'is a fourth-generation American ex-patriate. Her great-grandparents, Daniel Sargent Curtis and Ariana Wormeley Curtis, came to Venice from Boston in the early 1880s with their son Ralph, Patricia's grandfather.'

'Not only nice,' said Rose, 'but well liked.'

'The Curtises,' said Peter, 'were rich, old-line Bostonians, whose ancestry went back to the *Mayflower*. They bought Palazzo Barbaro, and their descendants have lived there ever since.'

'Carlo has a business in Malaysia,' said Rose. 'Manufacturing. I forget what.'

'In terms of seniority,' said Peter, 'the Curtises are way ahead of all the other English-speaking expatriates in Venice. They're in a class by themselves.'

'Tablecloths and napkins!' said Rose. 'That's what he makes. Carlo's company, I mean.'

'But why would a rich, socially prominent Bostonian pack up his family and leave America for good?' I asked.

'Aha!' said Peter. 'That's the curious part.'

Peter went on to explain that Daniel Curtis was riding in a commuter train from Boston to the suburbs when he got into an altercation with another man over a seat that had been saved for a third party. Words were exchanged. The other man declared that Daniel Curtis was 'no gentleman', and in reply Mr Curtis twisted the man's nose. The injured party turned out to be a judge, who thereupon brought suit against Daniel Curtis for assault. A trial followed, and Daniel Curtis was convicted and sentenced to two months in jail. Upon his release, according to the story, he indignantly gathered up his family, moved to Europe, and never came back.

'It is only fair to point out,' said Peter, 'that in all the years he lived in Venice, Daniel Curtis behaved like a consummate gentleman. From the moment he and Ariana set foot in Palazzo Barbaro, they made it a gathering place for the best-known, most-admired artists, writers, and musicians of their day. Robert Browning read his poetry aloud to the Curtises and their guests. Henry James, a frequent houseguest, used the Barbaro as the model for the fictional Palazzo Leporelli in his masterpiece *The Wings of the Dove*. John Singer Sargent was a distant cousin, and when he was visiting the Barbaro, he painted in the top-floor studio of his cousin, Ralph Curtis, who was also an accomplished painter. Monet painted views of Santa Maria della Salute from the Barbaro's water gate. Are you getting the picture?'

'I am,' I said.

'The Curtis family occupies a permanent place in the cultural history of nineteenth-century Venice. Their salon became known as the "Barbaro Circle", and it included James McNeill Whistler, William Merritt Chase, Edith Wharton, and Bernard Berenson.'

'And that madwoman from Boston,' said Rose, 'Mrs Gardner.'

'Isabella Steward Gardner,' said Peter, 'the eccentric Boston art collector, rented the *piano nobile* from the Curtises for several summers while she was acquiring important paintings for the museum she intended to build in Boston.'

'She not only rented the Barbaro,' said Rose, 'she copied it!'

'True,' said Peter. 'She built her Boston museum in the form of a Venetian palace, based loosely on the façade of Palazzo Barbaro. One can easily see why Mrs Gardner was so inspired. The Barbaro is one of the most important fifteenth-century Gothic palaces in Venice. Actually, it's two palaces. The Barbaro family bought the palace next to it in the late seventeenth century to provide themselves with a ballroom.

'One could go on and on about Palazzo Barbaro's architectural and decorative grace notes, but my point is that Patricia Curtis is, first and foremost, the inheritor and guardian of a considerable literary, artistic, and architectural patrimony. She is also, but only very incidentally, a woman who wears white.'

On the telephone, Patricia Curtis was reserved but friendly. She was leaving the next day, she said, for Malaysia, where her husband was part owner of a textile mill. However, if I could wait until her return a month later, she would be happy to show me Palazzo Barbaro.

Over the next few weeks, I educated myself about the Barbaro. I found a videotape of *Brideshead Revisited* and watched the Venetian episode, in which Laurence Olivier plays the ageing Lord Marchmain, living in self-imposed exile in a sumptuous Venetian palace. Palazzo Barbaro had been used for the filming of those scenes. Jeremy Irons and Anthony Andrews (as Charles Ryder and Sebastian Flyte) climb an exterior stairway to the *piano nobile*, saunter down the length of the polished terrazzo floor of the *portego*, and find Olivier standing at a window in the ballroom, looking out at the Grand Canal.

I reread *The Wings of the Dove*, keeping in mind that Henry James had been describing these same rooms as he wrote of the angelic, dying

Milly Theale ensconced in the 'palatial chambers' of her 'great gilded shell'.

As for Daniel Curtis's nose-twisting attack on Judge Churchill, accounts of it had appeared in a number of books, including Cleveland Amory's *The Proper Bostonians*, but they varied considerably. Amory's version had Daniel Curtis twisting a man's nose so violently he was disfigured for life. Another report said Curtis had bitten the nose of a streetcar driver; another had him knocking down a policeman who had insulted his wife; yet another claimed that the argument had been about giving a seat to a pregnant woman. The incident had taken on the character of a folk tale, changing with each telling. This may have been because Mrs Curtis had revised the story in order to put her husband in a better light. In any case, the real story had been reported in minute detail by the Boston newspapers, which reprinted verbatim transcripts of court testimony.

The confrontation had started when Judge Churchill took a seat being saved for another man, but it quickly turned into an argument about the bulky luggage – a carpetbag and a toy wagon – that Churchill placed on the floor in the tight space between himself and Daniel Curtis. The objects pressed against Curtis's legs, to his great annoyance, and Curtis brusquely told him to move them, which Churchill did. Moments later the third man arrived and claimed his seat, whereupon Churchill quickly got up and surrendered it. But before walking away, he leaned towards Daniel Curtis and said, in a low voice, 'If you are a gentleman, I have never seen one before.'

Stung by the remark, Curtis jumped up, demanded to know who Churchill was, and twisted his nose ('in a moderate and quiet manner', he later claimed). Churchill then angrily declared, 'Nobody but a blackguard would begin a fight in the presence of these ladies!' upon which Daniel Curtis hit him in the face, breaking his glasses.

Curtis was hauled into court, tried for assault, convicted, and sentenced to two months in jail.

The astonishing part is what happened next: more than three hundred of the leading citizens of Massachusetts petitioned the governor to issue a pardon for Daniel Curtis. Among the signatories were Harvard president Charles Eliot; future Harvard president A. Lawrence Lowell; the chief justice of the Massachusetts Supreme Court; the secretary of state of Massachusetts; the president of the Union Pacific Railroad; the naturalist Louis Agassiz; Charles Eliot Norton, who was Harvard's and America's first professor of fine arts; the historian Francis Parkman; the painter William Morris Hunt; the architect H. H. Richardson; the husband of Isabella Stewart Gardner (John L. Gardner); and an all-star roster of Boston blue-bloods, including Lowells, Saltonstalls, Adamses, Welds, Lawrences, Otises, Endicotts, Pierces, Parkers, Cushings, Minots, Appletons, and Crowninshields, to name just a few.

The story took an even stranger turn when Daniel Curtis then repudiated their petition by refusing to sign it. He likewise rejected Judge Churchill's offer to drop the charges in exchange for a sincere apology. Curtis said his own actions had been justified, given Churchill's provocations, and that he would not apologize. So Daniel Sargent Curtis spent the next two months in jail.

Curtis did not leave America in indignation as soon as he was released. He left eight years later. In fact, his jail term had had nothing to do with his leaving. He had expressed a desire to emigrate long before the nose-twisting incident. Ironically, his reason had been his unhappiness about the decline in civility in America. In a letter to his sister, written in 1863, six years before his confrontation with Judge Churchill, he had complained that 'American gentlemen are not exactly gentlemen. . . . [They have] a want of thorough self-contained self-respect, which belongs to men who are born gentlemen of good ancestors, educated properly, with sufficient estate and who know for certain their place and that of others . . . I do wish I had the means of quitting this land for ever with my children.'

Daniel Curtis's disenchantment with America was a sentiment shared by many people of his class at the time. It was in part a reaction to the social upheavals brought on by the Civil War and in part an alarmed response to the arrival of the first wave of immigrants from Ireland, who had little in common with long-established Americans. In any case, if Daniel Curtis had been irritated by Judge Churchill's thoughtlessness in cramming his baggage between the two of them, he would have found it intolerable to then be called ungentlemanly by the selfsame lout.

When Daniel and Ariana moved into the Barbaro, they took possession of a palace that had been renowned as a centre of humanist intellectual discourse for the four centuries it was occupied by the Barbaro family. The Barbaros had been true Renaissance men: scholars, philosophers, mathematicians, diplomats, scientists, politicians, military commanders, church patriarchs, and patrons of the arts. The best remembered was the sixteenth-century Daniele Barbaro, a diplomat, philosopher, and architectural translator of Vitruvius. Daniele Barbaro hired Andrea Palladio to design his summer estate – the Villa Barbaro at Maser – and engaged Veronese to paint the frescos. When he sat for his portrait, Titian painted it.

Palazzo Barbaro remained the Barbaro family's exclusive domain until the defeat and subsequent impoverishment of Venice at the hands of Napoleon. As their fortune dwindled, the Barbaros withdrew into a wing of the palace and divided the rest into apartments. When the last of the Barbaros died in the middle of the nineteenth century, the palace was bought by a succession of speculators, who stripped it of many of its paintings, hacked off carved marble figures, gathered up choice furniture and decorative items, and put them up for auction.

Daniel and Ariana Curtis became its saviours. They replaced rotting timbers, repaired broken stucco, and restored frescos and paintings. By creating their own cultural salon in the Barbaro, they even revived its humanist spirit. With the Curtises playing host to artists, writers, and musicians, Palazzo Barbaro came to be considered the most important American cultural outpost in Venice, if not in all of Italy. That was due in part to the profound influence of a grey eminence who remained largely behind the scenes – namely, Charles Eliot Norton, one of Daniel Curtis's Harvard classmates. An early appreciator of Italian art, Norton was a friend and literary executor of John Ruskin and Thomas Carlyle, a translator of Dante's *Divine Comedy*, a founder of the *Nation*, a teacher of Bernard Berenson and Ralph Curtis, and a friend and mentor to Henry James, Isabella Stewart Gardner, and others in the Barbaro Circle. (It was during one of Professor Norton's lectures in January 1876 that Ralph Curtis slipped a note to a fellow student inviting him to come to the room of a friend after class; they were going to start a college humour magazine along the lines of *Punch*. A few weeks later, Ralph Curtis and six of his friends published the first issue of the *Harvard Lampoon*.)

Because of their obvious devotion to Palazzo Barbaro and their energetic support of artists and the arts, the Curtises inspired an outpouring of goodwill in Venice that was so deeply felt it carried over to succeeding generations. Alberto Franchetti, whose family once owned the palace next door to the Barbaro, recalled that when he was growing up, long after Daniel and Ariana had died, the Curtis family was still regarded with admiration and gratitude.

'You have to understand,' Franchetti said, 'that they came to Venice at the lowest point in our history, when everyone was extremely poor and in despair. The Curtises were the one bright light in Venice at a very dark time. They did more than restore Palazzo Barbaro, they honoured it, and for this they won the lasting affection of Venice. Today we think of the Curtises as part of our history, and for foreigners this is a rare distinction. They are not Venetians, but we don't think of them as expatriates either. We see the Curtises as unique.'

There was every reason to expect that future generations of Curtises would continue to live in and safeguard the Barbaro, inheriting that same goodwill. But a problem had arisen.

For the first time in over a hundred years, the Curtis family was in danger of losing control of the Barbaro.

The source of the trouble lay in a provision of the Napoleonic Code, which was law in Italy: namely, that children shall inherit equal shares of their parents' property. That rule was thought to be more equitable than the British law of primogeniture, which allows the eldest son to inherit the entire estate. But in practical terms, the Napoleonic Code contributed to ferocious quarrels among heirs and to the breakup of large family properties.

Patricia and her two siblings, Ralph and Lisa, had inherited Palazzo Barbaro in the mid 1980s. Their mother had left it to them in equal shares, as required by the code, but her will did not specify which part of the palace would belong to whom. That question was left for the three heirs to settle among themselves.

Patricia, the eldest, was the only one of the three who lived in the Barbaro full-time. Lisa had married a Frenchman, lived in Paris, and was now the Comtesse de Beaumont. Ralph was divorced from his French wife and also lived in Paris.

'We tried everything,' said Lisa, 'every possible formula. We even thought of dividing the palace in thirds vertically, which would have given each of us an apartment on an upper floor and that part of the *piano nobile* that lay below. But it would have meant separating the *salone* from the *portego*, and the superintendent of fine arts would never have allowed it. In the end, we shared joint ownership of the *piano nobile* and took apartments elsewhere in the palace.'

As everyone knows, in any palace, the *piano nobile* is the grandest floor by far. It has the highest ceilings, the tallest windows, and the stateliest balconies. It is the floor where, for centuries, the money has been spent on such appurtenances as frescoed ceilings, wall-size paintings, gigantic chandeliers, and wave upon wave of sculpted stucco mounted above the doors, framing the paintings, surging across the ceilings. In some people's minds, the *piano nobile* is not merely the most valuable floor of a palace, it *is* the palace. In other words, if a person owned only that one floor, people tended to speak of the palace as *his* palace. Daniel Curtis had bought the top three floors of the Barbaro. Even though the two floors below were owned and occupied by other people, there was never any question that the Barbaro belonged to the Curtises, because they owned the *piano nobile*. In some quarters it was even known as 'Palazzo Barbaro-Curtis'.

The pre-eminence of the Barbaro's *piano nobile* over the other floors was especially pronounced, because it was the only floor that extended through both palaces. The other floors were all at different levels, so each was confined within the Gothic part or the baroque makes part. At ten thousand square feet, the *piano nobile* was not only much bigger than the other floors, it included the greatest prize of all – the grand ballroom with its monumental paintings and sumptuous swirls of stucco, a room of such elegance and majestic proportions that it was featured in virtually every photo book on Venetian palaces.

Because Patricia was the only one of the three Curtis siblings who lived in the Barbaro, she was also the only one who made regular use of the *piano nobile* – for receptions, parties, or as an incomparable guest flat. She looked after it with loving care, attending to its needs, while her sister and brother had barely any interest in it. Nevertheless, as joint owners, all three were obliged to make financial contributions to its maintenance.

'When the windows in the rear needed to be replaced,' said Lisa, 'we had to follow the guidelines of the superintendent of monuments, and it cost a hundred million lire [fifty thousand dollars]. When chairs need recovering, we can't use just any cloth. It has to be Fortuny. And the floors must be cleaned and polished properly, according to curatorial standards, because after all the Barbaro is a museum.'

As time went on, with the value of the *piano nobile* rising year by year to something over $6 million, Lisa and Ralph increasingly viewed it as a burdensome luxury. They wanted to sell, and the issue became emotionally charged. Patricia strongly resisted, and for a time they tried to make the *piano nobile* pay for its own upkeep by renting it out for private parties at a fee of $10,000 or more. But the parties also eventually became a source of disagreement among the Curtises, and they came to an abrupt halt.

The prospect of handing the *piano nobile* down to the next generation of Curtises loomed as an even thornier problem and only stiffened Lisa's resolve to sell. Ralph was divorced and childless, but Patricia had one son and one grandchild, and Lisa had two sons and six grand-children. Word had it that now, with the alternatives exhausted, Patricia had finally, reluctantly, given in to the two-to-one vote and agreed to put the *piano nobile* on the market. Prospective buyers were already coming to have a look. It was only a matter of time.

It occurred to me that the sale of the Barbaro might move faster than expected and that my visit might become an unwanted complication. In an idle moment, I looked in the telephone directory for the phone numbers of the other Curtises and found a listing for Ralph. I had intended at some point to seek him out anyway. What would be the harm?

After three rings, a recorded male voice said in American-accented English, 'You have reached the Earth liaison station of the Democratic Republic of the Planet Mars.'

I hung up, checked the number, and dialled again. The same voice answered with the same message and went on to declare that 'Qualified scholars will be admitted to the archives by appointment only. If you leave pertinent information, the librarian will return your call.' I left my name and telephone number and said I was trying to reach Ralph Curtis at Palazzo Barbaro. Two hours later, Ralph Curtis called.

'I thought I'd dialled the wrong number,' I said.

'Well, you know, we're inundated by people doing research on Henry James or John Singer Sargent or Tiepolo,' he said. 'It can be such a bore. They ask ridiculous questions. I couldn't care less whether Henry James wore a bow tie or a cravat when he wrote *The Aspern Papers*.'

'I know what you mean,' I said. 'So all that business about the Democratic Republic of the Planet Mars is just a ruse to put the academics off the scent?'

'Well, no,' he said. 'That happens to be real.'

'Ah . . .' I said, becoming wary.

'How do you feel about peace and nuclear disarmament?' he asked.

'I'm for it,' I said, weighing my words.

'Good,' he said, 'because that's the mission of the Barbaro Project.'

'The Barbaro Project?'

'World peace and nuclear disarmament. We're in touch with the heads of state of all the terrestrial nuclear powers. Our goal is to get them to surrender their nuclear fire codes to us so we can put them on a spaceship and blast them off to Mars, where they won't be able to get at them. What do you think of that?'

'It's a noble cause,' I said. 'But you keep saying "we". Who's in this with you?'

'Well, it's basically me. But I've talked to a lot of people, like you, who think it's a good idea.'

I took advantage of a pause in the conversation to explain my reason for calling. I mentioned my interest in the Barbaro, the Barbaro Circle, and life in the palace during five generations of Curtises. 'Would it be possible,' I asked, 'to visit Palazzo Barbaro?'

'It might be,' he said. 'I'll send you an application. Tell me your address.'

Three days later, a large envelope arrived with an application for admission to the 'R. D. Curtis Library and Research Center'. I filled it out, writing 'none' in the space provided for 'Affiliations with Alien Spirits and Movements'. The signature box called for a print of the big toe on my right foot. Even as I pressed my toe on to an open can of brown Kiwi shoe polish, I figured the chances were about even that I had become the victim of a put-on. But I sent in the application anyway, and in a matter of days, Ralph Curtis was on the phone again, asking if I was free to come to Palazzo Barbaro at three o'clock the next afternoon. I said I was.

'Good,' he said. 'We'll have a "liftoff".' He did not elaborate.

As agreed, I met him at a café in Campo Santo Stefano, immediately behind the Barbaro. He was seated at a table smoking a tapered green cigarette, the kind that usually had dried vegetables rolled into them. He was a man in his mid fifties, slightly built and deeply tanned. He wore blue-tinted aviator glasses, neatly pressed jeans, and a brown suede jacket over a crew-neck sweater. He snuffed out the cigarette and stood up. 'All set?'

A heavy wooden door at the rear of the palace opened on to an enchanting inner courtyard with walls of ancient brick and stucco and windows set at random intervals. To our left, a long, steep marble stairway with a vine-covered iron railing rose in two flights to the *piano nobile*. At the centre of the courtyard, a luxurious rhododendron sprouted from a large marble wellhead made from the capital of an old column. Directly in front of us, a darkened arcade led to the sun-sparkling water of the Grand Canal. An old gondola rested on stilts as if waiting to be launched. Its *felze*, a small black passenger cabin of the sort not seen for decades in Venice, was still attached. I asked how old it was.

'Over a hundred years,' said Ralph.

Which meant that Robert Browning, John Singer Sargent, and Henry James had probably gone for rides in it.

At the top of the stairs, we entered a tall, dim antechamber. A pair of polished doors stood to our right, and beyond them the formal *portego* and the storeyed rooms on the Grand Canal. But those doors remained closed. Ralph took a sharp left, towards a lesser door that led into his own apartment. It was a series of rooms, spacious but spare, at the back of the palace. Every room was painted plain white. The starkness of the place was heightened by its emptiness. What furniture there was amounted to a couple of chairs, a small wooden table, and some shelves. The apartment's chandeliers and wall fixtures were fitted with small cobalt blue bulbs, the same colour as those used to line airport landing strips. The name of each room was neatly stencilled on the walls: FLIGHT CONTROL CENTER, MOON ROOM, MARS ROOM, PEACE ROOM, EXTRATERRESTRIAL SEARCH ROOM.

'Welcome to the Starship *Barbaro*,' said Ralph, leading me on a brief tour of the apartment, which he referred to as 'the O.C. Wing of the Palazzo Barbaro'. O.C. stood for Odile Curtis, the name of his ex-wife.

In one room, three space suits were hung on the wall. A photograph of a stuffed animal, a monkey, was taped to the wall next to one of them, with a caption that read, 'Monkeyface, Flight Commander, Starship *Barbaro*'. In another room, an inflatable, life-size plastic female in a lacy black bikini sat on the floor, propped up against the wall. Ralph walked past each of these items without comment. In the Situation Room, there was a machine labelled 'Anti-Matter Reactor'. Ralph took a stack of audiotape cassettes from a shelf and went back into the Moon Room.

'Well,' he said, 'are you ready for liftoff?'

Ralph sat cross-legged on the floor next to a boom box. He shuffled through the cassettes.

'Let's see, what'll it be, *Apollo 11*? That's the first manned moon shot. You know, Neil Armstrong and "One small step for a man, one giant leap for mankind." Here's *Apollo 12* . . . pretty good . . . *Apollo 13* . . . I guess we'll skip that one – they had to abort the lunar landing, only orbited the moon and came home. We want a lunar landing as well as a liftoff, don't we?' He looked over at me.

'Sure,' I said. I had taken a seat on the floor as well.

'*Apollo 14*,' he went on, 'that's when Alan Shepard hit a couple of golf balls after he landed on the moon. *Apollo 15*, Shepard was back at the control centre in Houston. Let's do that one.'

Ralph put the cassette into the boom box, pressed the 'play' button, and leaned back against the wall. The tape began with the ultra-calm voice of Mission Control intoning the familiar mantra, 'T minus two minutes and counting . . .' We sat quietly, listening to the staccato back-and-forth between Houston and the astronauts. Then came the countdown: 'Ten . . . nine . . . eight . . . ignition sequence started . . . five . . . four . . . three . . . two . . . one . . . zero . . . Launch coming up . . . We have liftoff!'

'Damn!' said Ralph.

The roar of the rockets burst through the speakers with a massive violence that seemed likely to rupture them. Even so, Ralph turned up the volume. Throbbing sound waves pounded my eardrums and sent vibrations humming in the walls and floors. As the noise of the rockets began to fade, Ralph lifted his gaze from the boom box. My ears popped at the sudden drop in air pressure.

'How often do you do this?' I asked.

'Oh, I've had liftoffs at three in the morning. Telephones start ringing. The neighbours call. Occasionally my sister Pat freaks out.'

'Is that why you do it?'

'No, I do it because it gives me hope. I imagine it's the Starship *Barbaro* soaring out of the atmosphere and taking the nuclear fire codes to Mars. I wrote a letter to Bill Clinton offering to be the first person to go to Mars with the fire codes and not come back. It took a lot of courage to do that, you know, because people might have thought I was crazy.'

'Did Clinton write back?' I asked.

'Not yet. I sent Boris Yeltsin an artwork entitled *The Twelve Apostles from Planet Mars*. But I haven't had a response from him yet either. It can be discouraging at times. That's when I come here for a liftoff.'

On the tape, *Apollo 15* was drawing farther away from Earth. We sat in the blue-white glow of Ralph Curtis's Moon Room, listening to the conversations between Houston and the spacecraft interspersed with tiny beeps. *Apollo 15* would shortly be going into its Earth-orbit phase. Ralph pressed the 'fast-forward' button. 'Bear with me for a few minutes,' he said. 'We'll go right to the lunar landing.' When he resumed play, the voice of Mission Control was saying, 'They're at five thousand feet now.'

Fast forward.

'. . . twelve hundred . . .'

Fast forward.

'. . . eighty . . . forty . . . twenty . . . fifteen . . . ten . . . six . . . three . . . contact!'

'Damn!' said Ralph.

He sat quietly for a while, basking in whatever pleasure he was able to take from the replay of this trip to the moon. Then he gathered up the tapes, and while he was putting them away, I walked around the apartment again. The rooms were more barren than I had realized at first. There were no clothes in sight, no kitchen utensils, no towels or toiletries.

'But where are your belongings?' I asked. 'Where do you sleep?'

'Oh, I don't live here,' he said. 'I have no home, no fixed address. I prefer it that way.'

'You're joking.'

'Nope. I stay with friends. I leave my clothes in suitcases in various apartments.' He reached into his pocket and pulled out a key ring jangling with keys. 'I've got keys to the apartments of ten friends. These are my "house keys".'

Ralph Curtis's rooms could have made a very comfortable apartment. I ventured to say that it baffled me why anyone who could live in a palace on the Grand Canal would choose instead to live out of a suitcase in other people's apartments.

'I don't like possessions,' he said. 'I don't want to own anything.'

'But you're an owner of Palazzo Barbaro.'

'I prefer to think of myself as the Barbaro's "spiritual custodian".'

'In what way?' I asked.

'For four hundred years, the Barbaro family lived here. They were scholars, philosophers, diplomats, you name it – seekers of wisdom and harmony. That's the heritage of this palace, and it has to be protected.'

'Protected from what?'

'Well, anything inappropriate, offensive, debasing. For a while, we rented out the *piano nobile* for private parties, hoping it would be a harmless way to help pay expenses. We signed a contract with Jim Sherwood, who owns the "21" Club in New York and the Cipriani Hotel here, to do the catering. He went to great expense. He bought a lot of equipment and even installed a standard industrial kitchen, but it all got to be too much. He created a menu with really objectionable phoney names like "Tournedos Barbaro", and he commissioned sets of glasses and dishes that had the Barbaro insignia, which is a red circle on a white background.

'I said to him, "Jim, do you know where that insignia comes from?" He didn't know. I said, "It's from a battle during the Crusades when a Barbaro commander sliced an arm off a Saracen infidel and swabbed a bloody circle with it on a white cloth to make a battle flag." I said, "This is scandalous!" He'd spent eighty thousand dollars on the glassware and the dishes, and I made him throw them out. I told him, "You're lucky I didn't break them all!" And then finally I made him tear out the kitchen. Now the kitchen is being put to better use. It's the Peace Room.'

'And the *piano nobile* is up for sale,' I said.

'I'd rather not sell it. I'd prefer to donate the *piano nobile* to the National Gallery of Art as a symbolic gesture. I wrote them about it, but they said it would cost too much money to maintain.'

'But it is being sold, isn't it?' I asked.

'Probably,' he said. 'Pat isn't happy about it. She wrote a letter to my sister Lisa and me, accusing us of wanting to *smembrare* the family's artistic and cultural patrimony, which means, literally, to "dismember" it. She wrote the letter in Italian. She's very Italian at heart, which at times irritates me a little. Her dedication to the house is almost a sickness.

'Patricia's portrait was painted in the Barbaro when she was about twenty. It was done in the style of Sargent and Boldini, and I think it had a profound effect on her. It gave her a sense of not only having to live up to the house and the family but also the portrait. I told her, "It will destroy you." '

Ralph returned to his favourite topic as we put our coats on and went back out into the antechamber. 'If you like, I'll send you copies of the letters I mailed to the heads of state. They're on file in the Peace Room.' We were halfway down the courtyard stairs when I realized he had forgotten to show me the rest of the *piano nobile*, but I let it pass.

'I can send you other material, too, but only if you're really interested. I've written out the Martian National Anthem in Cyrillic lettering.'

We parted where we had met, in Campo Santo Stefano.

'You know,' he said, 'whoever buys the *piano nobile* will become the new spiritual custodian of the Barbaro. I just hope it'll be someone who understands what that means. We'll have to see what happens.'

He glanced around the *campo*, as if looking to see whether anyone was eavesdropping. 'Anyway,' he said, 'I have a plan. After the new custodians have had it for a while, once they've really settled in, I'll go over there and tell them about the Barbaro Project. You never know.'

A month after she had left for Malaysia, Patricia Curtis sent me a handwritten fax to tell me she was back in Venice and that, as promised, she would be happy to show me Palazzo Barbaro.

What I had learned in her absence about the impending sale of the *piano nobile* had put the palace and Patricia Curtis in a whole new light, and not just for me. Over the years, it had been Patricia, rather than her brother or sister, or all three for that matter, who had come to be viewed as the owner of the Barbaro. She was its *castellana*, and in the eyes of her fellow Venetians, she was now at the centre of a sad family drama. The sale of the *piano nobile* would be her loss, and her loss would be nothing less than the loss of the Barbaro itself. Local sympathies were with her, but in varying degrees of kindness. There were those who said, 'Patricia must fight for the Barbaro! Who would she be without it?' and others who understood that her passion for the palace had nothing to do with concern about social position but arose instead from an abiding sense of duty to preserve her family's heritage and the cultural history it embodied.

Patricia greeted me at the top of the courtyard stairs and ushered me into the *piano nobile*. She was cordial and relaxed and did not appear to be, in any sense, embattled.

As before, she was dressed in white, but I could see now that white, for her, was not a uniform white but rather a broad spectrum of whites: creamy white, milk white, linen white, bone white, dove white — her blouse, slacks, shoes, and jewellery were a mix and match of whites in a casual and oddly liberating way. White was, after all, the combination of all colours of light. Her oversized white-framed glasses stood out against her tanned face.

'I understand you've spoken with my brother,' she said.

'Yes, I have,' I answered, hoping she would not regard it as a transgression.

'That's all right,' she said, acknowledging in just three words everything I had heard about her struggles to hold on to the palace and at the same time letting me know she was past caring what her brother might have told me. She turned and led the way into a room with a lacquered Chinese slant-top desk and a view of the courtyard.

'This is the breakfast room,' she said, 'which we also call the Henry James Room, because Henry James wrote at that desk.'

In the preface to one of his books, Henry James had described this room as having 'a pompous Tiepolo ceiling and walls of ancient pale-green damask, slightly shredded and patched'. The walls appeared to be covered with the same worse-for-wear damask, but James had apparently been mistaken about the ceiling.

'He was looking at that,' Patricia said, casting a glance at a celestial scene painted on the ceiling. 'It's only a copy of the fresco Giambattista Tiepolo painted there in the eighteenth century. The original was peeled off and sold long before my great-grandparents ever came to the Barbaro. It's in New York now, at the Metropolitan Museum.'

Her American-accented English had European touches. She spoke the word 'Barbaro' in the Italian manner, softly rolling the *rs*.

We walked into the dining room and across a terrazzo floor that had a floral mosaic inlaid with mother-of-pearl. A life-size portrait of a young woman in a silvery pink, off-the-shoulder evening gown hung on the wall in a heavy gilt frame.

'That's Sargent's portrait of my grandmother,' she said. Lisa Colt Curtis had been an heiress to the Colt firearms fortune. Sargent had painted her standing with her hands resting lightly on the table behind her, a pose strikingly reminiscent of his controversial, and decidedly less demure, Madame X.

We walked into the long *portego*. At the far end, light poured in through four Gothic windows, casting a glow on the paintings and the stucco ornamentation along the walls. At the windows, which opened on to balconies over the Grand Canal, we turned left into a small drawing room with a fireplace and walls of warm red damask that was as shredded and patched as the green damask in the room where Henry James had worked. The furniture, the paintings, and the gold-leaf frames all had the patina of two centuries or more. A desk with an elegant ivory marquetry of vines and birds was worn at the edges, rubbed smooth, and polished through generations of use. Carved bookshelves were filled with aged volumes. A pride of figurine lions strode across the marble mantel below a creamy white bas-relief of children and musicians carrying flutes and tambourines.

'This is the *salotto rosso*,' she said. 'We also call it the Browning Room. It's where Robert Browning used to read his poetry aloud. When Browning was in Venice, he and my great-grandfather, Daniel Curtis, saw each other almost every day, sometimes twice a day, for three or four hours at a time. They went for long walks on the Lido, and Browning would talk the whole time. As soon as my great-grandfather got home, he would sit down and write notes about what Browning had said, while it was still fresh in his mind.'

Daniel Curtis's diary had been donated to the Marciana Library, and in the past few weeks, I had read portions of it. He had taken copious notes of his conversations with Browning, possibly with the intention of writing a book about him, although he never did. Browning spoke about things large and small. 'I get up always at 6.30,' he told Curtis, 'and dress by light of a stout gas-lamp in front. I take an hour and a half for my toilette and get a deal of exercise out of it. I put on my stockings standing up, in uno pede stans. At 8 I breakfast and at 9 I go to my study.'

Browning gave his last public reading for the Curtises and twenty-five of their guests in the *salotto rosso* on 19 November 1889, a month before he died. He read from *Asolando*, a new book of poems that was expected to be released shortly. In the days that followed, Daniel Curtis wrote entries in his diary that chronicled the poet's final days. Browning was staying at Palazzo Rezzonico, a huge baroque palace on the other side of the Grand Canal, then owned by his son, Pen Browning:

> December 1 . . . all this week Mr. Browning ailing and did not go to the Lido . . . dined out and went to the Opera, had taken blue pill and reduced diet and no wine.
> December 3 . . . Mr. Browning better: and so continued improving

as to bronchitis and breathing, but without strength, uneasy and at times wandering in mind.

December 8 . . . [Browning's doctors say he is suffering from] 'muscular weakness of the bladder' – no disease, no pain, but weakness which makes us anxious on account of his years.

December 9 . . . Went to Pal[azzo] Rezzonico – [Pen Browning] said his father was very weak and heart action weak. He had wished to get up and walk about, also wished to read – neither allowed. Said to his son, 'I will not get over this.'

December 11 . . . The English servant said they were up all night, expecting the worst! Dr. Munich called in. Pulse 160 over 130.

December 12 This morning Fernando saw [Pen Browning] – said the doctors give up hope! 6 pm My son just returned from Palazzo Rezzonico – Mr. Browning apparently much better and said to son, 'I feel a great deal better and would like to get up and walk about, but I know I'm too weak.' He was without pain of any kind. But at 8.30 pm came a note from Miss Barclay (stays in the house): 'Dear Mr. Browning is just passing away. He is still breathing – that is all' and asking my son to do what is necessary for having a cast made of Mr. Browning's head and hands, which his son feels to be a duty he owes to the public. Pen said that . . . a telegram was read from London reporting the demand already made for his new volume, issued today, [and Browning] said, 'Now that, I call good news! I am very grateful.' And so in few hours expires – in that Italy, whose name, he said, was written in his heart . . .

As Pen Browning requested, Ralph Curtis – grandfather of Patricia and the present Ralph Curtis – arranged for casts to be made of the poet's face and hands, and he found someone to take photographs of his body in repose. Meanwhile Daniel Curtis gathered branches of bay leaves from the Curtises' flower garden on the Guidecca, and Ariana made them into a laurel wreath that was placed on top of the coffin over Browning's head.

'And now we'll go into the *salone*,' Patricia said as we went from the intimate, denlike Browning Room into the soaring grandness of the ballroom. A lavish, rococo frosting of stuccoed leaves, garlands, and putti framed immense paintings by Sebastiano Ricci and Piazzetta, two eighteenth-century masters. Henry James had used this room as the centrepiece in his memorable description of 'Palazzo Leporelli' in *The Wings of the Dove*. It was Milly Theale's rented fortress, a 'thorough make-believe of a settlement' that would close her in and protect her from harm:

> . . . she felt herself sink into possession; gratefully glad that the warmth of the Southern summer was still in the high, florid rooms, palatial chambers where hard, cool pavements took reflections in their lifelong polish, and where the sun on the stirred sea-water, flickering up through open windows, played over the painted 'subjects' in the splendid ceilings — medallions of purple and brown, of brave old melancholy color, medals as of old reddened gold, embossed and beribboned, all toned with time and all flourished and scalloped and gilded about, set in their great molded and figured concavity (a nest of white cherubs, friendly creatures of the air), and appreciated by the aid of that second tier of smaller lights, straight openings to the front, which did everything . . . to make the place an apartment of state.

That typically Jamesian passage had come to represent the quintessential literary rendering of centuries-old Venetian interiors and the accumulated history that lives within all of them.

This was the room also where in 1898 Sargent had painted *An Interior in Venice*, his enchanting group portrait of the four Curtises — Daniel, Ariana, Ralph, and Lisa — four sunlit figures set into the magnificent gloom. In a few confident brushstrokes, Sargent had captured the spirit of the place as effectively as Henry James had managed to do in a paragraph of well-chosen words.

Sargent had originally presented the painting as a gift to Ariana Curtis in appreciation for her hospitality. But Ariana thought it made her look too old, and she objected to the casual pose of her son, who had one hand on his hip while half leaning against, half sitting on a gilded table in the background. So she refused it. Henry James wrote her a letter, begging her to change her mind. 'The Barbaro-saloon thing . . . I absolutely adored. I can't help thinking you have a slightly fallacious impression of the effect of your (your, dear Mrs Curtis,) indicated head and face . . . I've seen few things of S[argent]'s that I've ever craved more to possess! I hope you haven't altogether let it go.'

But she had. So Sargent submitted it as his diploma painting to the Royal Academy in London, where it has remained ever since. The irony is that *An Interior in Venice* has come to be recognized as one of Sargent's small masterpieces, and its value has kept pace with, if not surpassed, that of the entire *piano nobile* of Palazzo Barbaro. If only Mrs Curtis had accepted it . . .

Ariana Curtis's social fastidiousness was a well-known phenomenon and occasionally drew comment. After Claude and Alice Monet visited her for tea at the Barbaro in 1908, Alice Monet remarked in a letter, 'Tea went better than I would have imagined in spite of the great airs of the mistress of the house.' Matilda Gay, the wife of another painter, Walter Gay, wrote of Ariana that 'she is a wonder, this clear-minded and cold-blooded old lady of 80'. The Curtises took especial pride in their many titled visitors. Counts and countesses abounded. Don Carlos, the pretender to the Spanish throne, was a frequent guest, as were Olga of Montenegro and Empress Frederick of Germany (the daughter of Queen Victoria). The Queen of Sweden came to tea with her daughter, the crown princess.

But there was never any question that the Curtises were sincere in their appreciation of art and literature. Their dinner parties were built around cultural events: poetry readings, musical recitals, theatricals, art exhibitions, and *tableaux vivants* in which guests were costumed and arranged in poses as characters in famous paintings by Titian, Romney, Vandyke, Watteau, and others.

Ariana Curtis had once aspired to be a writer herself. Two of her sisters were published authors: Elizabeth W. Latimer wrote histories and novels, and Katharine Prescott was known for her translation of Balzac's novels into English.

For her part, Ariana tried her hand at playwriting. In 1868, before moving to Venice, she wrote a one-act play entitled *The Coming Woman, or the Spirit of '76*. It was a drawing-room comedy about women's rights, and over a period of thirty years, it enjoyed great popularity in Boston.

In spite of the intellectuals in their circle, the Curtises struck some people as a bit provincial and narrow-minded. Henry James, who admired the Curtises and considered them good friends, said of Daniel Curtis that he made all-too-frequent comparisons between Venice and Boston, and that he was 'doing his best to make the Grand Canal seem like Beacon Street'. James grew weary of Daniel Curtis's boring stories and bad puns. 'One calculates the time when one shall have worked through his anecdotes and come out the other side,' James wrote in a letter. 'Perhaps one never does.' Looking through the Curtis diary at the Marciana, I came across several of Daniel's witticisms, among them:

> A[riana] said one morning, 'Which shall be washed first, the baby or the tea-things?'
> D[aniel] replied, 'The baby is a-teething, so wash them all together.'

Patricia noticed that I was looking up at the large painting on the ceiling of the *salone*.

'Believe it or not,' she said, 'one of the previous owners covered that painting with tar, because she said she didn't like faces staring down at her. My great-grandparents put up a scaffolding and had the tar removed. There had also been a plan, years earlier, to detach all the stucco from the walls and the ceiling and ship it to the Victoria and Albert Museum, but they couldn't get it off without destroying it.'

A tea service had been set at a table in the centre of the room. We sat down in armchairs beside it. As I looked round the room, I tried to imagine what it would have been like to grow up in such a place.

'It was magic,' said Patricia. 'When we were children, we were taken to school in the gondola. There were always two gondoliers on duty downstairs in the *stanza di gondolieri*, a little room off the courtyard. They wore red-and-white-striped T-shirts, white jackets, a maroon neckerchief tied round the neck, white pants with a maroon sash, and a maroon armband with a silver Curtis-family crest.

'At a certain hour every morning, the gondoliers would dress the gondola. That meant polishing the brass and putting in the upholstery and pillows, which were white and maroon – the Barbaro colors. When my father wanted to go out, he would ring a gong from above to alert the gondoliers that their services would be needed soon. Then, in the evenings, they would undress the gondola upon receiving word that they would no longer be needed.'

Life in the Barbaro, when Patricia Curtis grew up there, was not typical of life elsewhere in Venice at that time, even in other palaces. 'It was the 1950s,' Patricia said, 'and by then no more than a dozen Venetian families were still using gondolas: the Cinis, the de Cazes, the Berlingieris, the Volpis, and Peggy Guggenheim.'

The Barbaro of Patricia Curtis's childhood was populated by a dozen servants or more. In addition to the gondoliers, there were two butlers, a major-domo, a cook, an assistant cook, two maids, a nurse, a handyman, and a laundress. The maids wore black-and-white uniforms and shoes called *friulane*, which were like espadrilles and made no sound as they moved around the palace.

'The servants were devoted to my parents,' she said. 'Rosa would always insist on waiting up for my mother and father when they dined out. She withheld the house keys from them, offering the excuse that they were far too big and heavy to be tucked into the pocket of a gentleman's dinner jacket. And when my parents returned home, she would insist on serving them hot lemonade.

'During the Second World War, the Italian government sequestered the Barbaro, and as "enemy aliens" we were not permitted to live here. But Rosa and Angelo stayed in the palace and looked after it faithfully. We were in Paris when the war broke out, and my father decided to take us directly to New York. We didn't know if we'd ever see the Barbaro again. The Venetian superintendents came, crated the art, and took it to the Doge's Palace, where it would be safe. The Japanese military attaché used the *piano nobile* for a headquarters and covered the dining-room walls with framed photographs of Japanese war planes in action – including kamikaze planes. But Rosa cleverly hid the silver and other valuables, and Angelo sealed off the entrance to the library on the top floor so convincingly that people who occupied the Barbaro during the war never even knew the room existed.

'When my parents came back to Venice after the war, Rosa proudly took them round the palace to show them that everything had been returned to its pre-war condition. She had even taken the photographs of the Japanese warplanes off the dining-room walls and stacked them away.'

We left the ballroom through an enfilade of doorways into the master bedroom suite on the corner. These were the royal chambers, majestic in scale and prospect: two tall, balconied windows on the Grand Canal; side windows looking out over a narrow rio along the side of the palace; brocaded walls, and furniture from the time of the Barbaros.

Before I left, Patricia took me through her own apartment one floor above – the apartment that would still be hers even after the *piano nobile* had been sold. It had the same floor plan as the *piano nobile*, minus the ballroom, which gave it a broad, sunny central hall with spacious rooms on both sides and, in all, eight windows on the Grand Canal. The ceilings were lower, the walls were decorated with simple but elegant mouldings, and yet by any standard, even for Venice, this was a superb apartment.

At one point, we walked into one of the guest bedrooms, and I became aware that Patricia was watching me for my reaction, now more than before. And immediately I saw why.

On the wall in front of us there was a full-length portrait of a young woman in a strapless white gown. The pose was the first thing that drew my attention. It was almost identical to the exuberant pose of Isabella Stewart Gardner in the famous portrait of her, painted at the Barbaro by Anders Zorn: arms outstretched to the sides as she pushed open a pair of double doors and came sweeping into the *salone* from one of the balconies on the Grand Canal. The brushwork in the painting was reminiscent of Sargent's style. I was fairly certain this was the portrait that Ralph had mentioned to me.

'Is that you?' I asked.

'Yes. I was wearing my débutante dress.'

'And who painted it?'

'A man named Charles Merrill Mount,' she said. 'Do you know him?'

Charles Merrill Mount was a name I did know. For years he had been a prominent Sargent specialist. He had written a biography of Sargent, and his expert opinion was often sought for the authentication of paintings thought to be by Sargent — that is, until it was discovered that he was authenticating Sargents that he himself had painted.

'You mean the Charles Merrill Mount who went to jail?' I said.

'Yes.'

I said that I thought it was pretty impressive to have a portrait of oneself painted by a master forger of Sargent paintings, based on a portrait by Anders Zorn, painted in the same place Zorn had painted his original. As I looked at the portrait, it occurred to me that Charles Merrill Mount had captured Patricia in more than one sense. He had pulled her into the artistic history of the house, back into the late nineteenth century, to the era of Sargent, Henry James, and Isabella Stewart Gardner. I could only guess how strongly she identified with that glorious past through this painting – and whether the white dress had anything to do with her always wearing white.

'There's another room on this floor that I think might interest you,' she said.

She opened the door to a long, narrow room with a low, vaulted ceiling. Bookcases lined the walls, and between them on three sides rays of sunlight streamed in and fell in pools of amber on the terrazzo floor. Much older and far more decorative than the rest of her apartment, this library was like a slice carved out of the *piano nobile* and brought up here for safekeeping. This was the room that the servant Angelo had sealed off during the Second World War so that nobody who lived in the palace knew it was there. It was a gem of a room, and it would still be hers even when the *piano nobile* was not. No two-to-one vote could take it away.

'One summer,' she said, 'when Isabella Stewart Gardner rented the palace from my great-grandparents, she had a houseful of guests, including Henry James, and she ran out of bedrooms. So she put an extra bed up here for James. He loved gazing up at the stucco and the paintings on the ceiling, and he wrote my great-grandmother a letter about it to tell her what she, the owner of the palace, had been missing if she hadn't slept in this room herself.'

She lifted a piece of paper out of a book and read: ' "Have you ever lived here? – if you haven't, if you haven't gazed upward from your couch, in the rosy dawn, or during the postprandial (that is after-luncheon) siesta, at the medallions and arabesques of the ceiling, permit me to say that you don't know the Barbaro." '

She slipped the letter back into the book.

'When I was fourteen, my father called us up here after school was finished for the semester – he sat at that desk over there – and handed out books he wanted us to read over the summer. He gave me *The Wings of the Dove*.'

'You were fourteen?'

'I'll admit I found it difficult, but, having read it, I can understand why, for some people, no matter who owns the Barbaro, it will always belong to Milly Theale. In fact,' she said as we started back downstairs, 'Milly Theale will be returning to the Barbaro in a few months.'

'How so?' I asked.

'An English film company is coming to make the movie of *The Wings of the Dove*.'

Patricia's mood seemed to brighten at the rightness of it. The Curtises had allowed footage for a dozen or more films to be shot inside the Barbaro, films that had no connection at all with the Barbaro. It seemed fitting that this one, which had everything to do with the Barbaro and the Curtises, would be the last under the ownership of the Curtis family.

I recalled a bit of dialogue from the book that made it all the more poignant, and I wondered if the thought had occurred to Patricia as well: Milly has moved into 'Palazzo Leporelli' and has fallen in love with it. She clings to it, never wants to leave. She tells Lord Mark, 'I go about here. I don't get tired of it. I never should – it suits me so. I adore the place . . . I don't want in the least to give it up.'

'. . . Should you positively like to live here?'

'I think I should like,' said poor Milly after an instant, 'to die here.'

'I've seen many actors, many directors, many film crews come to this house to make movies,' said Daniel Curtis, the son of Patricia and the namesake and great-great-grandson of the Daniel Sargent Curtis who bought Palazzo Barbaro in 1885, 'and every time it's been like being, not exactly stabbed in the back, but scratched badly.'

I had met Daniel Curtis for the first time outside the Barbaro during the filming of *The Wings of the Dove*. Tall, lean, and with a head of dark, curly hair, he was about forty years old and possessed of abundant charm and good looks, for which he had become celebrated in Venice.

'Because it's either a piece of duct tape on the terrazzo – you know that when they pull it up afterwards the whole bloody thing comes off, and it needs another twenty years of wax to make it as it was before – or it's something even more calamitous, as happened last year when a scene was being filmed here for *In Love and War*. A technician walked into the *salone* with a ladder over his shoulder and slammed the end of it into an eighteenth-century chandelier. Then, at the sound of the crash, he turned around to see what damage he had done and swung it into a second chandelier. I tell you from my heart, when something like that happens, it is, to me, like a rape of the house.'

The cast and crew of *The Wings of the Dove* came to Palazzo Barbaro, made their movie, and left. Crowds watched from the Accademia Bridge and Campo San Vio, fascinated as two mist-making machines on boats moored in the Grand Canal turned a sunny summer day into a drizzly winter afternoon and as a cherry-picker mounted on a barge lifted a cameraman high in the air to shoot a scene with Milly Theale and Kate Croy (played by Alison Elliott and Helena Bonham Carter) looking out from a balcony on the *piano nobile*. The director of photography used coral filters to give the scenes shot in Venice a warm golden glow, in contrast to the London scenes, which were shot with a cold blue motif. Inside the Barbaro, set designers draped bolts of dark velvet with gold threads over the furniture to create the chiaroscuro effect of a Sargent painting. In two months of shooting, the film crew caused no more harm to the Barbaro than the usual wear and tear, and advance word had it that the movie was very good.

When the filming was over, prospective buyers once again trooped through the palace, taking the measure of the *piano nobile*. Jim Sherwood was one of them. In addition to owning "21" and the Cipriani, Sherwood was the proprietor of a luxury empire that included the Orient-Express railway and a worldwide chain of thirty deluxe hotels.

Sherwood's catered dinners at the Barbaro had long since come to an end when he received a call from Patricia.

'Patricia asked me if I had any interest in buying the *piano nobile*,' Sherwood told me one afternoon as we sat on the terrace of the Cipriani. 'I wanted to go over and have a close look at it, but she was out of town, so I had to ask Ralph to take me through instead. Patricia warned me he'd object to the idea. I received a letter from him enclosing a form that I was supposed to sign with a print of the big toe of my right foot. The return address was "Mission Control, Spaceship *Barbaro*". I ignored it, and a few days later a second letter arrived in an envelope covered with blood. The message said, in effect, "Well, even though you haven't given us an imprint of your toe, you can come and look at the property." He was pleasant enough when we met with him.

'My thought was that we might create apartments on the *piano nobile* and advertise them as "A Night in a Venetian Palazzo on the Grand Canal". It would have been the only accommodation like it in Venice. I had a study done and found we could make six apartments, but with the asking price and the vast expense of restoration and repair, I concluded it wouldn't pay off.'

Finally a buyer emerged in the person of Ivano Beggio, the owner of Aprilia, the second-largest maker of motorcycles in Europe. 'Ivano Beggio is the new spiritual custodian of Palazzo Barbaro,' crowed Ralph Curtis. Patricia was depressed. Daniel was angry.

After the Beggio deal was done, I encountered Daniel again as he was walking over the Accademia Bridge with his girlfriend. He invited me to join them in his apartment in the Barbaro for a glass of wine.

High up in the baroque side of the palace, the apartment had windows running the length of its western wall, admitting a bright, warm afternoon sun. Daniel poured two glasses of white wine while his girlfriend made a cup of tea for herself.

'When the *piano nobile* was sold,' he said, 'I tell you, I felt so bad. Because I grew up in this house. It was at a time when we still had gondoliers and when my grandfather was still alive. Sometimes I dream of the cuddles and the love that my grandfather transmitted to me when I was six, seven, eight years old, because I still carry them inside me, together with the smell of whisky that always came out with his words as he was telling me enchanting stories at night about fishermen and sailors.'

Daniel spoke fluent, heavily accented English. His father, a Venetian named Gianni Pelligrini, was Patricia Curtis's first husband; they were divorced when Daniel was four. Daniel often used the surname Curtis.

'When I was a teenager, I used to lie on the floor of the *salone* and look at the plaster figures on the ceiling, the *stucchi*. If I looked long enough, faces and masks would begin to emerge, sometimes ugly, sometimes smiling, but always fantastic and always in the same corner, particularly with the change of light, because the *salone* was filled with light.

'But best of all, when I was eighteen, I had the palace all to myself. My stepfather was very busy setting up a new business in Malaysia, so my mother had to go there frequently, and when she was away, I had the run of the palace. The maids cooked my meals, and there was a major-domo living downstairs who was always drunk. He was called Giovanni, and he had a great many bottles of wine under his bed. As you can imagine, I had a lot of girlfriends who were attracted by the big house, and I became a bit of a playboy in those days.'

Just as Venetians had considered his mother to be the owner of the Barbaro, Daniel Curtis had been regarded as the heir apparent. To some degree, he shared that view.

'Selling the house – selling the *piano nobile* – has been a trauma for my mother,' he said. 'She is the sort of person who, like me, even though she lives among millions of beautiful things, if by accident she breaks a single glass, she is devastated. You know? And for us, selling the *piano nobile* was like breaking every beautiful thing in the house.'

He smoked a cigarette and leaned forward in his chair, elbows on his knees, as he spoke with intense feeling about the Barbaro.

'But my aunt Lisa and my uncle Ralph outvoted my mother, and that meant the end of the Curtis *piano nobile*. Then they had to divide all the *soprammobili* – the ornaments, the ancient boxes, glass bowls, ashtrays, all sorts of nice things. And, believe me, when you're dealing with a *piano nobile* of ten thousand square feet there's a hell of a lot of *soprammobili*. And they had to be divided fast, and nobody could call an antiques dealer to get an estimate of the value. They put all the objects on the floor of the big dining-room in three rows, and they made all of the rows equal. Then, once they all agreed that the rows were more or less the same, they drew lots to see who got which row. And afterwards, when everybody's standing around and thinking, "Well, what did I get?" I see my aunt go from her row to one of the other rows and take something from that row and put it in her own row, and then she puts something from her row into the other row. I said nothing. I stood there silently, thinking, "What an aunt I have."

'I tell you, if I had had the power I should have had, this house would never have been sold. But I could not say anything. As we say, "*Non ho voce in capitolo*", I had no voice in the matter. Because in this family, the Curtis family, the decisions have to be made by the leadership, not by the full membership. And the leadership is my mother and her husband; my aunt Lisa, *la comtesse*, and her husband, *le comte*, and my uncle Ralph and his fucking space astronauts and Monkeyface. But—'

He suddenly stood up, the better to make his point.

'There is a difference,' he said, 'between me and all the other Curtises – the five generations of Curtises in Venice, starting with my great-great-grandfather, Daniel Sargent Curtis. Do you know what it is? I am the only Venetian! In five generations, I am the only Curtis with any Venetian blood. My father was a genuine Venetian, born and raised in Venice.'

He walked to the window and looked down into the courtyard. Then he turned round and leaned against the windowsill.

'Do you know what it is to be a Venetian? Venetians are very tough, they are very quarrelsome. They argue seriously for honour, and the vocabulary of the ancient dialect is very earthy. Venetians have expressions that are so incredibly vulgar they cannot possibly be taken literally, because if you took them literally, you would have to kill the person who said it to you.

'But what Venetians have that is very good is that they don't get excited about whether you are a king, a queen, the president, or *la comtesse* or *le comte*. Venetians are very democratic. They are all brothers. They all help each other. And it is the same for me, because I am Venetian. To me the baker is my brother. But for my mother and my aunt and my uncle, the baker is the baker.

'I love this house as a Venetian, not just as a Curtis. It is part of me. If a piece of it breaks off, I save it. I have everything of this house. Look!'

He went over to a cabinet between two windows and started pulling drawers open, one after another. They were filled with broken pieces of marble, Istrian stone, bricks, shards of old glass, and iron ornaments.

He picked up a small, irregular piece of reddish stone.

'This stone broke off the step at the top of the stairs outside my door.' He picked up a brick. 'This was dislodged from a chimney during a storm, and this piece of iron came from an old window grille. Everything about this house is sacred to me.

'One day, I swear to you, I will buy Palazzo Barbaro from Ivano Beggio. I will get back every piece of the palace that was sold to him. He's a very smart businessman. He got a great deal, and he knows it. He will probably demand twice what he paid for it. Fine. I will earn the money, I will find it, I will borrow it from rich friends. And why not? It would not be the first time someone named Daniel Curtis bought the Palazzo Barbaro.'

9

The Last Canto

ON HIS FIRST VISIT AS a house guest at Palazzo Barbaro, Henry James was met at the water entrance by white-gloved servants, who led him from his gondola on to the carpeted steps of the landing platform and up the courtyard stairs to the *piano nobile*. He was enchanted by all of it: the luxury, the polish, the reminders of the distant past 'twinkling in the multitudinous candles'. But even as he gazed at the Barbaro's painted walls and sculpted ceilings, James had in mind a very different sort of palace.

At the time, June of 1887, he was deep in thought about a dilapidated ruin on a lonely canal in a melancholy, rarely visited part of town. The once-grand interior of this other palace was shabby, dusty, and tarnished. Its walled garden had become an overgrown tangle of weeds and vines. Two impoverished spinster ladies lived in the palace, rarely went out, saw no one.

James told nobody about this other, derelict palace or its two lonely inhabitants, because they were fictional. They were characters in a short novel he was just then composing – *The Aspern Papers*, the other of his two masterful novels set in Venice. In the mornings, he would go to the Barbaro's breakfast room, sit down at the Chinese lacquered desk beneath the 'pompous Tiepolo ceiling', and write a few pages. During his five-week stay at the Barbaro, he put the finishing touches on the manuscript and sent it off to his publisher.

James had come upon the idea for his story during a sojourn in Florence earlier in the year. A friend had told him of a recent discovery: Lord Byron's former mistress, Claire Clairmont – the half sister of

Mary Shelley and the mother of Byron's illegitimate daughter, Allegra – was living in obscurity in Florence. She was by then well into her eighties and a virtual recluse, tended only by her middle-aged niece. A Boston art critic and devotee of Shelley's named Captain Silsbee suspected that Claire Clairmont might have a collection of letters from Byron and Shelley, and he came to Florence to seek her out. He rented rooms from Miss Clairmont, 'hoping', as James recorded in his notebook, 'that the old lady in view of her age and failing condition would die while he was there, so that he might then put his hand upon the documents'. When Claire Clairmont did, in fact, die while Captain Silsbee was a tenant in her palace, he approached her niece and revealed his desire of obtaining the letters. In reply the niece said, 'I will give you all the letters if you marry me.' Silsbee fled.

The story fascinated James. He suspected that it might make the basis for a good novel. 'Certainly,' he wrote in his journal, 'there is a little subject there: the picture of the two faded, queer, poor, and discredited old English women – living on into a strange generation, in their musty corner of a foreign town with these illustrious letters their most precious possession. Then the plot of the Shelley fanatic – his watchings and waitings . . .'

In fictionalizing the story, James moved it to Venice in order to, as he put it, 'cover my tracks' and at the same time take advantage of the city's aura of mystery and its sense of a lingering past. He also altered the characters, creating an American Byron (Jeffrey Aspern) and an American Claire Clairmont (Juliana Bordereau). The covetous Captain Silsbee became the nameless narrator of *The Aspern Papers*, an American publisher, who worships the long-dead Jeffrey Aspern and comes to Venice hoping to gain possession of Aspern's love letters.

In James's version, the narrator goes to see Juliana Bordereau in her run-down palace in an out-of-the-way corner of Venice and asks to rent rooms on the pretext that he has a passion for flowers and must live near a garden; but gardens being a rarity in Venice, he would, if he lived in the house, hire a gardener, restore the weed-choked rear courtyard, and fill the house with flowers. The old lady agrees. He moves in, restores the garden, supplies the women with bunches of fresh flowers, and even takes the younger Miss Bordereau out for a chaste evening in St Mark's Square. Upon the old woman's death, he asks the niece for her aunt's letters, and she replies nervously that perhaps if he were 'a relation', he might have them. Stunned, he rejects her offer, but the next morning he tells her he has had a change of heart: he is ready to accept. But it is too late: she, too, has had a change of heart: 'I've done the great thing,' she says. 'I've destroyed the papers . . . I burnt them last night, one by one, in the kitchen . . . It took a long time – there were so many.'

More novella than novel, *The Aspern Papers* is a psychological thriller, a fraction the length of *The Wings of the Dove*, and far more readable. As different as the two stories are, they share at least one important theme: the feigning of love as a means of gaining something of value. In *The Wings of the Dove*, the prize is money; in *The Aspern Papers*, it is the letters of a famous poet.

The Aspern Papers had long been a favourite of mine, and on an earlier visit to Venice I had walked over to Rio Marin to have a look at Palazzo Capello, the faded pink palace that James had used as his model for Juliana Bordereau's crumbling abode. The building was forlorn and unoccupied. It also appeared to have been looted. From what I could see through a grimy windowpane, the interior had been stripped of mantelpieces and cornices. As I was peering inside, a door in the garden wall opened and a dour-faced woman came out. I asked if I might have a look at the garden.

'*Giardino privato*,' she said, closing the door abruptly and walking away down the canal.

The Aspern Papers came to mind about a month after the Fenice fire, when I read in the *Gazzettino* that Olga Rudge had died at the age of 101. Like the fictional Juliana Bordereau, Olga Rudge had been an American woman who had lived in Venice to an advanced age and had been the mistress of a long-dead American poet, in her case Ezra Pound. Like Claire Clairmont and Byron, she and Pound had also had an illegitimate daughter. But the similarity seemed to end there.

The remarkable relationship between Olga Rudge and Ezra Pound had lasted fifty years, despite innumerable obstacles: his marriage to another woman, the dislocations of the Second World War, Pound's indictment for treason, and his thirteen-year imprisonment in an insane asylum after being judged unfit to stand trial. The bond between Olga Rudge and Ezra Pound was not, like Clairmont and Byron's, just another brief, discarded affair.

Also, unlike Claire Clairmont and Juliana Bordereau, Olga Rudge had a life of her own. By the time she met Pound, she was already well known as a concert violinist. Later, while conducting research into the music of Antonio Vivaldi, she discovered 309 Vivaldi concertos that had not been performed for centuries, if ever. With Pound's encouragement and collaboration, she organized and played in Vivaldi festivals and was in large part responsible for the Vivaldi renaissance.

After Pound's death in 1972, Olga continued to live in their tiny house not far from the Salute Church. She lived alone (there was no spinster niece), but hardly as a recluse. She loved company and was, by all accounts, charming, bright, talkative, and energetic.

Curious to have a look at the house where Ezra Pound and Olga Rudge had lived, I went to Rio Fornace, a tranquil canal in the quiet district of Dorsoduro. There, a few steps off the canal in a shady cul-de-sac, I found 252 Calle Querini, a narrow, three-storey cottage. A marble plaque mounted above the door bore the inscription 'With unwavering love for Venice, Ezra Pound, titan of poetry, lived in this house for half a century.'

A pane of frosted glass made it impossible to look inside, but I heard stirrings in the house next door and saw figures moving about through the window. This, I remembered, was the house Rose Lauritzen's mother had bought as a summer retreat and later, Rose told me, sold to the Anglican Church as a vicarage. I knocked on the door and was greeted by a friendly-faced, white-haired man with the accent of an American southerner. He was the Reverend Mr James Harkins, the Anglican minister of St George's.

'Not at all!' he said when I introduced myself and apologized for showing up unannounced. 'I'd say you've come at just the right time! My wife and I were about to sit down to cocktails – weren't we, Dora? Won't you join us?'

A short, dark-haired lady stepped out of a closet-size kitchen and smiled as she removed her apron.

Reverend Harkins poured Beefeater gin liberally into a measuring cup. 'You like your martinis on the dry side, don't you?' He turned towards me, eyebrows raised in expectation of a yes. 'By the way, you can call me Jim.'

We settled into armchairs in a cosy living room. Politeness required that I not plunge immediately into questions about Ezra Pound and Olga Rudge, so I asked about St George's Church.

'Oh, we're very low key,' he said, 'very small scale.' He took a sip of his martini and paused to savour it. 'The Anglican ministry here is a retirement post. There's no salary. We live free in this house, and we get utilities and medical insurance.'

'When do you have services?' I asked.

'Sundays. Matins at ten thirty, Holy Communion at eleven thirty.'

'No evensong?'

'Mmmm . . . not regularly.' Reverend Jim swirled his drink pensively, no doubt recalling how, at some defining moment long ago, he had faced up to the necessity of choosing between evening prayers and cocktails, and chosen cocktails.

'How large is your flock?' I asked.

'We get twenty-five to fifty on Sundays,' he said, 'mostly visitors.

But if you're asking about permanent resident members . . .' He thought for a moment. 'Oh, I'd have to say we have no more than six, including Dora.' He smiled benignly. 'And of those six, most don't come on a regular basis.'

'So you have an intimate parish,' I observed.

'Yes, but it's a good ministry. We enjoy much more prestige and status here than we deserve. We're always invited to cultural events and RC events. I usually wear my clerical collar when I leave the house, even when I'm not on official business, to let people know I'm here, fly the colours, show the cloth. That's my purpose, really. To be here if I'm needed. I like to think of St George's as an ecclesiastical convenience store.'

Nearby church bells started pealing and were answered by another bell farther away.

Reverend Harkins cocked an ear. 'Salute and Gesuati.'

'Oh, no, Jim,' said Dora, 'I don't think we can hear Gesuati from here. It would have to be the Redentore.'

'Right, right,' he said.

'Let me ask you something,' I said. 'How well did you know your former next-door neighbours, Ezra Pound and Olga Rudge?'

Dora perked up at this. 'Well, Pound died years before we got here,' she said, 'and Olga was living up in the Tyrol with her daughter, Mary de Rachewiltz. But the minister who was here just before us knew Olga very well and told us about her. She was tiny as a bird. Delightful. She had sparkling eyes, and even in her nineties she wore very stylish clothes. She took an interest in everyone. She was curious about everything. But, you know, Venice is a terrible place to grow old in.'

'Why?' I asked.

'Old people have a harder time getting around here than anywhere else, because nobody can pick them up and drive them door-to-door the way they can in other places. You have to walk; you have no choice. And that means you have to climb over two or three bridges every time you go out. Even if you could afford water taxis, you'd have to walk to a place where a taxi could pick you up, and then you'd have to walk from wherever it dropped you to wherever you wanted to go.'

'We love Venice,' said Jim, 'but we'll have to leave as soon as we have trouble getting over the bridges.'

'Katherine, the minister's wife, would check up on Olga at least once a day,' said Dora, 'sometimes twice, just to see if she was all right. But, you know, at her age there were times she'd become confused. It got to the point that Olga needed constant care, and that's when Mary came and took her back to live with her. That's where Olga was when she died.

'No one is more vulnerable in Venice than old people living alone,' Dora went on, 'especially foreigners without family to look after them. They become dependent on outsiders; they have to put their trust in them. I'm told that's what happened with Olga, and that's when all the trouble started.'

'What trouble?' I asked.

'I'm not very clear about it,' said Dora, 'because it happened just before we got here. It seems that some friends of Olga's who'd been very kind to her for years gradually became deeply involved in her affairs. Olga had boxes full of letters and other documents – thousands of letters between her and Ezra Pound, and letters from dozens of other famous people. Some of the letters were valuable, some weren't. But before anyone knew it, the papers were gone.'

'So you've found out about the Ezra Pound Foundation,' said Rose Lauritzen, with a look that suggested I had uncovered a well-kept secret.

'Not really,' I said. 'Tell me about it.'

'I can't,' said Rose, 'because for once, thank God, I don't know enough about it to blather on like an idiot and get it all wrong!'

'The Ezra Pound Foundation,' said Peter, 'is, or rather was, a tax-exempt entity, the purpose of which was to promote the study of Ezra Pound and his works. Olga had often mentioned wanting to set up something like that to perpetuate interest in Pound. But the odd thing is that when she went ahead and formed this foundation, none of the people you'd have expected to be involved knew anything about it. Mary de Rachewiltz, the daughter of Olga and Pound, was largely in the dark, and she is her father's literary executor. James Laughlin, the founder of New Directions, Ezra Pound's publisher since the 1930s, didn't know anything about it, and neither did Yale, where the bulk of Pound's papers are housed.'

'How did it come to light?' I asked.

'Well, the first we heard of it,' said Peter, 'was from Walton Litz, who was my adviser at Princeton and a great Joyce and Pound expert. Litz often came to Venice to visit Olga, and on one occasion he came to see me and asked, "Who are these people called Rylands?"

'I told him, "Philip Rylands is the director of the Peggy Guggenheim Collection. He's English. Jane Rylands is his wife, and she's American. Why?"

'"Well," Litz said, "it seems they've created an Ezra Pound Foundation! And Olga has given her papers and her house to the foundation."

'Rose and I were shocked, because Litz and Mary de Rachewiltz had often discussed the idea of an Ezra Pound study centre along similar lines, with Litz running it.'

'What's become of the foundation?' I asked.

Peter drew a deep breath, as if preparing to deliver a detailed explanation. Instead he said, 'Why don't you ask Jane Rylands?'

As it happened, I had already met Philip and Jane Rylands. A friend had taken me to the Guggenheim Collection one evening just after closing time to meet them over a glass of wine. There were six of us altogether. We stood in a gallery that had once been Peggy Guggenheim's dining room on the ground floor of Palazzo Venier, her home for thirty years until her death in 1979. Philip Rylands was in his mid-forties and on the timid side, I thought. He had a pale, square face with a protruding chin. Large glasses magnified his eyes, which, together with eyebrows that lifted at the outer ends, gave him a look of perpetual alarm. Jane Rylands was short, sturdy rather than petite, and had a firm face and light brown hair. She appeared to be somewhat older than Philip. They were cordial but stiff. Several times Jane murmured comments to Philip, barely moving her lips, ventriloquist style.

Our meeting was perfunctory, and although I was neither charmed nor terribly impressed by the couple, they interested me. In a city like Venice, a museum with the cachet of the Guggenheim automatically conferred a certain status upon its administrator. The Guggenheim was an international nexus of art, society, privilege, money, and culture. The cool, spacious rooms with their white walls and terrazzo floors looked out on the Grand Canal in front and a lush, green garden, where Peggy and her dogs were buried, at the back. The palace itself was a curiosity. The Venier family, which had produced three doges, had started construction in 1749 and had completed only the first floor when work stopped for good. The floor of the unbuilt second storey served as a spacious roof-garden patio with the Grand Canal spread out before it and huge, towering trees rising up from the garden, providing a verdant backdrop. Inside and out, the truncated white palace offered itself as an elegant setting for receptions, lectures, screenings, gatherings of all types. In addition, the closing of the American consulate in Venice in the early 1970s had left the Guggenheim, by default, the most prominent American presence in Venice. At times the Guggenheim found itself in the role of a surrogate American embassy. The State Department called now and then to organize receptions and ask other favours. Clearly Philip and Jane occupied a position of prominence and power in Venice, and their evident self-consciousness made me all the more curious about them.

I had followed up our brief cocktail introduction by talking informally with each of them. Philip and I had coffee a few days later in the museum's café. He was friendly and good-humoured, though harried. He told me he had studied art history at Cambridge and written a thesis on the Renaissance painter Palma Vecchio. Alluding to his current work, Rylands mentioned that a small Picasso exhibition would be installed in the autumn, but he spoke mainly about the museum's expansion plans, which were being formulated by the Guggenheim executives in New York. He was hardworking and earnest, but he struck me as being a little on the dull side – the opposite of his wife.

I called on Jane at their apartment later in the week, and we had tea in a light-filled sitting-room. She was wearing a modish black-and-white tweed jacket, form-fitting blue jeans, and heels. I found her relaxed, engaging, and opinionated, especially on the subject of society figures in Venice. In the 1970s, she had been a Venice-based gossip columnist briefly for the *Rome Daily American* but had given it up when it started to raise hackles in Venice. Having observed Venetian society carefully, Jane had found ways of navigating in and around it. Venetians, she said, had a weakness for parties, and this enabled even a foreigner to wield a certain amount of power. How? Invitations! The invitation given, the invitation withheld. Certainly Jane was in a position to issue invitations, and to withhold them.

I liked her a good deal more this time. She was quick-witted and shrewd, which appealed to me. But she had a sharp edge and did not hesitate to show it. At one point, I made reference to a man, well known in art-world circles, who had been a close friend of Peggy Guggenheim's since the early sixties.

'Oh, him,' she said with a lighthearted laugh. 'What was he doing when you saw him? Serving drinks to all those rich men?' It was a cheeky remark, I thought, since she could not have known whether the man was a good friend of mine or merely an acquaintance. Nor, it later occurred to me, did she care.

'The name of Olga Rudge never came up?' Peter Lauritzen asked.

'Only once,' I said, 'as I was leaving. In a room off the parlour, I noticed a large painting of an old woman seated among various objects – books, I think. The colours were pastel. I liked the painting. I asked who it was, and Jane said Olga Rudge. Then she added, "Her archives are at Yale, you know!" She said it with a perkiness that seemed to say, "Isn't that wonderful?" which was odd, I thought, because I didn't think it was at all surprising that Ezra Pound's mistress of fifty years would have a collection of letters important enough to end up at Yale.'

'That's not where Jane Rylands had wanted them to end up,' said Peter.

I resisted the impulse to call Jane and ask to talk to her again. It seemed wiser to find out more about the Ezra Pound Foundation first. The Lauritzens begged off, saying their knowledge of the affair was too sketchy and that other people were closer to Olga when it was happening.

Meanwhile Olga's recent death had made her a frequent topic of conversation in Venice. What emerged from all the talk was a moving and dramatic portrait – of Olga Rudge, Ezra Pound, Mary de Rachewiltz and, in the background, Pound's legal wife, Dorothy Shakespear, and their son, Omar.

Both Olga Rudge and Ezra Pound had become expatriates shortly after the turn of the century: Olga in 1904, at the age of nine; Pound in 1908, at twenty-three. Olga had been born in Youngstown, Ohio; Pound was a native of Idaho.

Pound settled first in Venice, installing himself in a small apartment on Rio San Trovaso and, with his own money, publishing one hundred copies of his first book of poems, *A Lume Spento* (With Tapers Quenched). Three months later, he moved to London, where he became a driving force of literary modernism. He campaigned for a more austere, direct, and forceful style of expression – as summed up and exemplified by his rallying cry, 'Make It New'. He was a poet, a critic, an editor, and an unusually generous promoter of his literary friends and their work. He helped William Butler Yeats shed his Celtic romanticism, counselled Hemingway to 'distrust adjectives', and sang the praises of James Joyce to Sylvia Beach, who then published *Ulysses*. His editing of T. S. Eliot's 'The Waste Land' contributed so profoundly to the poem that Eliot dedicated it to him in gratitude and admiration: 'Ezra Pound, *il miglior fabbro*' – the better craftsman.

In 1920, Pound reviewed a concert for the *New Age* in which he praised a young violinist for 'the delicate firmness of her fiddling'. The violinist was Olga Rudge. Three years later, Pound and Olga met for the first time at the Paris salon of Natalie Barney. Olga, then twenty-seven, was possessed of exotic, black Irish good looks. Pound was tall, impressive in his signature brown velvet jacket, and married. They became lovers.

From the mid 1920s until the Second World War, Pound divided his time between his wife and Olga. The Pounds lived in a beachfront apartment in Rapallo on the Italian Riviera. Olga lived in Venice in the little house at 252 Calle Querini, given to her by her father in 1928 and nicknamed 'the Hidden Nest' by Pound. She also rented an apartment in Sant' Ambrogio, a hill town above Rapallo, that could be reached only by an arduous half-hour climb up a steep path of stone steps.

Olga gave birth to Pound's daughter, Mary Rudge, in 1925. She and Pound immediately placed the child with a foster family on a farm in the foothills of the Tyrolean Alps. Mary lived there, in the village of Gais, for the first ten years of her life, with visits from her parents on rare occasions and trips to see them in Venice. Omar Pound, born to Dorothy a year later, was sent to England and raised by his grand-mother.

Meanwhile Ezra Pound and Olga Rudge pursued their separate careers. Pound worked on his *Cantos*, the epic poem that was to occupy him for fifty years. Olga, proud never to have been financially dependent on Pound, continued touring as a concert violinist, published a catalogue of works by Vivaldi, and wrote the article on Vivaldi for *The Grove Dictionary of Music*.

The outbreak of war shattered the delicate Pound-Shakespear-Rudge ménage. The Hidden Nest in Venice was sequestered by the Italian government, and the Pounds were forced to evacuate their seafront apartment in Rapallo. That left Pound and Dorothy little choice but to move up the hill to Sant' Ambrogio, where they lived with Olga for nearly two years. The house was small and had neither electricity nor telephone. It was a difficult time for all. Pound loved Olga and Dorothy, and the women both loved Pound but loathed each other. As Mary later recalled, 'hatred and tension permeated the house'.

Pound began making twice-monthly trips to Rome to deliver pro-Fascist broadcasts over Italian radio, for which, in 1943, he was indicted by the United States government for treason. At the close of the war, he was arrested in Rapallo, held in an outdoor cage at a detention centre in Pisa for six months, and then sent back to America. Through the intervention of literary friends, the Department of Justice agreed to declare him unfit to stand trial by reason of insanity, and he was committed to St Elizabeth's Hospital for the Criminally Insane in Washington. During his thirteen years of incarceration, Olga wrote to him regularly but was not permitted to visit. That privilege was extended only to Dorothy, his legal wife. When, in 1958, the charges against him were dropped, he was released in Dorothy's custody. Pound was stripped of his legal rights; Dorothy was named his legal guardian.

Dorothy and Pound went to live with Mary in the South Tyrol at Brunnenburg, a medieval castle that Mary and her husband, the Egyptologist Boris de Rachewiltz, bought as a ruin and then restored. For the next two years, Dorothy and Pound lived with the de Rachewiltzes. In 1961, depressed and ill, Pound chose to put himself into Olga's hands. For the last eleven years of his life, he lived with Olga at 252 Calle Querini and withdrew into his shell of silence.

Undeterred by Pound's refusal to speak, legions of researchers, disciples, and the merely curious came seeking audiences. Olga could usually discern who among them was worth admitting to the Hidden Nest. She would simply ask them to quote a single line of Ezra Pound's poetry, of the thousands he had written, and many could not.

After thirty-five years as the other woman, without any legal rights whatever, Olga no longer had to share Pound with Dorothy. She had stood by him in dangerous and desperate times, and Pound was more than grateful. 'There is more courage in Olga's little finger,' he said of her, 'than in the whole of my carcass. She kept me alive for ten years, for which no one will thank her.' Pound died in Venice in 1972 and was laid to rest on the cemetery island of San Michele. Twenty-four years later, Olga would join him. (Dorothy died a year after Pound, in England, where she was buried in her family plot.)

In 1966, Pound composed a poetic tribute to Olga to be placed at the end of the last *Canto*, whatever he might write in the interim:

> *That her acts*
> *Olga's acts*
> *of beauty*
> *be remembered.*
>
> *Her name was Courage*
> *& is written Olga*

For twenty years after Pound's death, Olga lived alone in the Hidden Nest. Scholars, reporters, and friends kept coming, and Olga welcomed many of them, serving tea, engaging them in lively conversation, and concluding nearly every point she made with the word '*Capito?*' (Understood?) Her sole mission, as she saw it, was to tend Ezra Pound's eternal flame and to defend him against charges that he had been a Fascist and an anti-Semite — not an easy task, given his pro-Mussolini broadcasts during the war and the constant anti-Jewish ravings in his letters.

Despite her age, Olga was determined to continue living in Venice, even if it meant living alone. She treasured her independence. Mary, who was three hours away in the Tyrolean Alps, was therefore relieved when Philip and Jane Rylands befriended Olga and took a special interest in her welfare. They were young, bright, influential, and obviously respectable. Their attachment to the Guggenheim, which was virtually round the corner from Calle Querini, was doubly reassuring.

Jane and Philip Rylands doted on Olga. They looked in on her every day, took her to dinner, invited her to parties, ran errands for her, made sure the grocery shopping was done. In 1983, Jane organized a seminar at the Gritti Hotel entitled 'Ezra Pound in Italy', featuring talks by three generations of Pound's 'other family' – Olga, Mary, and Mary's son, Walter. Two years later, Jane arranged for a gala ninetieth-birthday party for Olga, also at the Gritti.

There was nothing Jane and Philip Rylands would not do for Olga. In the winter, they brought firewood from the Guggenheim and mopped up Olga's ground floor after it had been flooded in high water. If any problems arose – a leak, a stopped-up drain, a blown fuse – Olga knew that Jane Rylands could be counted on to take care of things quickly and efficiently. In time, however, there were signs that Jane Rylands's care of Olga had begun to verge on control.

In 1986, Olga offered a young American painter, Vincent Cooper, room and board at 252 Calle Querini in exchange for painting a *trompe l'oeil* mural of arches and columns on the ground floor. Olga wanted the mural as a reminder of one that had been on the walls when she and Pound lived there before the war. It had been removed when the house was sequestered. Cooper would live on the top floor in what had been Pound's studio and Mary's childhood bedroom.

'The morning I moved in,' Cooper told me, 'Mrs Rylands arrived at the house and came stomping up the stairs and made it very clear she didn't want me there. She walked towards me with her arms folded and looked me square in the face and told me I was in the home of a major twentieth-century literary figure. "There are very important objects in the house," she said, "and if anything were to go missing, you're the one who'll be blamed for it . . . and I don't think you'd want that."

'She informed me that she'd arranged to have Olga's portrait painted in that very room "by a very important artist from London who will be arriving very shortly". She began hauling various things up to the third floor – books, sculptures, objects – and arranging them to form a background for Olga's portrait. She advised me to leave and not tell Olga on my way out, because she would only tell me to stay.

'After Mrs Rylands had left, I went downstairs and told Olga I was leaving because Jane Rylands didn't want me in the way. "You will do no such thing!" Olga shouted. "This is my house, and I invited you here! How dare Jane Rylands tell you to leave? And anyway, I do not want to have my portrait painted!" She insisted I stay and finish the mural, and at least be there while "I'm having my portrait painted by a stranger."

'Then the doorbell rang, and it was the portrait painter Sir Lawrence Gowing. He had such a choking stutter that Olga couldn't understand a word he said and was visibly distressed by it. I helped him upstairs with his supplies, and when he saw Mrs Rylands's arrangement, he said, "I set up my own poses! Really! That Jane Rylands is quite a manager!" I then left the house.

'Gowing had already gone when I returned in the early evening. He'd made considerable progress on the portrait, but he'd moved Olga to another corner of the room and ignored Jane's instructions completely. Olga was not surrounded by Jane's objects at all but was posed in the middle of my belongings, including my suitcase and passport. An unfinished drawing of mine that I'd leaned against the wall was also now part of the background. It framed Olga's head.

'Olga had arranged for me to go to a party that evening, but I couldn't get to my clothes without disturbing Gowing's arrangement of objects. So Olga lent me a black velvet jacket of Pound's. I was just leaving the house when Mrs Rylands stopped by to inspect the portrait. She was beside herself when she saw it. "I told him where to paint Olga, and that's where she's going to be painted!" She turned to me and, speaking to me now as an ally rather than as somebody to be brushed aside, she said, "When Gowing comes back, tell him if he wants the commission, he must paint Olga where I've set up the pose and with the objects I've chosen." She said that since she had commissioned the painting and was paying for it, it would be done her way.

'Gowing left the pose as it was, but he satisfied Mrs Rylands by agreeing to include life casts of Ezra's and Olga's faces in the fore-ground. He did, however, complain that he was doing three portraits for the price of one. He and Mrs Rylands did not part on very good terms.

'When the portrait was finished, Mrs Rylands gave a dinner party at the Gritti to unveil it. Olga never said whether she liked the portrait or not, but she burst out laughing every time she looked at it.'

At about this time – the mid 1980s – Olga began to exhibit lapses of memory. She was then in her early nineties and would lose track of what she was saying, misplace things, forget appointments.

James Wilhelm, a professor of English at Rutgers and the author of *The American Roots of Ezra Pound* and *Dante and Pound*, talked with Olga at a centennial celebration of Pound at the University of Maine in 1985. He noticed signs of forgetfulness. The following year, while on a visit to Venice, he went to see Olga at the Hidden Nest to take her out to lunch.

'Before going out,' Wilhelm told me, 'Olga and I sat in the living room talking. She mentioned that guests were staying on the third floor, a young poet and his girlfriend, and that they were asleep, so unfortunately she couldn't show me the third floor where Pound used to work. Later in the conversation, I heard some noises above, and I said, "Olga, I hear footsteps above. The people upstairs must be getting up."

'Suddenly Olga's eyes narrowed, and she bent towards me, "Who *are* those people upstairs?"

'I said, "Olga, I don't know. You said they were a young poet – and his girlfriend."

' *"Yes . . . yes . . . who . . . is . . . that . . . girl?"*

'Once again I said, "I don't know."

'She sat back in her chair. "I wish they'd go!"

'I knew she didn't mean it. She wanted people in the house around her, but I could already see deep-rooted signs of memory loss.

'I told Olga that I was going to Bologna for a week and that I would see her when I came back to Venice afterwards. But when I called her house, a strange woman answered. Someone connected with the Guggenheim Museum, I believe. She told me that Olga had fallen ill and was unable to see anyone.' Wilhelm later wrote about these meetings with Olga, in much the same detail, for the scholarly journal devoted to Ezra Pound and his works, *Paideuma*.

It was at about this time also that Olga made mention of the Ezra Pound Foundation in conversations with friends, vaguely, without offering much detail. It was clear that Jane Rylands was involved.

'Mrs Rylands and Olga talked about the foundation all the time,' said Vincent Cooper. 'Olga had stacks of letters and papers around and was a bit overwhelmed by it all. She'd have important visits from publishers and lawyers and other people, and when they left, she'd ask me who they were. I thought it was risky for anyone to do serious business with Olga. She was full of enthusiasm but becoming forgetful and very easily confused.'

Jim Wilhelm recalled that 'there was suspicion in Venice that the aged Olga might be being used by others for some purpose'.

Christopher Cooley, a friend of both Olga's and Pound's, knew the contents of their library very well, having catalogued the books in it for them in the early 1970s. Cooley lived in a house on Rio San Trovaso. We spoke in his garden.

'When Olga told me about setting up a Pound foundation,' Cooley recalled, 'I said to her, "I hope you're not signing any papers having to do with this foundation without consulting your family." She was vague about that, neither affirming nor denying. She asked me if I'd like to be on the board of the foundation, and I told her I was uneasy about it. I said, "You know, Olga, if the house is going to be used by visiting students, there will be various expenses. The foundation will have to raise money. It could become very complicated." So I told her, very gently, no.

'The next time I saw Jane – it was at a party at Palazzo Brandolini – I asked her to tell me about the foundation. She said, all smiles and teeth, "I'm just helping an old lady do what she wants to do."

'Then I asked her pointedly who was on the board of the foundation, feeling entitled to do so, since Olga had invited me to be on it. She snapped, "It's none of your business!" and walked out of the room. It didn't smell right to me. I caught up with her a little while later and said, "That last remark of yours was the only revealing thing you've said about the foundation."'

Then came the incident of the disappearing papers. Olga had several large trunks full of papers stored on her ground floor. One Christmastime, Jane took the trunks away to make space for Olga, she said, and to put the papers out of danger from high water. Either Olga forgot where Jane had said she was taking them or Jane never told her; in any case, a short while later, Olga became anxious about them and complained to a number of people that Jane had taken her trunks and that she did not know where they were. Finally she asked Jane to return them, and Jane did. But, according to Olga, when she opened them, she found them empty.

At this point, Arrigo Cipriani, the owner of Harry's Bar, entered the story. Cipriani had grown up in a house on the corner of Calle Querini and Rio Fornace. The rear windows of Olga's house looked out on the Ciprianis' garden.

Without telling Cipriani what I wanted to talk about, I made an appointment to see him. As agreed, I stopped by Harry's Bar one morning at eleven. The waiters and barmen were rushing around the restaurant setting up for lunch. A postman came in and dropped a stack of letters at the bar. Arrigo Cipriani arrived a few minutes later. He was wearing a dapper dark blue suit with peaked lapels. He was in trim condition, still the agile black-belt karate expert.

'Do you mind if we walk while we talk?' he said. 'I have an appointment.' He led the way down Calle Vallaresso.

'What can you tell me about the Ezra Pound Foundation?' I asked as I walked alongside him.

Cipriani's face turned from cheery to serious. 'It is not a nice story,' he said.

A workman wheeling a cart called out, '*Ciao*, Arrigo!' as we passed him at a fast clip. Cipriani waved and then ducked into a narrow alley between buildings, still walking at top speed.

'Jane Rylands came to me,' he said, 'and told me she was cleaning Olga Rudge's house. She asked if she could put some things in a *magazzino*, a storeroom, that I own next door to Olga. Just a few boxes, she said. The ground floor was empty, so I said fine.'

Cipriani took another turn, and two businessmen smiled as we passed: '*Ciao*, Arrigo!'

'Some time later,' Cipriani continued, 'workmen on a job nearby told me Jane Rylands was going in and out of the *magazzino*. Then I happened to meet Joan FitzGerald in the street. You know Joan FitzGerald, the sculptor, a very close friend of Pound and Olga? She made a sculpture of the old man; it's in the National Portrait Gallery in Washington. I mentioned to Joan that I had some things of Olga's, and Joan told me that Olga was worried about her belongings. She said Jane Rylands had taken several boxes and returned them empty, and now Olga didn't know where the contents were. I said, "I think I know where they are. Let me check."

'Just to be sure,' said Cipriani, 'I went to the *magazzino*, and there they were: big stacks of papers wrapped in sheets of clear plastic. There were signs saying, "Do Not Touch", "Property of Ezra Pound Foundation". I called Joan and two businessman friends and said, "Come over!"'

'It was Easter Sunday. We took Olga into the *magazzino*, and as soon as she saw the papers, she said, "Those are my things!" She began picking up handfuls of stuff and carrying them back to her house, but there was no room. I said, "Wait! I have a better idea. I own another *magazzino* right across the *calle*, and I've got the keys with me." So we carried the papers and boxes across the *calle* into number 248 and locked the door. I was very angry now. I realized I had been an unknowing accomplice to whatever it was Jane had done, legal or illegal. It could have got me into serious trouble, and now, by moving these papers with the "Do Not Touch" signs, I was afraid I could be accused of stealing Jane's property. So I made everybody sign a piece of paper saying we had moved the boxes.'

Cipriani turned another corner, and we were suddenly in the bright sunlight at the foot of the Rialto Bridge.

'You know,' he said, 'I had a strange feeling from the beginning. After I told Jane she could put the things in my place, she asked me if I would like to be on the board of directors of the Ezra Pound Foundation. What did I know about the poetry of Ezra Pound?'

Two men standing in a doorway called out to Arrigo and waved him over.

'*Ciao! Subito, subito!*' (I'll be right with you) he said. Then, turning back to me, 'Well, that's it. As I told you, it's not a very nice story.'

The episode of the disappearing papers became a turning point in the fortunes of the Ezra Pound Foundation. Jane had told Olga she had moved the papers to keep them from being damaged in high water, but it was plain to everyone that the ground floor of Arrigo Cipriani's *magazzino* was at virtually the same level as Olga's and therefore no safer.

Harald Böhm, a sculptor, told me Jane had enlisted his aid in moving the papers. 'Jane asked me if I would help her move some furniture. It was Christmastime. I said okay, because she had a certain power in the art world. She could make connections between rich people and artists, and at the time I was hoping she would find me a big commission. But when I arrived at Olga's house, I found out we would be moving papers, not furniture. Jane said the papers were very valuable and that if they were left in Olga's house, someone might steal them, or Olga's family might sell them. Jane spoke as if we were doing something heroic. But I noticed that while Philip and I were moving the papers out of the house, Jane was keeping Olga occupied in conversation upstairs. I did not think Olga was aware of what we were doing, and it made me nervous. I knew she had a kind of Alzheimer's. Everybody knew it. I was afraid Olga was being duped, and that I had been duped into helping. I was worried I'd be arrested, especially when Jane said afterwards, "Be sure you don't tell anybody about today, or *peggio per te* − it will be bad for you."'

Friends of Olga's, their suspicions already aroused, became alarmed when the episode of the missing papers occurred. Several people called Mary de Rachewiltz and implored her to come down to Venice quickly and find out what was happening. Walter and his father, Boris de Rachewiltz, came in her stead and asked Olga to show them the foundation's legal papers. Olga said she had none; Jane Rylands had them. When Boris and Walter finally read the documents, they understood what Olga had done. And, finally, so did Olga. To Christopher Cooley, Olga said simply, 'What a fool I was. Oh, what a fool I was.'

Having discovered that the foundation was the instrument through which her mother had virtually disinherited her, Mary de Rachewiltz sought help from friends in Venice. One of the people she appealed to was Liselotte Höhs, an Austrian artist who lived near the San Trovaso gondola workshop, not far from Olga. Liselotte and her late husband, the lawyer Giorgio Manera, had been friendly with both Olga and

Pound and had made it a tradition over the years to invite them for Christmas dinner. After Pound's death, Olga had expressed a desire to create a foundation in Venice dedicated to Pound's memory, and Liselotte had tried to help her. She accompanied Olga to a meeting with the head of the Cini Foundation and on Olga's behalf went on her own to see the heads of the Marciana Library and Palazzo Grassi. But she was not able, at the time, to secure any commitments.

Mary had given Liselotte copies of the foundation's legal papers, and Liselotte had been incensed by what she saw. I was told that she still had the copies, and when I called her she invited me to come and have a look at them.

We sat in her living-room, a large studio with a double-height ceiling and a northern skylight. Liselotte was a passionate Valkyrie with flashing eyes and blonde hair flowing in waves down her back.

'Mary didn't know what to do,' she said. 'She begged me to please help her find a lawyer. Olga had always wanted control to remain in Venice and always with her grandson, Walter, involved. He was her favourite.'

Liselotte handed me the foundation's incorporation papers. They were in English. The foundation had been recorded as a not-for-profit corporation on 17 December 1986 – in Ohio. The principal office was located in Cleveland, not in Venice.

'Why Ohio?' I asked.

'A good question,' said Liselotte.

Jane was from Ohio, I recalled. And Olga had been born in Youngstown, but she had not lived in Ohio for more than eighty years at the time these papers were signed.

The foundation had three officers: Olga Rudge as president, Jane Rylands as vice president, and a Cleveland attorney as secretary. The foundation's bylaws stated that two of the three could outvote the third. This meant that from the outset Olga had ceded control of the foundation to Jane Rylands and a lawyer from Cleveland, neither of whom had ever met Ezra Pound or had any expertise in his life and works.

Liselotte now handed me a contract between Olga and the foundation, this one in Italian, documenting Olga's donation of her house to the foundation, outright, free of charge. At the time she signed it, Olga was ninety-two.

Liselotte then handed me a second contract. In this one, Olga had agreed to sell the foundation all of her 'books, manuscripts, diaries, private correspondence, newspaper clippings, writings, papers, documents of any kind, drawings, books and albums of drawings and sketches, photographs, tapes and magnetic cassettes, and any objects that might be added to the collection before her death' — all for the sum of 15 million lire, or seven thousand dollars, which, according to the contract, Olga had already received.

The significance of this contract was very clear. For a pittance, not only had Olga sold fifty years' worth of her correspondence with Ezra Pound, she had also sold letters to her and to Pound from T. S. Eliot, Samuel Beckett, e. e. cummings, H. L. Mencken, Marianne Moore, Robert Lowell, Archibald MacLeish, William Carlos Williams, Ford Madox Ford, and other literary figures, as well as drafts of the *Cantos*, books that bore marginalia and annotations by Pound, and first editions of books inscribed to Pound by their authors. The total value of the collection could have approached $1 million, the market for Poundiana being what it was at the time. Any number of items were, by themselves, worth more than the sale price of the whole lot. Among the most valuable would have been the notebooks of the sculptor Henri Gaudier-Brzeska, a founder, along with Pound, of the vorticism movement. Gaudier-Brzeska died during the First World War, at twenty-four, rendering his notebooks particularly rare and valuable.

'Did Olga have her own lawyer with her when she did all this?' I asked.

'I don't think so.'

When Olga finally realized what had happened, she became hysterical. She called Joan FitzGerald at night, saying she wanted to dissolve the foundation and, in tears, rushed over the Accademia Bridge to see her. Liselotte handed me another page. It was a photocopy of a letter handwritten in Olga's large, clear script, addressed to the Cleveland attorney:

24 April 1988

Dear [Sir],

I wish to inform you that it is my firm intention to dissolve the 'Ezra Pound Foundation.'

I have revoked the donation of my house at Dorsoduro 252, Venice – I would like to make it very clear that I never knowingly sold my archive to the 'Foundation' or to anyone. Any deed to this effect can only be due to some misunderstanding.

Cordially yours,
Olga Rudge

The reply, which was sent seven weeks later, informed Olga that the Ezra Pound Foundation could not be dissolved just because she wanted it to be; it would take a majority vote of the trustees. And even if the trustees did vote to dissolve the foundation, its property could not be returned to Olga, but it would have to be passed on to another tax-exempt institution. That was the law, he said.

Olga apparently wrote several letters declaring her desire to dissolve the foundation. Liselotte handed me another one, dated 18 March 1988. This one was not addressed to anyone in particular. 'My intention,' Olga wrote, 'has always been that any foundation formed in the name of Ezra Pound would include Trustees from the Cini Foundation, Ca' Foscari University, the Marciana Library and my grandson Walter de Rachewiltz . . .' The handwriting was clearly Olga's, but there was no way of knowing whether the letters were in her own words or had been composed by someone else and then copied by Olga.

Given all this commotion – friends of Olga's rallying against the foundation, Olga herself declaring she wanted to dissolve it – one would have thought that Jane Rylands might have backed off a bit, saying, 'I'm so sorry. I only meant to help.'

But it was not until two years later that she finally transferred custody of the papers to Yale. Then she dissolved the foundation. There were rumours that Yale had paid Jane Rylands a considerable sum of money for title to the papers, but they were only conjecture.

For whatever reason, the Venetian press never covered the story of the Ezra Pound Foundation and the uncertain fate of Olga Rudge's house and papers. News of it spread through word of mouth, however, raising questions about Jane and Philip Rylands.

When the Rylandses arrived in Venice in a Volkswagen camper in 1973, this much was known about them: Jane had been born in Ohio, graduated from the College of William and Mary, and moved to England, where she taught freshman composition at the American air base in Mildenhall, near Cambridge. She was outgoing, ambitious, well read in English and American literature, a dedicated Anglophile, and popular with the boys in Cambridge for serving fried-chicken dinners bought from the PX at the air base. Philip was a student at King's College, Cambridge, when he met Jane. He was shy, serious, and best known for being the nephew of George 'Dadie' Rylands, a distinguished and influential Shakespearean scholar, actor, and director. Dadie Rylands was a surviving link to the Bloomsbury group, a protégé of Lytton Strachey, and still a beloved fellow at King's, where he had been living in the same rooms since 1927. His apartment had been decorated by Dora Carrington and visited by countless intellectuals. Virginia Woolf described a luxurious lunch there in her book *A Room of One's Own*.

Word had it that Philip's parents were less than enthusiastic about his marriage to Jane, who was ten years his senior.

When they arrived in Venice, Philip had long hair held back at the sides by two bobby pins, and Jane wore 'frumpy' clothes and her hair in a bun. Philip was still writing his dissertation, which would take him the better part of twelve years to finish. Meanwhile Jane supported both of them by teaching at the American air base in Aviano, an hour north of Venice.

At first they knew no one in Venice, but Philip regularly attended St George's Church, then the focus of Anglo-American expatriate social life. There he met Sir Ashley Clarke, the former British ambassador to Italy who headed Venice in Peril, the British counterpart of Save Venice. Sir Ashley and Lady Clarke took a liking to the Rylandses, who in turn were attentive and helpful to the Clarkes. Philip became involved with Venice in Peril, and it was reported that he would eventually succeed Sir Ashley. The two collaborated on a small booklet commemorating the restoration of the Madonna dell'Orto Church. Before long, Jane and Philip underwent makeovers: Philip cut his hair respectably short, and Jane began to fashion her hair and clothes in a more up-to-date style.

As the bright new young couple in town, they were taken up by established expatriates, notably the sculptor Joan FitzGerald, who introduced them around. They met John Hohnsbeen, a friend of Peggy Guggenheim's since the 1950s. Hohnsbeen in turn introduced them to Peggy, and almost immediately Philip and Jane began to ingratiate themselves. Jane bought Peggy dog food and various supplies at a discount from the PX in Aviano, walked Peggy's dogs, volunteered for household chores. In short, they made themselves indispensable to Peggy.

John Hohnsbeen was at first relieved that Philip and Jane were being so helpful to Peggy: it lifted some of the burden from him. For years Hohnsbeen had come to Venice from Easter to November to stay with Peggy and act as the unpaid curator of her collection. After Peggy's death, he continued his Venetian summers in a rented apartment. It had always been Hohnsbeen's custom to spend most of the day at the Cipriani pool, which was where I found him having a spartan lunch and chatting with friends among the rich international set. Residents of Venice could, for a stiff fee, enjoy daily pool privileges all summer.

'I was a house guest who sang for his supper,' said Hohnsbeen, whose white hair was combed straight across his tanned brow so that he resembled Pablo Picasso. 'Peggy and I were sort of a couple. I'd owned a gallery in New York and knew most of the Old Guard of the New York art world. I would hang Peggy's exhibition at the beginning of the season and take it down at the end, which would involve all sorts of unpleasant duties, like scraping the maggots off the back of the Max Ernst *Antipope* canvas, because it had been in the surrealist gallery, off the canal, which was very humid. The maggots loved the glue.

'The first few years with Peggy were marvellous, but then her arteries began to harden, and it was awful. I'd come in late at night and navigate around the artwork – through the Calder, past the Giacometti match-stick people, whose arms got broken all the time but not by me, then turn right, dodging the Pevsner, and into the bedroom. I was with her when she had her first heart-attack, and her face went all funny. After that, Peggy kept a fifteen-pound cowbell by her bed, and I'd leave my door open with the understanding that if she clanged, I would leap up and run to her assistance. It was a twenty-four-hour-a-day job.

'I liked Jane and Philip,' Hohnsbeen went on. 'We spent hours together, and Jane's a terribly good cook. They had won Peggy over, too. It was the frozen corn on the cob that did it. Jane brought it from the PX in Aviano, and it went straight to Peggy's heart. But people kept telling me, "Watch out for Jane Rylands!"'

'Who told you that?' I asked.

'Oh, everybody. And then Jane and Philip began to invite Peggy to dinner and not invite me. They wouldn't say anything about it to me. They'd sneak her out. Peggy was a semi-invalid by then, so it would have been a huge effort for them to pick her up, take her out, and bring her back. Peggy was hard work, and not many people would put up with her. The mischief went on behind my back during the summer. It clicked into high gear when I left in November, and continued until I returned in the spring.'

By the time Peggy reached her final illness, in the autumn of 1979, Philip and Jane Rylands had become her virtual keepers. They had keys to her house. They looked after her affairs. They took her to the hospital in Padua. The day after Peggy died, the director of the Guggenheim Museum in New York, Thomas Messer, arrived in Venice to take possession of the premises. He found Philip Rylands in the flooded basement, moving paintings to keep them from getting wet. Needing someone on hand to carry out the orders of the New York office, Messer asked Philip to act as temporary supervisor. Later he appointed Philip permanent administrator. The rise of the Rylandses had begun.

It was clear from the start that Jane Rylands intended to have a role in the running of the museum, to the irritation of Messer. 'On one occasion,' Messer told me, 'I was giving instructions to Philip in Jane's presence, on some probably minor procedural matter, and she blurted out, "No! That cannot be done!" I thought she really had a nerve interfering like that. I became very angry and let her know she was not to consider herself part of the management of the museum. But she dug her heels in and went right on exercising authority that no one had given her. She dominated Philip. I thought he was the most henpecked husband I ever saw.'

Once the Rylandses had their Guggenheim bona fides firmly in hand, Jane levered her position in ways that could only be called brilliant. She took over a lecture series at the Gritti and invited such luminaries as Stephen Spender, Arthur Schlesinger, Peter Quennell, John Julius Norwich, Brendan Gill, Adolph Green, Hugh Casson, and Frank Giles, editor of the *Sunday Times* of London. She gave dinner parties, and among the people signing her guest book were the speakers at the Gritti and such others as Adnan Khashoggi, Jean Kirkpatrick, and Queen Alexandra of Yugoslavia. 'When I looked at her guest book,' said Helen Sheehan, an intern at the Guggenheim in the 1980s, 'I realized Jane was putting a lot of energy into making a social life for herself. She used to tell me, "One moves forward in society." '

With the implied imprimatur of the Guggenheim enhancing her stature and influence, Jane acted informally as an artists' agent, putting wealthy patrons together with painters and sculptors in Venice. This gave her a certain power among artists in Venice. She asked the American painter Robert Morgan to paint a small portrait of Olga for her, just Olga's head. When it was finished, the matter of Morgan's fee came up. Jane proposed a very low fee, little more than an honorarium, pointing out that Morgan's reputation would be greatly enhanced when people saw his work hanging on her walls.

On at least one occasion, Jane counselled an artist about his work. 'She told me that the Fascists were going to be on the rise in Italy,' said Harald Böhm, 'and that I should make my art more figurative, to be in line with the times, I guess. I thought that was very strange.'

Mary Laura Gibbs was an art historian from Texas who moved to Venice in 1979 and became a good friend of the Rylandses. 'Jane does deserve credit for enlivening the intellectual scene in Venice,' she told me. 'It seemed to me that early on she saw that life in Venice was actually pretty dull. She looked around and thought, "I can be something socially and intellectually here." I think she saw the possibility of setting up something like a salon.

'But there were times she took herself a bit too seriously. I remember quite vividly the time the Prince and Princess of Wales came to Venice. They were scheduled to attend services at the English Church, and members of the congregation were given tickets. I had two. My maid, Patrizia, who was very nice, was eager to go, and I told Jane I was going to let her use my other ticket. Jane flew into a rage and said, "No, you're not!" I said, "Excuse me?" She said, "Well, I think it would give offence. Unless giving offence to the prince and princess is what you want to do! Is that what you want to do?"

'Jane had an odd facility for alienating people. Two camps formed: the anti-Rylands group and the Rylandses themselves. There wasn't really a pro-Rylands camp.'

Vincent Cooper, the young American painter, once asked Jane Rylands why so many people disliked her. 'I just spark animosity in people,' she told him. 'I don't know why. I'm not very subtle, I guess. No soft soap.' According to Cooper, 'Mrs Rylands had little or no consideration for Olga's old friends, many of whom had known Pound, too. To her they were merely unworthy and annoying characters who might just walk off with something. I took Mrs Rylands's concerns for the preservation of the contents of the house to be genuine.'

These concerns, though no doubt genuine, would not have been entirely altruistic. At the time, Jane Rylands was about to come into control of Olga's books and papers, so any theft from Olga would have amounted, in a way, to a theft from Jane Rylands as well.

On a literary level, Jane valued Philip's kinship with his uncle, the Cambridge don Dadie Rylands, and, through Dadie, a link to the Bloomsbury group and half of literary England. To honour and proclaim the connection, she commissioned Julian Barrow – an English artist who lived in John Singer Sargent's studio at 33 Tite Street in London – to paint a portrait of Dadie in his rooms at King's College. When the painting was finished, Jane asked Barrow to paint Philip into the portrait. Reached on the telephone, Barrow told me he had been appalled and had politely refused. 'I told her it would be . . . a distraction.'

Philip Rylands's ascension at the Peggy Guggenheim Collection was accompanied by a few grudging comments, mainly complaints that as a student of the Renaissance, he was hardly qualified to oversee a gallery of modern art. There were murmurs also that Jane had manoeuvred Philip into a position that had been meant for John Hohnsbeen. But, in fact, according to Messer, Peggy had never indicated any preference at all as to who should run the museum after she died. Not John Hohnsbeen and not Philip Rylands. At the time, Philip's appointment caused very few ripples.

When the Olga Rudge imbroglio surfaced almost ten years later, however, the Rylands–Peggy Guggenheim connection came in for something of a reassessment. Some people thought they detected a pattern, a serial courtship of the elderly in Dorsoduro: first Sir Ashley and Lady Clarke, then Peggy, then Olga.

'Selective gerontophilia' was what Mary Laura Gibbs called it. 'Before the Rudge thing,' she said, 'I would have defended Jane and Philip against any criticism about their intentions regarding Peggy. They were very good to her, especially Jane. But when it all happened again with Olga Rudge, it made me wonder.' Thinking back on it, Mary Laura Gibbs recalled that at a certain point Olga began to voice displeasure at Jane's meddling. 'Olga would make vaguely negative remarks in passing, like, "I'd like to show you a piece of music, but Jane Rylands has taken all of that away." She was becoming suspicious and uncomfortable.'

Once the substance of the foundation was known, friends of Olga's wrote letters and made phone calls on her behalf. Joan FitzGerald, whose early sponsorship of Jane and Philip had long since turned sour, called the American ambassador in Rome, Maxwell Rabb. Rabb looked into the matter and reported back, 'Jane and Philip Rylands seem to have many friends.'

James Laughlin, the founder of New Directions and Pound's publisher since the 1930s, tried to pressure Jane Rylands from the other side of the Atlantic. 'It was a big deal getting rid of that woman!' he bellowed over the telephone when I reached him at his home in Connecticut. 'She had no business doing what she did! It took Donald Gallup thirty-five years of backbreaking work, starting in 1947, to assemble the Pound Archives for the Beinecke Library at Yale. Gallup was the director. He tracked down scraps of paper all over the world, had to deal with five teams of lawyers and endless lawsuits between Pound's two families over who owned rights to what. Yale received fifteen big boxes of Pound's papers in 1966 from Mary, but those boxes had to stay in the basement of the Beinecke for seven years unopened until the lawsuits were over and done with. I'll bet Mrs Rylands didn't know anything about all that!

'Now, let me tell you something else she probably didn't know: Pound wrote a will in 1940 leaving everything to Mary. Books, property, everything. But because he didn't file the will with an Italian court at the time he wrote it, it was not technically valid, even though he reiterated his wishes in writing later on. After Pound was released from St Elizabeth's, Dorothy was given sole authority for his legal affairs by the American authorities. Pound could not legally write another will unless Dorothy signed it, and Dorothy simply rejected the 1940 will. She and Omar hired lawyers. Mary had to bow to necessity and hire a lawyer herself; she ended up having to divide the estate with Omar. Then, after all that, along comes this Rylands woman with no Pound credentials whatever. She leaps in with both feet and causes more heartache and expense for a family that's already suffered for decades over this kind of thing.'

The pressure that made the difference came from the trustees of the Guggenheim Foundation in New York, the controlling entity. One of the trustees was Jim Sherwood, owner of the Cipriani Hotel.

'From Jane and Philip's perspective,' Sherwood told me, 'they were saving Olga's papers. From the point of view of people in Venice, they were trying to steal them. The matter of the Ezra Pound Foundation came up at a board meeting in New York. The trustees were worried that the controversy might break out into the open and become an embarrassment to the museum. Furthermore, Peter Lawson-Johnson, who was the chairman and a cousin of Peggy's, felt that because of Pound's anti-Semitism, Jane's involvement was in dubious taste, in light of her connection to the Guggenheim through Philip. The board told Philip he had to choose between the Ezra Pound Foundation and his continued role at the museum.'

It was time, I thought, to talk again with Philip and Jane Rylands. I reached Philip by telephone at his Guggenheim office. Given the number of people I had already spoken with on the subject of the foundation, I was not surprised by his reaction to the mere mention of my name.

'We're not interested in talking to you!'

'I'd like to ask you a few questions.'

'I'm not interested in hearing your questions.'

'About the Ezra Pound Foundation.'

'I know very little about the Ezra Pound Foundation, and, anyway, we have an agreement with Mary de Rachewiltz not to talk to you about it.'

'Then, to be fair to you and Jane, I will send you written questions so at least you'll have an opportunity to respond.'

'I will view the submission of written questions as an invasion! We are not about to be tried by the press.'

'That is not my intention.'

'Anyway, it's only gossip!'

'No,' I said, 'it's not gossip.'

'What is it, then?'

'It's history. Because when you attach yourself to famous people, as you and Jane seem to like to do, then you become part of their story.'

Mary de Rachewiltz was somewhat more agreeable when I reached her at Brunnenburg Castle. But she, too, was reluctant to talk about the Ezra Pound Foundation.

'I felt embarrassed when the Rylands episode happened,' she said.

'They were very nice people. Very nice to my mother for many years. They relieved me of worry.'

'Have you all agreed not to talk to me about the Ezra Pound Foundation?' I asked.

'No,' she said, 'but we are not permitted to talk to anyone about the terms of the settlement with Yale.'

'Why?'

'We were obliged to sign statements saying we would keep the terms confidential. Jane Rylands insisted on it. We also had to agree not to bring legal action against Jane, the Ezra Pound Foundation, or Yale, and none of them would sue us.'

'Did Jane receive any money from Yale?'

'We were never told. That was part of the arrangement. Jane Rylands doesn't know our part of the settlement either.'

'Did you receive any money?'

'Of course, but it was a financial loss for us. The open market would have fetched ten times what Yale paid for the papers.'

Mary suddenly realized she had let slip a note of resentment and quickly reversed herself, as if pulling her hand back after touching a hot pan. 'But, really, there's no rogue in this play. My mother simply changed her mind. Philip and Jane meant well.'

'As helpful as they were to you,' I said, 'do you think at some point Jane and Philip might have gone just a little bit too far?'

'When it was over, my mother said to me, "Oh, these people. Now I see why I was invited to lunch."'

This time Mary let the negative comment stand.

'Was there a moment when you began to feel that things were not quite right?'

Mary hesitated for a moment. 'Well, yes. Jane Rylands was starting to take control of events. A lot of little things made me wonder. There was a pamphlet printed. A lecture being given. Copyright materials not properly handled.'

'Culminating,' I said, 'with a house being given away. Papers sold without your knowledge.'

'Well, yes. For us the house is a family shrine.'

'Would you mind if I came up to Brunnenburg to talk to you for an hour or so?'

'Tell me,' said Mary, 'why does all this interest you?'

'To be perfectly honest,' I said, 'I was struck by the similarity between what happened to your mother and the story in *The Aspern Papers*. Are you familiar with that novel?'

'We've been living with *The Aspern Papers* for forty years,' she said.

Before setting out for Brunnenburg, I read Mary de Rachewiltz's 1971 autobiography, entitled *Discretions*, a play on the title of her father's early autobiography, *Indiscretions*. Apart from being a surprisingly moving story, the book introduced me to two new elements in the saga of the Ezra Pound Foundation: the strained relationship between Mary and her mother, and Mary's near-obsessive adoration of her father.

Because Mary's first ten years had been spent with a foster family on a farm in the South Tyrol, just a few miles from the border with Austria, she grew up milking cows, shovelling dung, and speaking a Tyrolean dialect of German. She acquired habits learned from her foster father: spitting a great distance and blowing her nose with her thumb.

Olga was appalled to discover that her daughter was growing up as a peasant with dirty fingernails, primitive table manners, and teeth that were brushed only occasionally. Mary resisted Olga's attempts to reshape her into a well-mannered, sophisticated young lady. She felt like a doll in the fashionably short dresses Olga wanted her to wear. She was bored by a violin Olga gave her and slammed it against the chicken coop, confiding in her memoir that she would rather have had a zither or a mouth organ. Mary was intimidated by Olga's insistence that she learn Italian and speak it all the time when she was in Venice. 'Her stern attitude handicapped me more than the language barrier had done,' Mary wrote. There were times when Olga was 'majestic and beautiful like a queen towards me; soft and willowy, smiling like a fairy towards [my father].' And when Olga played the violin, 'I saw no shade of darkness, no resentment . . . I [had] a glimpse of her great beauty and my fear of her changed into a kind of veneration.' But as soon as the music stopped, Olga once more became distant, impenetrable, authoritarian.

In her late teens, Mary learned all at once not only that she was illegitimate but that Olga had wanted a son. At that moment, she wrote, she felt the impossibility of ever winning her mother's affection.

Olga was deeply hurt by *Discretions* and did not speak to Mary for several years. Olga had a copy of the book, and Christopher Cooley noticed that it was heavily annotated. 'Whenever the subject of the book came up,' he recalled, 'she would grab it angrily from the shelf and start thumbing through it. "I've put this right," she'd say, "and I've put that right." And then she'd slam it back on the shelf.'

Although the situation had improved over time, a geographical and emotional distance remained between the two women. The Rylands episode, whatever else it proved, made it clear, to Mary's embarrassment, that she had ceded much of her mother's care to Philip and Jane.

Mary's love of her father stood in contrast to her feelings towards her mother. 'The image of my [father] always presented itself as a huge glowing sun at the end of a white road,' she wrote. When Pound took her to see the sights in Verona, his image dimmed the monuments in the background. Mary recalled how he tap-danced all the way home from a Ginger Rogers–Fred Astaire movie. And she remembered sitting in her room on the third floor of the Hidden Nest, listening for the sound of his return – first the tapping of his black malacca cane as he entered Calle Querini and then, as he approached number 252, the sound of a loud, prolonged 'Miaow,' answered by Olga's 'Miaow' from her room on the second floor, after which Mary would run down two flights of stairs to greet him at the door.

When she was fifteen, her father – the man who had given literary counsel to Yeats and Eliot – sent her a letter about learning how to write:

CIAO CARA

To learn to write, as when you learn tennis. Can't always play a game, must practice strokes. Think; how was it different to go to the Lido to play tennis? I mean different from when one went to play in Siena?? Write that. Not to make a story but to make it clear.

It will be very LONG. When one starts to write it is hard to fill a page. When one is older there is always so MUCH to write.

THINK: the house in Venice is not like ANY OTHER house. Venice like no other city. Suppose Kit Kat or even an American needed to be told HOW to find the Venice house? How to recognize you and me going out of the door to go to the Lido. He gets off train, how does he find 252 Calle Q.?

Describe us or describe Luigino arriving at ferrovia? has he money, have we, how do we go?

A novelist could make a whole chapter getting protagonista from train to front door. Good writing would make it possible and even certain that Kit Kat could use the chapter to find the house.

ciao.

THINK about this quite a good deal before you try to write it out.

While Mary was still in her mid teens, Pound asked her to translate the *Cantos* into Italian, as an exercise. Thus began her lifelong study of her father's work. '[T]he Cantos slowly became the one book I could not do without,' she wrote. 'My "Bible", as friends have often teased me.' In the 1960s, when Yale bought a substantial collection of Pound's papers, they created the Ezra Pound Archives and named Mary as curator. Once a year for twenty-five years, Mary spent a month at Yale organizing and annotating her father's papers.

Mary's transformation from a dialect-speaking farm girl into a beautiful, refined, educated, multilingual adult was complete by the time she had reached her twenties. But her love of the mountains and farms of her childhood remained undiminished, and her home in the South Tyrol was, in effect, a return to her foster roots.

The trip from Venice to Brunnenburg Castle took about three hours, first the drive to Merano, then up to the village of Tirolo by means of a funicular lift. I walked the final quarter-mile along 'Ezra Pound *Weg*' towards Brunnenburg Castle, a vision out of *Grimm's Fairy Tales* with turrets and crenellations. The castle clung to a steep hillside terraced with grapevines; it commanded a spectacular view of the valley and distant mountains. Mary lived in one of the castle's two towers. Walter and his wife, Brigitte, lived in the other with their two sons. As I came through the gate, I noticed a cluster of American college students in a courtyard. They were attending one of the month-long, live-in seminars at which Mary lectured on the writings of Ezra Pound and Walter taught classes on medieval saints and heroes.

I continued up a series of outdoor steps, at one point passing a replica of Gaudier-Brzeska's sculpture of Pound's head, set into a small garden. A few steps above that, I came face-to-face with Mary de Rachewiltz. She was tall and smiling; her blonde hair was brushed back from her face, accentuating high cheekbones. There was a quiet pride in her bearing: she was, after all, despite all the sadness in her life, the daughter of one of the greatest literary figures of the twentieth century.

We sat down at a large table on a terrace, where a few moments later we were joined by Walter. He was dark-haired, angular, and dressed in a black T-shirt and jeans. He had just come from the vineyard, he said, where he had been netting the vines to keep the birds away. He put a bright red binder stuffed with papers on the table and started flipping through the pages. I saw letters, bank statements, legal documents, but they were all upside down from my perspective, and moving so quickly I could not make them out.

'We're not allowed to show anybody most of these,' Walter said. 'But I can tell you about some of them. The whole story is right here.'

Mary looked at the notebook and sighed. 'There's really no rogue in this play,' she said, just as she had done on the telephone. Before I could respond, Walter spoke up, saying with some impatience, 'Jane Rylands took advantage of your grudge against your mother.'

Mary said nothing.

Turning to me, he continued, 'The wheels were set in motion by my grandmother. She wanted to perpetuate the writings of Ezra Pound, but she never mentioned to us that she was giving her papers and her house to a foundation.

'We were finally alerted when Liselotte Höhs and Joan FitzGerald called my mother from Venice and told her we should come down right away and find out what was going on. My father and I went to the office of the notary and read the contracts. We were quite surprised to see how much Olga had given away.

'My father then went over to the municipal building and found that the Comune bureaucracy had not yet transferred ownership of the house, so we were able to have it put back in my grandmother's name. But the sale of her papers was a *fait accompli*.

'When we showed the contracts to my grandmother, she said, "I never saw this piece of paper. I never signed such a document."

'We noticed also that the contract for the sale of her papers said that she had already received the fifteen million lire, the equivalent of seven thousand dollars, and perhaps she did, but we've never been able to find any record of it. When we tried to have a meeting with Jane to discuss all of this, she became evasive. She didn't come to appointments.'

Walter flipped some more pages.

'Here, for example,' he said. 'My father and I had an appointment to meet Jane at her house one day, but when we arrived, she was not home. We found this note.' He held up a three-by-five card. 'It says, "I am sorry you had to cross the *ponte* for nothing."'

'My grandmother was ninety-two when all this happened,' Walter went on. The implication in his remark was that if Jane's delaying tactics went on long enough, matters would resolve themselves biologically. Olga would die, and Jane would be in control. 'The biggest joke,' said Walter, 'is that my grandmother lived to be a hundred and one!'

'No,' said Mary, 'the biggest joke is that I got fired from Yale!'

'Olga Rudge and her family were twice the victims in this affair,' said Walter. 'First, the loss of my grandmother's papers to the foundation. Then, in the course of negotiations with Yale, the family received less than the true value of the papers, and Ralph Franklin, who had become the director of the Beinecke Library, fired my mother as curator of the Pound Archives. Mr Franklin had never really liked the arrangement; it had been set up by the previous director.'

Walter turned more pages. 'Here's a cheque for six hundred dollars made out by my grandmother to the law firm in Cleveland, Ohio. Six hundred dollars! My grandmother never had any money. I don't understand why she had to pay the law firm anything. The gift of her house and her papers should have been enough.

'My grandmother may have been president of the foundation, but it was in name only. Jane Rylands assumed certain exclusive powers for herself. She put my grandmother's Gaudier-Brzeska notebooks in a safe-deposit box, which actually seemed a wise thing to do, because they were very valuable. But when my grandmother and I went to the bank to retrieve them, we were turned away. The bank official told us that Jane Rylands was the only person who had authority to open the safe-deposit box of the Ezra Pound Foundation. My grandmother said, "But I'm president of the Ezra Pound Foundation!" The bank officer said, "I'm sorry, we have our instructions from Mrs Rylands."'

Walter turned more pages in the red notebook. 'Ah, I found it,' he said. It was a small piece of light blue writing paper on which was written, in large letters, as if for a child to read, words to the effect of

'Look in the safe-deposit box. Count the notebooks. How many notebooks do you see? 1 2 3 4 5 6.' It seemed the written equivalent of speaking slowly and with exaggerated clarity to a child, or perhaps to an old person who was a bit confused. The piece of paper was unsigned, and whoever was intended to circle a number did not.

'What is the significance of this?' I asked.

Walter shrugged. 'I am sure Jane Rylands wrote it. I think it's indicative of my grandmother's state of mind and Jane's caution once the gossip had begun.'

He slipped the piece of paper back into its clear plastic sleeve.

'Sometimes Jane involved herself in matters that had nothing to do with the foundation,' he went on. 'My grandmother owned two important paintings – by Fernand Léger and Max Ernst. Jane took them to the Guggenheim to be framed, she said, and for safekeeping. When we asked Jane to give them back, it took her months to return them, and when she did, they were still unframed.'

'Did you ever ask Jane why she got into all of this?' I asked.

'Yes,' said Mary, 'and she said, "I'm in it for business reasons." She spoke about setting up Ezra Pound libraries in major cities around the world. There would be symposiums, conferences, publications.'

'She repeated that comment several times,' said Walter. 'That she was "in it for business reasons". '

'Why didn't you sue to have your grandmother's contracts declared invalid?'

'We were told the only way the contracts could be nullified was through criminal law,' said Walter. 'We would have had to make accusations of fraud, or *circonvenzione d'incapace*, which means "deception of the disabled", and we were not prepared to do that. Anyway, we were told that no lawyer in Venice would take a case against another Venetian lawyer or notary. We'd have to find a lawyer in Milan or Rome.'

Walter closed the notebook and pushed it aside.

'Well,' I said, 'in spite of everything that's happened, Jane and Philip still seem to have fond recollections of Olga Rudge. They have a portrait of her.'

'Oh?' Mary looked surprised. 'Where is it?'

'In their apartment,' I said.

'I would like to know who paid for it.'

'I gather Jane commissioned it and paid for it herself,' I said.

Mary smiled a sardonic smile. 'I would like to know who paid for it.'

On a brief return to the United States, I spent a day at the Beinecke Library in New Haven. There I found the Olga Rudge Papers filed in 208 boxes, taking up 108 feet of shelf space. I read dozens of letters and other documents, each providing a fragmented glimpse into the world of Ezra Pound and Olga Rudge.

One letter was of particular, if ironic, interest. It was from Mary in Brunnenburg to Olga in Venice, in August 1959. Disciples and scholars had been coming to the castle and foraging through Pound's papers like 'hogs after truffles'. Mary was growing weary of it and wrote to her mother, 'Have re-read *The Aspern Papers* last night, God I have a mind to make a big bonfire and burn up every single scrap of paper.'

Nearly thirty years later, on 24 February 1988, Mary again wrote to Olga from Brunnenburg:

Dearest Mother,

You asked me to 'put it in writing.' Time is precious, hence briefly: DEfund your 'Foundation' and make sure that the only place we can call home will be kept up by one daughter, two grand-children, four great-grandsons of whom you carry photographs around. If you want to entrust the 'technicalities' to Walter, I am sure he'll be ready to assume responsibility. At present you are tending the fire in a place that does not belong to you.

With love,
Mary

THE CITY OF FALLING ANGELS

My most curious discovery at the Beinecke, however, was not something I read, but something I was not permitted to read. All but one of the 208 boxes of the Olga Rudge Papers were available for perusal. One box, number 156, was off-limits, 'restricted' until the year 2016. Box 156 contained the papers of the Ezra Pound Foundation.

I would have liked to ask Jane Rylands what the sealed box contained and why it was sealed. There were a number of other questions I would have put to her as well, but since Philip had warned me that he would view even the submission of written questions as an 'invasion', I did not. Instead I called the Beinecke's director, Ralph Franklin, and asked him why this box, and only this box, was sealed.

'That was one of the conditions upon which the Ezra Pound Foundation agreed to the sale.'

'Why the year 2016, which is twenty-six years after the deal was signed?'

'I don't know.'

'Did you pay Jane Rylands any money?' I asked.

'We never dealt with Jane Rylands directly,' he said. 'We dealt with the Ezra Pound Foundation. There were two competing parties, both claiming ownership of Olga Rudge's papers: Olga Rudge on the one hand and the Ezra Pound Foundation on the other. We bought out both claims and thereby bought the papers.'

'At that point, of course,' I said, 'the foundation consisted only of Jane Rylands and a lawyer in Cleveland. Shortly after making the deal with Yale, they dissolved the foundation. What happened to the money?'

'I don't know what the foundation did with the money it was paid.'

'Would that information be revealed in the box that's sealed until 2016?'

'Even I don't know what's in the box,' he said.

Upon my return to Venice, I went directly to Calle Querini and knocked on the door of the Reverend and Mrs James Harkins.

Reverend Harkins greeted me warmly and handed me the key to the house next door. Mary had left it for me. I had made arrangements to rent the Hidden Nest for the next six weeks. The interior had been renovated recently, Mary said, and no longer had any of her parents' effects in it, but the idea of seeing Venice from the perspective of the Hidden Nest, however briefly, appealed to me.

'Don't forget,' said Reverend Jim, 'we generally sit down to cocktails at five thirty!'

I thanked him and walked next door, turned the key in the lock, and opened the door.

The house was sixteen feet square, broom clean, and spare of furniture. Its white walls had been freshly painted. On the ground floor, where Olga's papers had once been stored in trunks and where, before he lapsed into silence, Ezra Pound read his poetry aloud to friends, there was now a dining-room table, four chairs, and a small kitchen behind sliding doors. Two windows on either side of an open fireplace looked out on the Cipriani garden at the back and, on the far side of the garden, the high brick wall of the old Customs warehouse. A framed poster from a 1920s concert, featuring Olga Rudge and George Antheil, hung on the wall. But there were no books or bookshelves and no mural.

Up a flight of wooden stairs, the second floor, once Olga's bedroom, was furnished now with a table and two chairs.

On the third floor, which had been Pound's studio, there was a bed and a bathroom. A simple wooden writing table had been built into the stair rail in front of the window.

An object on the table caught my eye. It was a book, the only book in the house: a paperback copy of *The Aspern Papers*. I turned to the title page and read the inscription: 'May the "hidden nest" inspire an equal masterpiece – M. de R.'

10

For a Couple of Bucks

'Y OU'RE SURPRISED?'
　　Ludovico De Luigi peered down his aquiline nose at me, greatly amused at my response to the day's news. We were sitting at an outdoor café in Campo San Barnaba, and the newspaper on the table in front of us bore a headline that contained the word 'arson'. The experts looking into the Fenice fire had changed their minds. Back in February, they had decided the fire had been caused by a combination of accident and negligence. Now it was June, and they had come to the conclusion it was arson.

'Why shouldn't I be surprised?' I said. 'Months ago they ruled out arson with "near-mathematical certainty". Have you been sure all along it was arson?'

'No, and I'm not even so sure now,' said De Luigi. 'But it was inevitable that someone would be accused of arson. I knew it would happen as soon as Casson said he was going to prosecute a lot of very important people for criminal negligence – the mayor, the general manager of the Fenice, the secretary-general of the Fenice, the chief engineer of Venice. These are men of means. They've hired the best defence lawyers in Italy. These lawyers know they can't prove their clients weren't negligent, because it seems obvious to me they *were* negligent. But if they can persuade the court that it was a case of arson, then all charges of negligence are automatically dropped by law.'

'Are you suggesting that the experts have been pressured into changing their minds?'

De Luigi shrugged. 'It's never that blatant. It's more subtle than that.'

I was about to ask De Luigi what kind of subtlety he had in mind when a woman sitting at the table next to us gasped. A seagull had landed in the midst of a cluster of pigeons pecking at breadcrumbs and had seized one of the pigeons in its beak. The pigeon was flapping and wriggling, trying to free itself from the much bigger seagull. In short order, the seagull had the pigeon pinned to the pavement and was jabbing its chest with its long, sharp beak. After a few moments, it pulled out a bloody morsel the size of a large grape – the pigeon's heart, no doubt – juggled it in its beak, and swallowed it.

The seagull left the dead pigeon lying on the paving stones and strutted towards the edge of the San Barnaba Canal (towards the very spot, as it happened, where many years earlier Katharine Hepburn fell backwards into the canal in *Summertime*). The other pigeons, having flown away in panic during the attack, fluttered back and resumed pecking at the breadcrumbs only a few feet from the seagull, sensing perhaps that its appetite had been satisfied. The woman at the next table shuddered and turned away. De Luigi chuckled silently.

'There you have it,' he said, 'acted out before your eyes. An allegory: the strong versus the weak. It's always the same. The powerful always win, and the weak always come back to be victims all over again.' He laughed.

Now that the experts had ruled the Fenice fire a case of arson, it was up to Felice Casson to identify the guilty party or parties. 'All that remains to be done is to put a face on the monster or monsters who did this,' Casson was quoted as saying. Speculation focused once again on the Mafia. Casson let it be known that he was in active pursuit of the Mafia theory. He had received a phone call from a prosecutor in Bari, where the Mafia had burned down the Petruzzelli Opera House in 1991. After comparing photographs of the two fires, the Bari prosecutor noticed a disturbing similarity: in both the Petruzzelli and Fenice fires, flames started on an upper floor and spread quickly in a lateral direction, indicating arson. Could the two fires be related? The close rapport between the Mafia boss who had ordered the Bari fire, Antonio Capriati, and the Mafia boss of the Veneto region, Felice 'Angel Face' Maniero, lent weight to a possible Bari-Venice connection. Over the years, the two men had met frequently in Padua. Furthermore, in 1993, while he was on trial for robbery and drug trafficking, 'Angel Face' Maniero had admitted under oath that he had considered setting fire to the Fenice as a way of intimidating the men prosecuting him.

Despite Mayor Cacciari's oft-repeated insistence that there was no Mafia presence in Venice, it was generally understood that 'Angel Face' Maniero and the Mafia controlled the water-taxi business in Venice and that until recently Maniero ran the moneylending racket in front of the Casino, charging the usurious rate of 10 per cent a day.

The youthful, forty-one-year-old Maniero was one of Italy's most daring and outrageous mafiosi. He once boasted of having ordered the theft of a jewel-encrusted reliquary containing St Anthony's jawbone from Padua Cathedral to use as a bargaining chip later on, in the event that he or any of his men were ever arrested. Maniero cultivated an image of urbane nonchalance. He wore ascots, owned a fleet of luxury cars, and was often seen consuming champagne and caviar in the company of tall, blonde women. While being hunted by the police in 1993, he bought a thirty-six-foot yacht and brazenly set off on a cruise around the Mediterranean. Police caught up with him off Capri, boarded the yacht, and arrested him. Though convicted and sentenced to thirty-three years in jail, Maniero made a spectacular prison break after only a few months behind bars. Seven of his henchmen, disguised as *carabinieri* and armed with assault rifles, strode into the high-security prison in Padua and held the guards at gunpoint while he and five other members of his gang escaped. When he was recaptured five months later, Maniero turned informer. In exchange for his release under the witness-protection programme, he provided information that led to the arrest of more than three hundred Mafia figures. At the time of the Fenice fire, Maniero was in Mestre testifying against seventy-two fellow mafiosi in trials involving a pair of million-dollar robberies, the sale of hundreds of kilos of heroin, and a double homicide.

Maniero's collaboration with the anti-Mafia prosecutors had made it entirely possible that if Maniero had not been responsible for the Fenice fire himself, other Mafia figures might have ordered it to make it look as though he had done it.

Another Mafia theory presented itself when a Sicilian mob informer told Casson that the top Mafia boss in Palermo, Pietro Aglieri, had confided to an associate that he had set fire to the Fenice in order to save face. A government witness in a Mafia trial in the Veneto had declared himself to be both a homosexual and a great friend of Aglieri's. Deeply embarrassed, Aglieri sought to redeem himself among his underworld peers by flexing his muscles and pulling off a cataclysmic stunt in Venice. He would torch the Fenice. According to the informant, Aglieri and another clan member drove up to Venice from Palermo and set the Fenice on fire with a cigarette lighter. Casson pursued this story until he began to have doubts about the source. But rather than reject the story out of hand, he passed it on to the anti-Mafia unit in Venice for further investigation.

Meanwhile Casson's experts did their best to explain why they had changed their minds about how the fire had started. They had originally believed that a spark or a carelessly tossed cigarette had ignited the resin-coated flooring in the *ridotto*, the lobby on the third level of the entrance wing. The burning resins would have started a slow fire in the floorboards, one that smouldered for two or three hours before bursting into flame. A smouldering fire was typical of an accidental fire.

But subsequent lab tests had shown that even with the resin coating, the flooring would not catch fire except at a much higher temperature than a spark or a cigarette could have provided. The experts were forced to conclude that the floorboards would have caught fire only if someone had poured flammable liquid on to them first. Eight litres of the highly combustible solvent Solfip had been stored in the *ridotto*, and traces of it were found in charred remnants of the floorboards.

The single piece of evidence that had originally led the experts to conclude that the fire had been accidental was the discovery that the beams supporting the floor of the *ridotto* had burned all the way through. This, they believed, had indicated a slow, smouldering start, and therefore an accidental fire. In keeping with the new arson scenario, the experts now said that because the beams had been coated with resin and saturated with solvent, they had kept on burning throughout the fire, despite being doused with water from the firemen's hoses.

So the fire had not smouldered for two or three hours. It had become a roaring blaze within ten or fifteen minutes of being set. This would mean that the fire had been set some time between 8.20 p.m. and 8.50 p.m. and not at six o'clock, as the experts had thought at first. But then what about the eight witnesses who said they had smelt something burning outside the Fenice at six o'clock? The experts pointed out that nobody inside the Fenice had smelt anything at that hour and that, furthermore, none of the witnesses to the six-o'clock smell had reported it when they said they smelt it. The six-o'clock smell, the experts suggested, had most likely come from a restaurant kitchen or a wood-burning oven.

The fire's transformation from negligence to arson meant that Felice Casson had to go back and re-examine all the information that had been gathered in the past several months. Casson now took greater interest in three young men in their twenties who had been seen running towards Campo San Fantin shouting, *'Scampemo, scampemo!'* (Let's get out of here!) in the Venetian dialect shortly before the fire broke out. They had been laughing. It seemed to witnesses that they might have pulled a prank of some sort that had perhaps been taken the wrong way. Two other young men had been seen running away ten minutes later. They had all come from the direction of the Fenice's stage door on Calle della Fenice.

Twenty-five people had been working on the restoration of the theatre on 29 January. Casson wanted to know who had been the last to leave.

Gilberto Paggiaro, the Fenice's sad-eyed, fifty-four-year-old caretaker, came on duty at four o'clock on the afternoon of 29 January 1996. From his chair in the small porter's office next to the stage-door exit, he saw most of the people leave between 5.00 p.m. and 5.30 p.m. Three more people left the building during the next half-hour: a set designer, a press officer, and the snack-bar lady whose coffee machine would briefly be blamed for the fire. At 6.30 p.m., the Fenice's house electrician went home. Ten minutes after that, an executive of one of the firms doing work in the Fenice left, and he was followed by a work-crew foreman. At 7.30 p.m., the Fenice's staff carpenter walked out with four other employees who had joined him in the carpentry shop to celebrate the birthday of a former colleague.

That left nine people still in the theatre at eight o'clock: the caretaker Paggiaro; the Fenice's photographer, Giuseppe Bonannini, who was taking pictures to document the renovation work; and seven young electricians employed by Viet, a small electrical contractor. Viet was behind in its work. All seven of the company's electricians, including the owner of the company, had lately been putting in twelve-hour days. Three of the men had been hired within the last week to help make up for lost time. On 29 January, they were working on the ground floor. At eight o'clock, they finished work and went up to the dressing room on the fourth floor to shower and change.

Enrico Carella, the twenty-seven-year-old owner of Viet, told investigators that he left at 8.30 p.m. with his cousin Massimiliano Marchetti, who was also one of his employees. Within the next five minutes, three more electricians left, one of whom later told investigators that he and the other two were probably the three young men seen running down Calle della Fenice. 'We'd been joking around,' he said.

A sixth electrician left a few minutes later, saying goodbye to the remaining electrician on his way out. The last Viet electrician to leave had been asked by the Fenice's house electrician to turn off lights throughout the theatre. After doing so, he stopped by the porter's office on his way out; not finding Paggiaro, he left a note to the effect that he had turned off the lights as asked. The note was found after the fire, but this man, Roberto Visentin, was the only one of the seven Viet electricians whose departure had not been witnessed by anyone else.

Now only two people remained in the theatre: the caretaker Gilberto Paggiaro and the photographer Giuseppe Bonannini.

Paggiaro set off on a security check at 8.30, picking his way through the darkened theatre with a torch. This tour generally took upwards of half an hour, given the size of the opera house, its many levels, and its labyrinthine layout. Paggiaro first walked upstairs, crossed the stage, and went into the south wing, where he looked through the rabbit warren of offices and meeting rooms. He found everything in order. He then walked back across the stage and checked the offices in the north wing. Still nothing amiss. From there he moved along the horseshoe corridor behind the second tier of boxes towards the rear of the auditorium and the Apollonian rooms. It was at this point, as he approached the middle of the horseshoe corridor, that he smelt smoke. Believing that the smell was coming from the outside, he opened a window and saw a woman across the *calle* shouting, 'Help! The theatre is on fire!'

Now Paggiaro was alarmed. He knew that the photographer Bonannini was still in his office on the fourth floor, because Bonannini had asked him to call in at his office while he was on his rounds and guide him downstairs through the dark with his torch. Paggiaro raced upstairs and found Bonannini in his office, still sorting photographs.

Out of breath, Paggiaro shouted, 'Beppe, Beppe, I smelt smoke down on the second tier! Come and give me a hand. We've got to find out where it's coming from. Come on. Hurry!'

The two of them left Bonannini's office and started down the stairs. 'The second tier, the second tier!' Paggiaro shouted, leading the way.

They opened the door to the horseshoe corridor on the second tier and immediately smelt smoke. Paggiaro turned on his torch and illuminated a thin haze. They proceeded further along the corridor, passing the doors of the individual boxes, towards the rear of the hall. They were just behind the royal box when, looking through the door into the Apollonian rooms, they saw heavy black smoke rolling down the stairs from the *ridotto*, smoke so acrid they were forced to cover their noses and mouths with their handkerchiefs. Reflections of flames flickered on the walls. They heard the crackling sound of a fire burning furiously. Then suddenly there was a burst of flames. They turned and ran back down the corridor and up to Bonannini's office to call the fire department. Bonannini fumbled with the keys and could not find the right one. Meanwhile Paggiaro saw a phone outside the messenger centre, ran to it, picked it up, and made the call. The dispatcher told him they had already been informed about the fire and to run downstairs quickly and open the front door for the firemen. When the two men reached the ground floor, Bonannini left immediately. Paggiaro darted into his office to put on his overcoat and a beret-style cap. Then, thinking there might be someone else left in the theatre, he called out, 'Fire! Fire! Is anybody there?' But there was no answer. Then he, too, ran out through the stage door and down the *calle* to Campo San Fantin. At exactly 9.21, his torch still in hand, Paggiaro presented himself to the first policeman he saw and announced that he was the caretaker of the Fenice.

The policeman looked at him in amazement. For the past twenty minutes, he had been banging on the front door, shouting for someone to open it. 'Where have you been all this time?'

*   *   *

Casson asked Paggiaro the same question over and over again in the course of no fewer than ten interviews. Casson did not suspect Paggiaro of direct complicity in the fire, but he thought it likely the man had gone out for something to eat, abandoning his post at a crucial moment. Paggiaro swore he had never left the theatre, that he had brought something to eat from home that day, though whether it was fruit or sandwiches he could not recall. In spite of his protestations, Casson was not convinced. So he kept Paggiaro on the list of people to be charged with negligence.

Casson had no suspicions about the photographer Bonannini. His story checked out, and he had no discernible motive.

The seventh and last Viet electrician to leave, the thirty-two-year-old Roberto Visentin, the one nobody actually saw walk out of the door, was Casson's first serious arson suspect. It had been Visentin's fourth day on the job for Viet, but he was familiar with the layout of the theatre, having worked there previously for three years as a full-time employee. One of the other electricians had privately voiced suspicions about Visentin, citing his disappearance from the dressing room at about 8.15, when he said he was going to turn off lights in the theatre. Casson questioned Visentin closely and went over the route he said he took while turning out the lights. Visentin's story did not conflict with anyone else's — it was corroborated by the house electrician, who confirmed that he had asked Visentin to turn out the lights — and Visentin had no likely motive. Casson crossed him off the list.

Casson now concentrated on Enrico Carella, the owner of Viet, and his cousin, Massimiliano Marchetti, aged twenty-six. He examined the transcripts of their earlier interviews. Both had said they had left the Fenice at 8.30 p.m. and stopped briefly next door at the Bar del Teatro La Fenice to have a spritzer with three of the other electricians. Then they had taken the *vaporetto* to the Lido to have dinner with Carella's girlfriend, arriving at her house at 9.15. It was while he was at the Lido, Carella said, that he had received a call from a friend who had just seen a report on television that the Fenice was on fire. Carella told Marchetti and his girlfriend about the fire, and the three of them called a water taxi and came back to Venice.

Over the next several months, Casson summoned all seven electricians for repeated questioning, together and separately. He broke down their stories, compared the details, drilled them on contradictions to determine whether these were honest lapses of memory or outright lies. When their answers did not satisfy him, they knew it: his face turned bright red. He was unrelenting. He had detectives follow them; he bugged their cars, tapped their telephones and cell phones, tapped the telephones and cell phones of their parents and girlfriends, and he secretly videotaped them while they sat in holding rooms at the police station waiting to be questioned. Then, on 22 May 1997, sixteen months after the fire, Casson pounced.

Shortly before dawn, a squad of policemen knocked on the door of the apartment on the Giudecca where Enrico Carella lived with his mother and her second husband. For the next four hours, the police searched the apartment; then they told Carella to get into the police boat. The same scenario was being played out simultaneously in Salzano, a small town on the mainland, where Massimilliano Marchetti lived with his parents and younger brother.

At noon TV news programmes showed footage of Carella and Marchetti being led out of police headquarters in handcuffs on their way to jail. They had been interrogated and formally arrested on suspicion of burning the Fenice. Casson had obtained a court order invoking a new law that allowed 'preventive detention' for ninety days. He had based his request on the concern that if Carella were to remain at large, he might try to tamper with the evidence by exerting psychological pressure on the other Viet electricians. As their boss, Carella still owed them money for salary and overtime.

The motive for burning the theatre, said Casson, had been to avoid having to pay a penalty for lateness in completing the electrical wiring.

The deadline had been 1 February, only two days away, and the penalty was $125 a day for every day beyond the deadline. An estimated two months' work still remained to be done, which meant the total charge against Viet would have come to $7,500. That seemed like a ludicrously small amount of money, hardly enough to cause someone to burn down an opera house. But added to the $75,000 in debts that Casson said Carella had outstanding, it might have seemed daunting. According to Casson's theory, Carella and Marchetti had meant to set a small fire that would have interrupted their work and released them from the deadline. But things had got out of hand.

Viet was working at the Fenice as a subcontractor for Argenti, a big construction firm in Rome. Carella's father, Renato Carella, had brokered the deal with Argenti and then set up Viet for his son. The electrical subcontract for the Fenice was Viet's first job. Renato Carella served as Viet's foreman and liaison with Argenti in Rome, which made him, in effect, his son's employee.

Of the two cousins, Enrico Carella was the more outgoing and self-assured. He was smart and articulate. He dressed in expensive clothes, even on the job. 'He'd show up wearing Fratelli Rosetti loafers,' said one of the Viet electricians. The dark-haired, handsome Carella had a string of overlapping girlfriends. He would move in with one girl and, after a period of time, announce that he was seeing someone else. Alessandra, the girlfriend he and Marchetti visited on the Lido the night of the fire (and who had loaned Carella $8,000), was replaced by Elena, who was told by Carella that he was going on vacation with another girl, Michela, but not before Elena, shortly after meeting him, had loaned him $3,000. By the time he was arrested a year and half later, Carella was engaged to Renata, who owned an ice cream shop in Crespano del Grappa and whose father had graciously loaned Carella's father $12,000. During this period, Carella bought a BMW for $25,000 and an Acquaviva motorboat for $7,000.

Massimiliano Marchetti was, by comparison, a tongue-tied wallflower. He was not interested in the high life; he did not appear to be ambitious; he was shy and inarticulate, and had only one girlfriend, his fiancée.

With the two cousins in his crosshairs, Casson showed himself still to be an unusually aggressive prosecutor. He not only booked them for arson, he threw in a charge of attempted murder – worse than murder, actually: the term Casson used was *strage*, which means 'slaughter' or 'massacre'. Casson had in mind the scores of people who might have died if the fire had swept through a large swath of Venice, as it could easily have done. Moreover, he bluntly announced that he was also investigating three other arson suspects still at large: Renato Carella and two Sicilian mobsters – Aglieri, the Mafia boss in Palermo who had allegedly boasted of burning the Fenice, and the man who had supposedly helped him do it, Carlo Greco.

Renato Carella had left the Fenice at least two hours before the fire and was not thought to have had a direct hand in it. Casson suspected he might have been the connection between his son and persons unknown for whom a destroyed Fenice would be worth a considerable sum of money. For Casson the most likely suspects were companies that expected to play a significant, lucrative role in rebuilding the theatre.

Thus, there were really two arson theories: the small-fire theory, in which the two cousins, acting alone, attempted to set a minor, contained fire to avoid paying a $7,500 penalty, and the total-devastation theory, in which the cousins were secretly paid to burn the theatre to the ground. Casson had the luxury of pursuing both theories at once.

The shift to the arson theory came as a relief to the fourteen people Casson had earlier cited for negligence, but their relief was short-lived. Within days Casson announced he would still seek indictments for negligence. Even if the fire had been the work of arsonists, he argued, negligence had created conditions that made it impossible to extin-

guish. In any case, if he failed to get a conviction for arson, Casson
could fall back on the easier-to-prove case of negligence.

'I never excluded the possibility of arson,' Casson told me shortly after
the arrests. 'I gave the experts a written report at the very start, saying
that evidence of arson should not be overlooked. But they kept telling
me, "Negligence, negligence, negligence." From time to time, I'd ask,
"What about arson?" and they'd answer, "Negligence." '
 We met in Casson's office in the fifteenth-century Tribunal building
at the foot of the Rialto Bridge. The building's interior had been
partitioned haphazardly. Snaking hallways were lined with battered
metal cabinets and stacks of legal documents, giving the place the
ambience of a cluttered warehouse. Casson's office looked out on the
Grand Canal, but it was drab and felt more like borrowed space than
the central nervous system of a busy anti-crime division.
 'When the experts decided it was arson after all,' Casson went on, 'I
had to review months' worth of interviews, looking for clues.'
 'Did you find any bombshells?' I asked.
 'One of the first things I verified,' said Casson, 'was Enrico Carella's
statement that after he and his cousin had left the theatre, they went to
have a spritzer next door at the Bar del Teatro La Fenice and then went
to the Lido. This may sound foolish to you, but I wanted to know if it
was true that they had had a spritzer at the bar. So I went there and
asked to talk to the bartender who had been on duty the night of the
fire. It turned out the bar was closed that night.'
 Casson allowed himself a modest smile.
 'I immediately called in one of the other electricians who had
confirmed the story about the bar, and I confronted him with the news
that the bar had been closed. He backed down and admitted it was a lie.
Then he told me that the day after the fire Carella had tried to persuade
all of the electricians to agree on a consistent story to tell the police.
Carella had set up meetings to talk it over, once at a pizzeria near St

Mark's Square and another time at his girlfriend's house on the Lido. He wanted them to say they had all left together at seven thirty, an hour earlier than they really had.'

Casson paused to see if I understood the significance of the change in time.

'Only a person who set the fire,' he said, 'would have known that leaving the building an hour before it burst into flame would have put him in the clear.

'When I looked carefully at their statements, I found that Carella and Marchetti had told conflicting stories. In separate interviews, they had both said they went up to the dressing room together, but each described taking a different route through the theatre.

'The times they cited were frequently contradicted by the evidence. For example, Carella said he had arrived at his girlfriend's house at nine fifteen. But phone records show that she had called him at nine twenty-one, when he was supposedly already there. Why would she have called him if he was with her?'

'Could Carella merely have been mistaken about the time?' I asked.

'Possibly,' said Casson, 'but there are other time conflicts. For example, Carella said he learned about the fire from a friend who called him after hearing the news on television. We checked: the first mention of the fire was at ten thirty-two p.m., but at ten twenty-nine p.m., Carella called the fire department, identified himself, and asked if it was true the Fenice was burning. At least one hour before that, he had called one of his workers and left a mysterious message asking if the man had left a blowtorch burning. The worker had not used a blowtorch all day.'

Casson recited these points without having to consult notes or files. It was clear that he was intensely, intimately involved with the case.

'Carella had been exhibiting strange behaviour in the days leading up to the fire,' Casson continued. 'Nine days before, late on a Saturday evening when the theatre was empty, one of the watchmen was surprised to find Carella up in the *soffitone*, the attic, in his street clothes. This is the location where one of the experts believes that a second fire was set, and Carella had no work-related reason to be there. Carella tried to explain his presence by telling the watchman he was hoping to catch a glimpse of a woman taking her clothes off in a window across the *calle*.'

Casson raised an eyebrow.

'About a week before that, someone working for Viet had left a blowtorch turned on with a ten-centimetre flame burning all night. It was connected to a fifteen-kilo cylinder of propane gas.'

'Do you have any notion of when and how they set the fire?' I asked.

'I was just coming to that,' said Casson. 'Several witnesses said that Carella and Marchetti had both absented themselves from the Viet work site on the ground floor more than once during the afternoon and evening. Some time between seven and eight o'clock, Carella was seen walking away from the work site in the direction of the *ridotto* upstairs.

'This is when I believe he set things up for later on. He went up to the *ridotto*, knowing that the crews working there that day had already gone home. He opened a cabinet, took out the cans of solvent, opened them, and poured the solvent on to the floor and on a pile of raw planking. He then went on to the dressing room, where he joined the others and changed his clothes. After getting into street clothes, Carella and Marchetti came downstairs with the others. Carella went into the caretaker's office to make a phone call, and Marchetti waited for him outside the office. The first three electricians said goodbye and went out of the door. Carella and Marchetti then hid somewhere in the building until the last electrician, Visentin, had left. After Visentin was out of the door, they slipped back upstairs to the *ridotto*, unseen. With Marchetti standing lookout, Carella picked up a blowtorch, lit it, and trained the flame on the floorboards. As the fire began to spread, they ran back downstairs and left through the stage door at eight forty-five.'

'Nobody saw them during all that activity?' I asked.

'Well, yes: Carella and Marchetti were probably the two young men seen running down Calle della Fenice ten minutes after the first three had gone by.'

Lawyers for Carella and Marchetti immediately attacked Casson's case, Speaking for Marchetti, Giovanni Seno argued that almost all of Casson's evidence involved the attempt by Carella and Marchetti to make it look as though they had left the Fenice at least an hour before the fire broke out.

'Of course they did!' said Seno. 'They were frightened. It's only human that a person would try to distance himself from unfounded suspicion in a horrific event like this. Casson's case is all conjecture, nothing more.'

Carella's lawyer added that Casson had got it all wrong as to motive: Viet was not really late; the Fenice had given them a six-week extension, until 15 March. Furthermore, if there had been a penalty, it would have been paid by the company that had given Viet the subcontract, Argenti. Carella's lawyer also claimed that Enrico's personal debt amounted to only $7,500, a tenth of what Casson had estimated. The $75,000 figure, he said, had probably come from a wiretapped conversation in which Carella's father mentioned to a friend that his son's debts had mounted after the fire. That was because much of his equipment had been destroyed in it.

I asked Casson if there had been a single moment or a single piece of evidence that tipped the scales and convinced him that Carella and Marchetti were guilty.

'Yes,' he said without hesitation and again with a sly smile. 'It happened on April the twelfth to be exact. I summoned Marchetti and his girlfriend, Barbara Vello, to answer some questions. During the interview I handed her a notice informing her that she was under investigation for lying to us about a phone call Marchetti had made to her on the night of the fire. We had found out from a wiretap of a conversation between them that Marchetti had tried to get her to change the time of the call. He said, "I called you at eight thirty that night." She said, "You called me at six o'clock," and he kept telling her, "No, eight thirty. I called you at eight thirty."

'I had purposely scheduled the interview at the Santa Chiara police station in Piazzale Roma,' Casson went on, 'rather than in my office at the Rialto, because I knew they would be driving in from Salzano in Marchetti's car. I told them they could park right in front of the police station, which is usually not allowed. What they didn't know was that a few days earlier we had planted a tiny radio transmitter in their car. After the interview, they got back into the car, and Barbara Vello was furious because now she was under investigation for perjury. She turned to Marchetti and screamed at him in dialect, "For a couple of bucks, and that other one up to his ears in debt! So, to make a little money they agree to set the Fenice on fire. If only some money had come out of it, or if at least that cousin of yours had ended up with some of the cash he was supposed to get."' (*Per quattro schei e quell'altro coi debiti i se ga messo d'accordo per fare un pochi de schei e i ga dà fogo aea Fenice. Almanco che ghe fusse vegnui in scarsea quei schei, almanco che ghe fusse vegnui in scarsea a to cugin.*)

'That's when I became certain,' said Casson. 'I called her in again and asked her to explain her statement. At first she said she didn't remember saying it, so I offered to let her listen to herself on tape. Then she became vague. She said she had been very angry. Her comment hadn't been meant as an admission. She had merely been letting off steam, talking haphazardly.'

The police had been listening to tapes for months without finding anything useful. When they heard this one, however, they were elated. Casson, too, was clearly pleased about it. He released Barbara Vello's remark to the press, and it made predictable headlines. But doubts were raised in certain quarters about what the young woman had really meant to say.

At noon one day, I stopped in Gia Schiavi, one of the wine bars frequented by the locals, near the Accademia. I found four men standing at the bar. One of them had a copy of the *Gazzettino*; he was reading Barbara Vello's words aloud to the others.

'The way it's written,' one of the men said, 'it sounds like a statement: "They burned the Fenice for a couple of bucks." But it depends on her inflection. She could have meant it as a question: "They burned the Fenice for a couple of bucks?" meaning, "How could the police think anyone could be that stupid?"'

The other men chorused their agreement. 'Yes, yes . . . Of course . . .'

'Then there's the second part: "If at least your cousin had made some money out of it." She could have been saying, "Well, if they *did* do it, at least your cousin should have got some money out of it."'

Five months after the arrests, both cousins were still in jail. Barbara Vello was at home in San Donà on the mainland, despondent and pregnant.

'She's blaming herself for what happened to Massimiliano,' said Marchetti's mother. 'She shouldn't. It wasn't her fault. They're trying to twist her words.'

Signora Marchetti and her husband were sitting at their kitchen table in Salzano, a small town half an hour north of Venice. At the end of the three-month preventive detention, Casson had asked the judge for a three-month extension, and it had been granted. He kept the pressure on, putting Marchetti and Carella in solitary confinement for weeks at a time. No one knew when they would be released.

'I wouldn't wish this hell on anybody,' said Signora Marchetti, her youthful face drawn and sombre. She had close-cropped grey hair and wore a zippered sweatshirt over a pair of slacks. Her husband, a plant manager at a chemical company in Marghera, sat quietly by her side. She poured Coca-Cola from a plastic litre bottle.

'The police pounded on the door at six in the morning,' she said.

'They had a search warrant, but they wouldn't tell us what they were looking for. We all sat here in the kitchen for two hours while they looked under every object and every piece of furniture in the house. They opened every drawer, every cupboard, every closet. They even searched Massimiliano's car.'

'They asked us if we wanted to call a lawyer,' said Signor Marchetti. 'I said, "No, look wherever you like. We've got nothing to hide." '

'We were thinking it might have something to do with marijuana,' said Signora Marchetti. 'A year ago, Massimiliano was arrested for possession and got a one-year suspended sentence. But that's all over and done. The police didn't find any marijuana. They took his samurai sword, though, and they still have it.'

Signora Marchetti dabbed her eyes with a handkerchief. 'Then, at eight o'clock, they asked Massimiliano to get into the squad car. They said they were going to take him to sign some papers. Just a formality. He took his tools with him, expecting to go to work afterwards. We got into our car and followed them to the Questura in Marghera. Then we sat and waited. At nine o'clock, they told us he'd been arrested for setting fire to the Fenice. We were dumbfounded. We didn't see him for two months after that. I went to court every day asking for permission to see him.'

Signor Marchetti took his wife's hand.

'And to think,' she said, 'the night the Fenice burned, we sat up watching it on TV and crying. We love Venice. Massimiliano loves Venice. He couldn't have done this. He's a good boy. He told me they were going to give him two free tickets when the renovation was finished. He asked me if I would go with him. We were hoping to see Woody Allen.'

'How have the neighbours reacted to this?' I asked.

'Our friends have no doubt he's innocent, and that is a comfort to us. But I have lost faith over this. I've been going to church for thirty years. I don't go very often now.'

✳   ✳   ✳

223

Lucia Carella, Signora Marchetti's older sister, worked as a housekeeper at the Cipriani Hotel. She had been divorced from Renato Carella for many years and was now married to his brother, Alberto Carella. They lived at Sacca Fisola on the Giudecca with her son, Enrico. Twenty years of exposure to the Cipriani's high-end clientele had made Signora Carella a bit more worldly than her sister. Her face was set in defiance rather than worry, but the look in her eyes revealed an enduring sense of humour.

'The police got us up at five in the morning and went through everything,' she said, 'but they wouldn't tell us why. I asked Enrico what they were looking for, and under his breath he said, "The bastards are just trying to bust my balls. They're probably looking for drugs." He didn't suspect that it had anything to do with the Fenice. He didn't seem nervous at all.'

'The prosecutor,' I said, 'claims that Enrico was the one who set the fire, and that your nephew, Massimiliano, was merely acting as lookout for him.'

'Casson!' she said. 'Let me tell you about Casson. The first time he called me after he arrested Enrico, he asked me to come down and answer some questions. He said I had the right to refuse. But I said, "I'm perfectly willing to come and answer your questions." I went to his office and told him everything I knew and everything I was able to remember. That was that.

'Then Casson decided to keep Enrico in jail past the three months' detention period, and, as you can imagine, I was not only desperate but very angry. Right after that, Casson called me again and asked me to come back and answer more questions. But this time I said no. I said I had nothing more to tell him. And he said, "Oh? You won't co-operate? Well, in that case you will not be allowed to visit your son." And during the seven months Enrico spent in prison, I was able to visit him only twice. My sister went to see her son every other week.'

'Why do you think Enrico has been charged?'

'He's a scapegoat. Casson says he burned the Fenice to avoid paying a penalty. Really? Because of the fire, Enrico lost equipment that was worth ten times what the penalty would have cost. That alone should be enough to prove he didn't do it.'

'Your son had been questioned about the Fenice repeatedly before they arrested him,' I said. 'Didn't it occur to you or him that he might be a suspect?'

'Our biggest mistake was not hiring a lawyer right away,' she said. 'We underestimated the gravity of it. We underestimated Casson, that idiot who has ruined our lives.'

'Casson says your former husband, Renato Carella, is also an arson suspect,' I said.

'Casson! Casson is one of those people who loves to be on TV, who is never wrong, who knows everything, who always gets the guilty ones. An important person told me he knows a magistrate here in Venice who says Casson does more harm than good!'

Signora Carella leaned towards me. 'I shouldn't repeat this,' she said, lowering her voice, 'but he told me the magistrate thinks Casson is a dickhead.'

Signora Carella suddenly clapped her hand over her mouth, aware she might have stepped over the line, but when I laughed, she did, too.

The investigation was still in progress when Casson released the two cousins – Marchetti after five months, Carella after seven. Enrico Carella went to live with his fiancée in Crespano del Grappa and was passing the time working in her ice-cream shop. I gave him a call.

'Sure, I'll talk to you,' he said, 'but you'll have to pay me.'

'I'm sorry,' I said, 'but I don't work that way.'

'I'll tell you things I haven't told anybody else,' he said.

'You've already been interviewed by the *Gazzettino* and *Oggi*,' I said. 'Why would you tell me things you wouldn't tell them?'

'You'll see.'

I wished Carella well and instead called Marchetti through his lawyer, Giovanni Seno. Seno said I could talk to Marchetti in his office as long as I understood he might not be able to answer certain questions. Fine, I said. The subject of payment never came up.

Seno's law office was located in a shopping mall above a hardware shop in the town of Spinea, a half-hour drive from Venice. He had a moustache and salt-and-pepper hair, artfully combed to disguise an encroaching baldness. Seno's glove-leather sports jacket was, I later learned, his trademark item of apparel. It gave him a touch of natty informality, in keeping with his casual manner. He was brimming with an amiable confidence that stopped just short of a swagger. When I asked at the outset what sort of cases he usually handled, he answered matter-of-factly, 'Mafia.'

'Have you ever represented Felice "Angel Face" Maniero?' I asked.

'Yeah,' he said, 'but that was twenty years ago, when he was just a kid, before he became a *capo*. It was for some minor crime. I don't remember what.'

Seno's most famous current client, Massimiliano Marchetti, arrived at Seno's office accompanied by his father. The young Marchetti was short, solidly built, and had long blond hair, thinning on top. He was wearing a windbreaker, faded jeans, and jogging shoes. There was a small gold ring in his left ear.

'What was it like to be in isolation for forty-two days?' I asked him.

Marchetti considered the question for a moment. 'You're in there alone,' he said. 'No TV, no newspaper . . . you never see anybody.'

'What did the room look like?' I asked.

'They call it the Lion's Mouth,' he said, speaking haltingly. 'It's like . . . I mean . . . you can't see out . . . You only see sky.' He paused.

'Why did they put you in isolation?'

'Umm . . . they . . .' Marchetti seemed at a loss for words.

Seno spoke up. 'It was a way of trying to get what they wanted out of him. But he didn't have anything to give them, so it was really just a form of torture. I've seen them put some guys in isolation for eleven months. They had to be pulled out by psychiatrists.'

'Yeah, I was lucky,' said Marchetti.

'How do you think the fire started?' I asked.

'I don't know,' he said. 'Really . . . I have no idea.'

'Well, how did you find out about it?'

Marchetti looked at his father and then at Seno. 'I told them . . . uh . . . what I remembered, which . . . Not everything . . . I mean . . . the times weren't right. And I didn't think that the fact that . . . And also, because . . . I mean . . . knowing I hadn't done anything, you didn't stop to think about it . . .' Then he fell silent.

'But how did you actually find out?' I asked.

After a long pause, Marchetti said, 'From my cousin. That evening . . . it was after . . . what was it? . . . Ummm . . . it was—'

'How did you find out?' Seno cut in, visibly exasperated. 'Don't be so fucking vague! He wants to know exactly how you found out! What happened! Who told you?'

Marchetti's father gave his son a worried look. 'Someone called them,' he said, trying to help.

'No!' said Seno. 'Carella says that. He' – pointing to Massimiliano – 'he didn't hear the telephone call.'

'I wasn't . . . um . . . in the same room,' said Marchetti.

Seno leaned towards me, palms up. 'What can I do? That's the way he talks. Understand? He's trying to defend himself, and he talks like that. He pulls out one word a minute. No way can I let him testify.'

'What's going to be your main line of defence?' I asked Seno. 'What's your most powerful argument?'

'Motive!' said Seno. 'Casson hasn't even suggested Massimiliano has a motive. How could he? Massimiliano was only an employee of Viet. Viet wasn't his company. He had no worries about any penalty or fine. He couldn't possibly have had a motive.

'When Casson talks about a motive,' Seno went on, 'he always says it was the penalty. That's Carella, maybe, but not Massimiliano. So Carella is really his main suspect. But there is absolutely no evidence to implicate Massimiliano at all except that he told Casson that he and his cousin were never out of each other's sight. That ties him to Carella; so if Carella set the fire, then Casson figures Massimiliano had to be there, too. If Massimiliano hadn't said that, Casson would have severed him from the case, and he wouldn't be going through any of this. But, look, Massimiliano didn't think he was a suspect until he was arrested sixteen months after the fire. He didn't have a lawyer, me, until the day he was arrested, and by then he'd been interrogated five times.'

'So do you think Carella might be guilty?' I asked. 'Or at least do you think he might know what happened?'

'I didn't say that,' Seno said. 'I only meant that of the two boys, Carella would be the more likely candidate.'

'Do you think they've been set up?'

'Absolutely. This whole thing stinks. It's been very dirty from the start. The police, the press, the whole thing. When we come to trial, I'm going to show that these two kids didn't have enough time to set the fire, between the time Casson says they were last seen in the theatre and a few minutes later, when I can prove they were outside. I won't go into all the details now, but they'd have had to run through the theatre at top speed to do it, and in the dark, too.'

'But if it's arson,' I said, 'what other suspects are there?'

'Are you kidding? With all the oddball characters they had over there at the Fenice, they didn't have to pick on these two guys. There was actually one guy working there — listen to this — who used to say, "Fire! Fire!" every time he walked by. No joke! And I heard about another guy who, wherever he worked, a fire would break out. They ruled that guy out almost immediately.

'No, the only evidence Casson has is who "officially" left the theatre last. And "officially" it was Carella and Marchetti. Now, what kind of evidence is that? What does it prove? Anybody could have walked into that theatre! Anybody! No one was checking. Doors were unlocked, some doors were even left open! Nobody was standing guard. The caretaker wandered off and didn't even show up at the fire until twenty minutes later. But who needed an arsonist anyway? The place wasn't a theatre. It was a cowshed, ready to go up in flames any minute.'

Despite Casson's confidence in his case against Carella and Marchetti, the public remained dubious, at least as far as I could tell from casual conversations and overheard remarks.

A vendor at the Rialto food market said to a housewife buying tomatoes, 'Who but a fool would believe two Venetians burned the Fenice? Venetians, no less!'

The housewife nodded. 'It's crazy.'

'And for so little money!' said the vendor. 'But even if it was for a fortune. No. To burn down the Fenice? It's unthinkable.'

The Venetian penchant for conspiracy theories was not satisfied by the notion that two young men had torched the Fenice to avoid a small penalty. There had to be something much bigger, and more secretive, behind it. The Mafia was still a prime suspect for many people, if they believed it was arson at all.

One person who did not believe it was arson was the man whose photographs had, ironically, been used by the experts to prove that it *had* been. The photographer, Graziano Arici, had been walking through Campo San Fantin on his way to dinner the night of the fire when he smelt smoke, saw flames, and ran home to get his camera. His pictures were studied not only by Casson's experts but by the prosecutor in Bari who had compared them with pictures of the fire that had been set by arsonists at the Petruzzelli Opera House and found an eerie similarity.

'It was only because I had broken up with my girlfriend a few hours earlier that I happened to see the fire,' Arici told me. 'I walked her to the *vaporetto*, and instead of going with her to Mestre, I came back home and was on my way to having dinner alone.'

Arici invited me to look at his photographs at his studio on the ground floor of Count Girolamo Marcello's palace, barely one hundred yards from the Fenice. An engaging, grey-bearded man, Arici sat at a computer nimbly manipulating a keyboard and mouse, arranging and rearranging his images of the fire on his monitor, zooming in and out. The photographs showed the fire spreading rapidly from left to right.

'They claim these pictures prove arson,' Arici said, 'because there was a fire wall dividing that floor in two, and it didn't seem to slow down the "flashover". So one of the experts figured that the fire must have been set in at least two places – possibly even three places – and of course that would have meant arson. But I think that's nonsense. What if the fire doors had been left open? What about the stacks of wood and the heaps of sawdust and wood chips? They could easily have caught fire in an accident.'

'So what do you think happened?' I asked.

'Well, maybe the electricians wanted to dry something and used a heater or a blowtorch. They had an accident. Maybe they tried to put the fire out and couldn't, and then they got scared and ran. That would explain why they tried to make people believe they had left the theatre an hour earlier than they did. Casson probably accused them of arson hoping they would tell him about the accident if there was one, and get a lighter sentence – for negligence, fleeing the fire and not reporting it. But who knows? I'm only a photographer.'

Ludovico De Luigi was only an artist, but *he* had it all figured out. 'It always comes down to money in the end,' he said, 'and the end is nowhere in sight. A lot more money has to pass through many more hands before this will be over.'

I mentioned that I had been impressed by the apparent thoroughness of the scientific tests made by Casson's experts. De Luigi's response, after having a good laugh, was to insist that I meet a friend of his. 'I'll show you a real expert,' he said. 'Come with me.'

At the rowing club on the Zattere, De Luigi introduced me to a man who was standing next to a gondola tied up at the landing platform. The man had a thick black beard without a moustache, like Abraham Lincoln's. His name was Gianpietro Zucchetta, and he was a chemist who worked for the Ministry of the Environment. His gondola was an exact replica of Casanova's gondola, *circa* 1750.

'It looks like the gondolas you see in paintings by Canaletto,' said Zucchetta, 'which are noticeably different from modern gondolas.'

Zucchetta's gondola had a removable cabin, or *felze*, attached to its midsection, and its front-to-back line was straight instead of curved at the bow, which made it necessary for two gondoliers to row it instead of one. Most tellingly, the prow rose higher out of the water, and Zucchetta said that the first time he took it out at high tide, he was surprised to find it would not fit under a number of bridges that Casanova had passed under with ease. 'It was a dramatic demonstration of how much the water level has risen in Venice over the past two hundred and fifty years,' he said.

Zucchetta knew more about water and Venice than most people did; he had written a history of *acqua alta* in Venice. He was also an authority on Venetian bridges, having catalogued all 443 in his book *Venice, Bridge by Bridge*. In the course of conversation, I learned also that Zucchetta had written several other books: two about the canals of Venice, one about the 'lost canals' that have been filled in (the *rii terrà*), one about Casanova, one about Casanova's gondola, one about the history of gas in Venice, and yet another about the Venetian sewer system. 'When you pay a gondolier to row you on the canals,' said Zucchetta, 'he's rowing you through the sludge of Venice.'

But none of these specialities was the reason De Luigi had brought me to see Zucchetta, as I discovered when I asked, 'What will your next book be about?'

'A history of fires in Venice,' he said.

De Luigi beamed. 'My friend Zucchetta is an expert on fires. He's investigated – what? – six hundred, seven hundred fires?'

'Eight hundred,' said Zucchetta, 'including the fire at the Petruzzelli Opera House in Bari. I'm a member of the International Association of Arson Investigators.'

'Have you been called on to consult on the Fenice fire?' I asked.

'Yes,' he said, 'but I've refused.'

'Why?'

'Because it's a political fire, and I don't investigate political fires.'

'What do you mean by that?'

'Politicians are involved. They are among the people being charged with negligence. Now, there are two conflicting charges: negligence and arson. Naturally the negligence suspects all want the verdict to be arson, and the arson suspects want it to be negligence. Each side will try to find experts to prove their point. Two of the negligence suspects have offered to give me a blank cheque if I would testify as an expert for them. They told me I could fill in the figures. Obviously they wanted me to say it was arson, even if I didn't think so. That's why it's a political fire, and that's why I refused.'

'Who were they?'

'That I won't say. But the defendants are not the only people who have a stake in the outcome of this case. A lot of people lost property. The apartments of some of the neighbours were damaged, other people had equipment or personal belongings that were destroyed in the fire, and they all want to recover losses not covered by insurance. If the verdict is arson, none of them will collect anything by suing the electricians, because they have no money. However, if it's found to be negligence, then these people have a choice of rich targets to sue: the city of Venice, the Fenice Foundation, and the fifteen individuals charged with negligence. Two of the defendants for negligence have already put their property in their wives' names.'

Signor Zucchetta's rowing partner arrived. They prepared to board the gondola.

'I assume you've been following developments in the case,' I said.

'Yes, I have,' Zucchetta replied, stepping into the gondola and steadying it as his rowing partner climbed in.

'Do you have an opinion about how it happened?'

'Certainly,' he said. Zucchetta untied the mooring line and pushed away from the platform.

'Do you think the electricians did it?'

Zucchetta shook his head. 'If the electricians burned down the Fenice,' he said with a smile, 'then plumbers are responsible for *acqua alta*.'

II

Opera Buffa

A FEW DAYS AFTER THE arrests of the two electricians, I was riding in a *vaporetto* headed for St Mark's when a water taxi fell in behind us. Five men in business suits were standing on the taxi's foredeck behind the pilot, and even from a distance of fifty feet, I could tell there was something important about this group. A robust, elegant, white-haired man in sunglasses was clearly the leader of whatever pack this was. He had strong features, a florid complexion, and a regal bearing. I assumed the other men were business associates or even bodyguards. Then the head man removed his jacket, and I could see he was wearing his wristwatch over his shirt cuff. I knew immediately who he was. Nobody did that but Gianni Agnelli.

Agnelli, the chairman of the automotive giant Fiat, could have been in Venice for any number of reasons. In the 1980s, he and Fiat had bought the neoclassical Palazzo Grassi, restored it, and converted it into a magnificent exhibition space for major art shows. One of Agnelli's sisters, Cristiana Brandolini d'Adda, lived directly across the Grand Canal from Palazzo Grassi in Palazzo Brandolini. Another sister, Susanna Agnelli, owned a vacation apartment in San Vio. It was likely, however, that Gianni Agnelli's reason for being in Venice had something to do with the rebuilding of the Fenice.

Reconstruction of the opera house had been thrown open to competitive bidding, and six consortiums had submitted plans. Fiat had entered a bid through Impregilo, a group of construction companies headed by Fiat Engineering. The announcement of the winner was expected soon. Impregilo was the odds-on favourite, thanks largely to Agnelli's magisterial presence and to the fact that Impregilo had successfully renovated Palazzo Grassi, making it the only company in the Fenice competition that had already experienced the logistical nightmare Venice imposed on construction projects. The difficulties were unique to Venice, and prodigious. Giant cranes essential for construction would have to be disassembled and floated to the Fenice through a narrow, heavily travelled canal on barges that would be unable to pass under the canal's two bridges during especially high tides. Bricks, structural steel, wood planks, metal pipes, blocks of marble, and other building materials would all be brought to the Fenice by the same route, but since there would be no room to store these things at the Fenice, off-site containment areas would have to be created in the nearest open spaces – in Campo Sant'Angelo, for example, or even on platforms erected on the Grand Canal.

Agnelli, who was known affectionately to the public and the press as 'L'Avvocato' (the Lawyer), had assembled the same team that had worked so well on Palazzo Grassi ten years earlier. That included the architects Gae Aulenti in Milan and Antonio Foscari in Venice.

Gae Aulenti would be the senior architect on this project. She was best known for her transformation of the nineteenth-century Parisian railway station Gare d'Orsay into the Musée d'Orsay, and for designing the modern-art gallery at the Pompidou Centre in Paris.

Antonio (Tonci) Foscari and his architect wife, Barbara del Vicario, lived in Palazzo Barbaro in an apartment directly beneath the Curtis family's ornate *salone*. Tonci Foscari, a professor of architectural history at the University of Venice for the past twenty-five years, was the current president of the Accademia di Belle Arti. At present, the Foscaris were working together on the restoration of the seventeenth-century Malibran Theatre near the Rialto. That project had suddenly taken on a new urgency, because the loss of the Fenice had left Venice without a major theatre for live performances.

Of all Tonci Foscari's architectural projects, the one best known to the public was his and Barbara's restoration of their country house along the Brenta Canal: the Villa Foscari, also known as La Malcontenta. Andrea Palladio had designed the villa in the sixteenth century for two Foscari brothers, and it was a model of perfect simplicity and harmony. *House & Garden* had featured it in an article entitled 'The Most Beautiful House in the World'.

On the night the Fenice burned, the Foscaris were at home when a friend called to tell them a fire had broken out near them. They had rushed to the roof of the music conservatory next door, the tallest building in the area. Tonci Foscari had stood with his camera in hand, horrified, feeling as if he were watching a murder, unable to bring himself to take a photograph. Now he was part of a team hoping to rebuild the Fenice.

We sat in the living-room of the Foscaris' apartment in Palazzo Barbaro. The white walls were decorated with a chaste eighteenth-century pastel stucco trim, a minimalist treatment compared to the riot of baroque embellishment in the Curtises' old *salone* one floor above. Large windows looked out on to the Grand Canal. Portraits of Foscari's ancestors – a Venetian admiral and a pope – stared down at us from the walls. The portrait of the fifteenth-century Doge Francesco Foscari, who was immortalized in the Byron play and the Verdi opera *The Two Foscari*, was hanging in the Correr Museum in St Mark's Square.

'A French group asked me to participate in a bid to rebuild the Fenice,' said Foscari, 'and then a Spanish group. But I hesitated. Finally L'Avvocato Agnelli began reassembling the Palazzo Grassi team. It was almost inevitable that he would. Having restored Palazzo Grassi, he could not *not* compete for the contract to rebuild the Fenice. And, being Agnelli, he could not fail to win. And if he won, he would be able to guarantee absolutely, as no one else could, that the job would be completed on schedule and at the cost he promised. He called me and said, "You are with us!" And at that point, I had to become very pragmatic. It seemed like a secure situation, more so than the others, so I accepted.'

Foscari was under no illusion that his architectural contribution could be much more than seeing to the details in making a new version of the original theatre. His real value to Impregilo would be his familiarity with Venice's complicated building procedures and his experience in dealing with the local bureaucracy.

'Theoretically,' he said, 'all the designs submitted should be essentially the same. It's really just a competition between construction companies, or at least it should be. But – and this is very Italian – it has become a competition among architects with endless debates about their relative gifts.'

'Has Agnelli made an offer Venice won't be able to refuse?' I asked.

'It will be a good deal for Venice, if Venice chooses it,' he said. 'L'Avvocato certainly won't make any money from it. In fact, he could well lose money. But he'd doing it as a matter of pride and prestige, not for the profit. Furthermore, when you build in Venice, any anticipated profits could disappear, because the most unexpected events can cause very expensive delays.'

'Like what?' I asked.

'Well, for example, when you're digging a foundation, you might uncover an architectural relic of historical value. That happened just recently at our restoration of the Malibran Theatre.' Foscari's eyes brightened. This was apparently a delay he relished.

'Do you know what lies beneath the Malibran? Marco Polo's house! It was built in the thirteenth century. We knew this before we started, of course, and when we dug down, we found it exactly where the documents said it would be. We came to the ground floor of the house two metres below the level of the ground today. That was exciting, but there was more to come, because we kept digging. Soon we came to an eleventh-century floor, and below that an eighth-century floor, and farther down, finally, a *sixth*-century floor! This floor was laid at the time of the invasion of the Lombards, and it represents the original foundations of Venice itself. We have very little knowledge of that period in Venetian history. The written record goes back only as far as the eighth century.

'Seeing those floors was an intensely emotional experience for me. It was dramatic evidence that the water level has been rising, and Venice sinking, for fifteen hundred years, and that the Venetians have been dealing with this problem the same way for all that time, by raising the level of the city. We're still doing it today. You can see workmen all over the city tearing up the paving stones along the canals and relaying them seven centimetres higher. This will reduce the number of floods for thirty years or so, but we can't keep doing that for ever.

'Excavating Marco Polo's house and all those floors below it was considered a big "problem", because it caused a delay in restoring the Malibran. It took us five months. Five very interesting months. Meanwhile all the Venetians were saying, "Oh, but you're five months late! It's always like this, no one can ever get anything done on time in Venice." And I said, "I'm sorry, it's very rare that you have the opportunity to do excavations of this sort. It's important."'

'What's under the Fenice?' I asked.

'I've found a map of the site, drawn before the Fenice was built, so we know where the previous structures were. Fortunately, there's nothing as important as Marco Polo's house.'

On the night of the Fenice fire, while Tonci Foscari stood on the roof of the music conservatory, transfixed, unable to take a photograph, Francesco da Mosto, also an architect, mingled with his dinner guests on his *altana* on the other side of the theatre, watching the blaze through the viewfinder of his whirring video camera.

Francesco and Jane da Mosto had been giving their first dinner party as a married couple when their landlord called to ask if they were burning down his house. He had seen smoke rising over the house from across town. Francesco went up to the *altana* to investigate, and when he got there, it all became abundantly clear. The da Mostos' rooftop afforded a close, unobstructed view of the fire, and as the evening wore on, friends and family members came over, among them Francesco's father, Ranieri da Mosto. Count da Mosto was a member of the Venice city council, which had abruptly adjourned its evening session upon receiving news of the fire.

Francesco had been working as an auditor for the Public Works Department, and in the days that followed the fire, he was pressed into service with a group seeking to reconstruct the dynamics of how the fire started and to assess the stability of the Fenice's surviving outer walls.

One afternoon the Milanese architect Aldo Rossi came to the Fenice to look at its remains. Rossi, who had designed the restoration of the Carlo Felice Opera House in Genoa, had recently joined Holzmann-Romagnoli, the German-Italian consortium preparing a bid for the reconstruction. As he was being escorted round the site, Rossi mentioned that he was looking for a Venice-based architect to work on the Fenice with his group. The head engineer suggested Francesco da Mosto.

Meeting the next day, Rossi and da Mosto had coffee and discussed the Fenice. Rossi found da Mosto to be well informed and engaging. 'I want you on the team!' Rossi said, adding that he preferred informal working relationships. 'When you address me,' he told da Mosto, 'use the *tu* form.'

Informality suited Francesco da Mosto perfectly. At thirty-five, he had a shock of unruly, prematurely white hair and an inclination to wear comfortable, usually rumpled clothes – a sports shirt open at the collar, a loose-fitting jacket, and cargo pants with big pockets. He could often be seen riding in his outboard motorboat through the canals or out into the lagoon.

The da Mosto family was one of the oldest in Venice, its ancestry traceable for more than a thousand years. The contemporary da Mostos lived in Palazzo Muti-Baglioni, a huge Renaissance palace tucked into the narrow streets near the Rialto food market. Francesco had an office in a studio on the mezzanine floor.

'The doorbell is out of order,' he told me on the phone. 'When you get to the front door, look up. You will see a string hanging down from a window above it. Pull the string. It will ring a bell in my office, and I will buzz you in. Then come up one flight.'

Da Mosto greeted me at the landing of a red-carpeted stairway. As we turned to go into his office, he gestured towards a marble bust on a pedestal by the door. 'Meet Alvise da Mosto,' he said, 'my favourite ancestor. He discovered the Cape Verde Islands in 1456 at the age of twenty-nine.'

Da Mosto's studio was a dark, cavernous space with a high, beamed ceiling, shelves filled to overflowing with books, videotapes, and files. Computers, printers, and a drawing table were half buried amid piles of papers and journals. The walls were crowded with charts, photographs, masks, and souvenirs. It was clutter on a grand scale.

Da Mosto scooped a stack of papers off a chair, clearing a place for me to sit. I found myself facing a densely drawn family tree hanging on the wall.

'How many generations is that?' I asked.

'You know, I'm not really sure,' he said, laughing. 'I'd have to count. Anyway, I think it's about twenty-seven.'

'All nobility?' I asked.

'Nobility, yes, but not all of them noble. One of my female ancestors, a courtesan, gave Lord Byron the clap! Another, Vido da Mosto, was caught printing counterfeit money. They considered gouging his eyes out and hanging him between the columns in San Marco, but instead they gave him the job of printing the official money of the Venetian Republic. The theory, I guess, was that if somebody had a particular talent, the republic should make use of it. There was a da Mosto whose wife ate so much he went broke. Another da Mosto went to prison for insulting Doge Andrea Gritti, and three or four others were excommunicated. We've had a doge's wife, but never a doge, one da Mosto narrowly lost to a man who was beheaded after he became doge, so maybe it's just as well he lost. Anyway, da Mostos have always preferred being the power behind the throne. It's a safer place to be.'

'And now,' I said, 'a da Mosto is coming to the rescue of Teatro La Fenice.'

'Everybody expects Agnelli to win,' he said, 'but we'll find out in a day or two.'

Da Mosto pulled a thick file out from under a stack of papers and handed it to me. 'These are the specifications the Comune gave us for the new Fenice. It's the preliminary plan,' he said, 'what you call "bid documents".'

I leafed through the pages. The Fenice was laid out in a mixed-media presentation: floor plans, drawings, sketches, photographs, paintings.

'Fortunately,' said da Mosto, 'someone discovered the architectural plans that were drawn up in 1836, after the first fire. They were found in an archive along with detailed written instructions by the Meduna brothers. So we have all the correct measurements for the auditorium, which means we can re-create the Fenice's acoustics exactly. The Medunas even described how the pieces of wood should be cut. Sound waves travel along the grain of the wood, so if it is cut properly and positioned at the correct angle, the sound will be carried evenly from the stage to every point in the theatre. The Medunas personally signed every piece of wood!' Da Mosto clearly took delight in this last detail.

'It seems pretty clear what's expected,' I said.

'Yes, but not completely,' he said. 'When I received these documents from the Comune last September, I sat down and studied them several times. And something didn't seem right.'

Da Mosto turned to the Comune's floor plans. 'Here, look at this area.' He pointed to the south wing, a complex of small buildings attached like barnacles to the south wall of the theatre.

'According to this drawing,' he said, 'the old south wing has been enlarged so that it now incorporates a two-storey building the Fenice doesn't own. It's this blank space right here. It covers three hundred square metres in all, but it's never been part of the Fenice. Right now,' he said, pulling out an old map of the theatre, 'you can see there's a *magazzino* on the ground floor. It contains a laundry used by the restaurant Antico Martini; on the floor above, there are a couple of privately owned apartments. It's very strange. There's no mention of this new space in the written instructions we were given. If we were supposed to rebuild the theatre exactly as it was – *com'era* – this space doesn't belong in it.'

'Then why is it on the drawing?'

'That's what I wondered. Signor Baldi, the owner of Antico Martini, says he needs the laundry for his table linens, and no alternative space is available, so he won't sell his *magazzino*. I didn't know what to do about it, so I asked some of the engineers and architects who worked on the preliminary plan for the prefect. When they realized what I was talking about, they turned white as a piece of paper. So I immediately called Aldo Rossi and told him to stop work, because there was some confusion about the south wing.

'I was apparently not the only one who raised the question. One of the other competitors had already written a letter asking about it. So the prefect sent faxes to all the bidders, but the wording of his fax only made it more confusing. He told us we were to build "the entire south wing of the theatre, from the ground to the roof". But what does "the entire south wing" mean? Does it mean the footprint of the old south wing as it was before the fire, or the footprint of the old south wing plus the additional building? Now I was more confused than ever. So I went over to the office of the city council and talked with some of my friends there who had worked there for years. Those are the people who always know what's going on. They told me no one had said anything about it to them, but, with a little smile, they said we should include the new space.

'We had a big meeting in Milan, and I explained what was going on in Venice. We decided to take a bit of a risk and go ahead with Rossi's plan for the enlarged south wing.

'The Comune probably assumed everybody would design the south wing with more of the same kind of offices that were there before. But Rossi had another idea, and it was brilliant. He moved the rehearsal hall from the top floor down here to the ground floor in the new space. He made it big enough to hold rehearsals for a full orchestra and chorus. It could also be used for chamber-music concerts or conferences. The beautiful thing is that this rehearsal room becomes a new medium-size theatre that could be in use at the same time as the main theatre. It's isolated acoustically, and it has its own entrance on the street. With two theatres operating at once, the Fenice's total capacity would be increased by about ten per cent.'

Da Mosto put the file back down on the sea of papers on his desk. 'I'm curious to see what the others have done with the south wing.'

On the way out, da Mosto took me one flight up to the *piano nobile*. The central hall was a vast space, seventy-five feet in length. It had tall leaded-glass windows at each end and stuccoed walls hung with portraits of da Mosto ancestors, one of whom had been a paymaster of the Venetian military and was surrounded by stacks of gold coins. Off the main hall, an elegant salon with walls of gold brocade led to a small, frescoed chapel and beyond it a dining room where, da Mosto said, a scene from Visconti's *Senso* had been filmed.

'The producers of the movie *The Talented Mr Ripley* also want to shoot a scene in the house,' said da Mosto. 'It's very expensive to keep the *stucchi* repaired in these humid conditions, so we said yes.'

As I was looking at the family portraits, da Mosto's father came into the room. He was a courtly gentleman, soft-spoken and impeccably dressed in a suit and tie in muted colours. I had read that he was a leading proponent of the movement to restore the Republic of Venice as an independent state, separate from the rest of Italy. He was a separatist, an *indipendista*. I asked him about it.

'Most people don't realize,' he said, 'that the Venetian Republic never really died. When Napoleon's army was approaching in 1797, the Grand Council voted in a panic to dissolve the republic. But the vote was illegal, because there were not enough people in the council chamber to make a quorum. Napoleon's savage and despicable occupation of Venice was only a military operation, and the Austrian occupation that followed was, again, nothing more than a military holding action. The unification of Italy in the referendum of 1866 was a sham, a trick by the Savoia family, with ballots that were filled in beforehand, and with the police and the *carabinieri* spying on people at the polling station. It was shameful.'

'But what can possibly be done about it now?' I asked.

'We hope to bring all of this to the attention of the Hague Tribunal. I don't know what will happen. It won't be an easy battle.'

Somehow I doubted that any tribunal would feel it had the authority to undo the unification of Italy 130 years after the fact, but that seemed to be Count da Mosto's hope.

'How do you feel,' I said, 'knowing that if Francesco's team wins the Fenice contract, he'll be helping to resurrect not just the Fenice but the Fenice's royal box, which was originally built for Napoleon and later rebuilt by the Austrians?'

'For the last fifty years,' the count said with a genial smile, 'a large, gilded lion of St Mark has adorned the pediment over the royal box. It's not Napoleon's royal box any longer, nor is it Austria's. It's ours.'

Six bids were submitted for the reconstruction of the Fenice. One, entered by Ferrovial of Madrid, was disqualified immediately because it lacked a mandatory anti-Mafia letter for one of its subcontractors.

Anti-Mafia letters were documents stamped by the police, confirming that a check of the criminal database had turned up no mob connections for the company, either past or present. Despite furious protests that it had indeed submitted such a letter, Ferrovial's application was rejected. Five candidates remained.

The results of the competition were announced on 2 June 1997, a year and a half after the fire. No one was surprised when Agnelli's Impregilo was declared the winner; Holzmann-Romagnoli had come in second. Curiously, however, the breakdown of scores revealed that Aldo Rossi's design had been judged the best. Impregilo had earned enough points to take first place by promising to finish two months earlier than Holzmann-Romagnoli and at a cost of $45 million – $4 million less.

Despite his disappointment, Francesco da Mosto seemed in good spirits when I encountered him on the street a few days later. 'The losing bidders all have the right to examine the bid that finished just above them in the competition,' he said. 'So I am going to have a look at Impregilo's bid. I'm on my way to the Prefecture now. I don't think I'm allowed to take anybody in with me, but if you'd like to come along, I'll ask.'

I accompanied da Mosto to the Prefecture, the huge Renaissance palace formally known as Palazzo Corner della Ca' Grande, and we learned that indeed he alone would be admitted to view the Fenice bid materials. A porter ushered him into storage rooms on the ground floor, and I contented myself with a walk upstairs and a tour of the magnificent rooms of state on the Grand Canal. Half an hour later, we met again downstairs. Francesco had a strange look on his face. I could not tell whether he was amused, perplexed, worried, or angry.

'What did Impregilo design for the new space?' I asked.

'When I saw it,' he said, 'I didn't believe it. I thought, "This cannot be true!" They had nothing. They left it blank.'

✻   ✻   ✻

Three weeks later, Campo San Fantin came alive after nearly a year and a half of bleak, funereal stillness during which the Fenice's charred shell had stood in silent rebuke to passers-by, a depressing symbol of hopelessness. As the weeks passed, three towering cranes, standard-bearers of restoration and renewal, rose high in the air over the Fenice. Workers on scaffolding reinforced the theatre's outer walls. The sound of jackhammers and earthmoving equipment signalled that excavation and the sinking of concrete pilings for a new foundation were under way.

Out on the Grand Canal, a four-thousand-square-foot platform was mounted on wooden pilings and enclosed by an eight-foot plywood wall. It was for storage of equipment and supplies. Cement mixers on the platform pumped liquid cement through underground tubes to the construction site. A brightly coloured mural of the Fenice was painted on the plywood wall, reflecting the optimism that had suddenly taken hold in the city. On the second anniversary of the fire, January 1998, eight months into the reconstruction, a jubilant Mayor Cacciari held a press conference to announce that work was proceeding on schedule. As promised, the Fenice would reopen in September 1999.

The mayor's expressions of joy turned to a cry of anguish when, barely two weeks later, the State Council ruled on an appeal by Holzmann-Romagnoli and revoked Impregilo's contract. According to the council, the preliminary plan had clearly indicated that the south wing was to include the new space. They quoted from the preliminary plan itself to show that bidders were not required to rebuild an exact replica of the Fenice: 'It will be impossible to reproduce the theatre as designed by Selva, rebuilt by Meduna, or modified by Miozzi. Nor can it be exactly as it was just before the fire. Even if painstakingly rebuilt, the new Fenice can only be, at best, an evocation of its former self.' Impregilo had been the only bidder to omit the new space, thereby giving itself an unfair advantage over the others by lowering the cost of its bid.

Work on the Fenice stopped.

'The ruling is demented!' Mayor Cacciari declared. 'The merits of this decision are way out of proportion to the damage done to the city and the country.'

The construction site was a shambles; no one in authority knew what to do. Officials in Rome and Venice, operating in near-panic mode, pleaded with the outgoing Impregilo and the incoming Holzmann-Romagnoli to co-operate with each other so as to achieve a quick and smooth transition. But that seemed unlikely, as events quickly became snarled in a tangle of complicated questions and disputes.

Would Impregilo be reimbursed for the $15 million it had spent already? Would Holzmann-Romagnoli honour the hundreds of contracts Impregilo had already signed with suppliers and craftsmen? Who would be responsible for the cranes, the leases for which were costing thousands of dollars a day, even with the site lying idle? Ditto for the scaffolding. And finally, could the partially built foundation designed by Gae Aulenti be adapted so that Aldo Rossi's Fenice could sit on top of it? Or could Rossi's design be altered to fit the foundation?

The man who could have answered the last of these questions most easily was, tragically, unable to do so. Aldo Rossi had been killed in a car accident in September. He had run off a winding road while driving to his house at Lago Maggiore. His associates in Milan would carry on. Francesco da Mosto, who had initially alerted Holzmann-Romagnoli that grounds for an appeal existed, would serve as liaison between the Rossi studio, Holzmann-Romagnoli, and the Comune of Venice.

Gae Aulenti's reaction to the news of her unexpected expulsion from the Fenice project was to issue a terse comment: 'To my successor, good luck.' It was, word for word, a proper thing to say, but in its brevity it carried the message that she was throwing up her hands in disgust.

Tonci Foscari's response was somewhat more graceful. He wrote a letter to the *Gazzettino* praising Aldo Rossi's design. He complimented Rossi on his decision to place the rehearsal hall on the ground floor, which could double as a small concert hall and enlarge the Fenice's audience. Foscari volunteered a few suggestions to the Rossi studio, in line with increasing the profitable uses of the Fenice. He proposed, for example, adapting the Apollonian rooms so they could function independently for parties and after-theatre dinners. This would require planning for extra bathrooms, a catering suite, and emergency exits. Foscari offered his proposals 'as a natural evolution of Aldo's thinking, and – in the memory of that faraway smile that lighted his face – they seem to me almost an act of respect'.

Gianni Agnelli said nothing at all about the court's decision, and this was true to form. 'L'Avvocato is the owner of Juventus, the Turin soccer team,' said Foscari. 'Some weeks he wins, some weeks he loses. Complaining is not his style.'

Meanwhile, upon close inspection, Rossi's architectural plan was found to be in violation of certain Venetian building codes. In order for the construction to go forward, either the laws would have to be changed or exceptions granted. The relevant officials, however, promptly declared it would not be a problem.

A more difficult issue was the privately owned building with the two apartments. The owners still refused to sell.

'All it will take is money,' Ludovico De Luigi said with a shrug. 'Keep watching. Many more hands are going to reach into this pie before it's over.'

De Luigi was sitting in front of his easel dabbing paint on to an image of the Church of Santa Maria della Salute as an oil platform suspended above a roiling sea confined within St Mark's Square. It was one of his familiar surrealist views of Venice. De Luigi's studio occupied the ground floor of his house, and his windows looked out on to the small canal, the Rio di San Barnaba.

'The Fenice is putting on an opera,' he said. 'An *opera buffa* – a comic opera.' He paused, reconsidering his words. 'No, a tragicomic opera. But this opera is not on the stage. It's in the audience. The spectators have become the performers. Politicians, building executives, architects. Everybody says they want to build the theatre. But nobody really wants to build it. They are only interested in the fees. They want this opera to go on and on. They come in, they get some money, they do nothing, then they leave, and on the way out, they get some more money. Then other people come in, and they get some money, and so forth. They all make impressive designs, but you have to know what's beneath. Ruthless people. Politicians.'

It was vintage De Luigi cynicism, but the real story was beginning to bear a resemblance to his vision of it and to the madness of his art.

'That's why I paint the Apocalypse,' he said, applying white-caps to the waves in the sea that filled St Mark's Square. 'I am a *svedutista*, a painter of negative landscapes, interior landscapes. I paint them as they exist in the mind. They are not abstractions. They are composed of recognizable features arranged in a surreal vision. They are portraits of our nightmares.'

De Luigi drew back and studied his darkly beautiful painting for a moment.

'They had to find somebody to blame for the fire,' he went on, putting brush to canvas again. 'But not the politicians, of course. First they accused the Mafia. It took two years for them to decide it was not the Mafia. And now they've found the two poor electricians.' De Luigi shrugged. 'Whoever burned down the Fenice did not do it for political or philosophical reasons. It was for money.'

'If it had been out of anger at the Fenice,' I said, 'I suppose the perpetrators would have made that known.'

'The Fenice does have its faults,' said De Luigi, looking up from his canvas. 'The whole focus of performances at the Fenice has changed, and for the worse. It's shifted from the love of art to narcissistic protagonism. Exhibitionism. It started the first time they put a spotlight on the conductor. It was for Herbert von Karajan. He was the first movie-star conductor. Conductors used to be in the dark. But von Karajan insisted on a spotlight, or there wouldn't be any music.'

Ludovico De Luigi himself was no stranger to the spotlight. He bathed in one of his own devising. It illuminated his shoulder-length white hair, his imperial profile, and his outrageous antics. Tonight he glowed more than ever in his personal spotlight. He was wearing a tricorne hat edged in ermine, a ruffled shirt, red silk breeches, and a dinner jacket on which he had painted lifelike red-and-orange flames. It was Carnival time again. Costumed revellers could be seen passing outside his window.

'For Carnival this year,' he said, 'I am dedicating myself to the second anniversary of the night the Fenice became an empty shell. It may remain an empty shell for ever. Who knows?'

We were joined shortly by Gianpietro Zucchetta, the bearded expert on bridges, canals, *acqua alta*, sewers, and fire. Zucchetta was accompanied by his wife, both in masks and eighteenth-century costumes, and a blonde woman who was dressed as a courtesan. After a drink, we climbed into Zucchetta's gondola, the replica of Casanova's, which he had tethered to a pole in the canal in front of De Luigi's house. De Luigi carried a small satchel on board and put it under the *felze*, out of sight.

'That's for later,' he said, with a look of bemused expectation. 'We're going to do a *scherzo*, a joke.'

He turned to me. 'Have you ever been arrested by the *carabinieri*?'

'I haven't had the pleasure,' I said.

'Then this could be your night!'

'Why?' I asked.

'Because I'm going to break the law, and anyone with me might be considered an accomplice.'

De Luigi seemed to enjoy keeping me in suspense, so I did not ask what his *scherzo* entailed.

'Being arrested is good for the soul,' he said. 'I was arrested for committing "obscene acts in public". It happened when I invited the porn star Cicciolina to inaugurate my horse sculpture in St Mark's Square, and she arrived topless. In a court of law I was declared an immoral person – a disreputable person!' De Luigi chuckled at the thought of it. 'But for an artist, a reputation and a *dis*reputation are the same. An artist wants to be recognized, to attract attention.

'I became famous in Chicago,' he went on. 'The police removed my paintings of nudes from a gallery on the grounds that I had painted "aggressive nipples". Of course, this made me very popular in Chicago.' De Luigi had another laugh, then looked up at me. 'Does the thought of being arrested worry you?'

'Not if it's for a good cause.'

'It's for the Fenice.'

'Well, then, fine,' I said.

With Zucchetta rowing in front and a professional gondolier handling the stern oar, we made our way to the Grand Canal, where we turned right and headed toward St Mark's. De Luigi was laughing and joking, but I noticed he was looking up and down the canal, his eyes darting from boat to boat, looking to see who else was on the water, police boats in particular. We were passing the Peggy Guggenheim Museum.

'After the war,' said De Luigi, 'Peggy Guggenheim used to give big parties. The servants would come out when it was over and give us ice-cream and cigarettes. Whenever she had a party, my friends and I would stand on the Accademia Bridge and watch her guests dancing on the terrace. One night, Peggy re-enacted the sinking of the *Titanic* – her father had died on it. She walked from her terrace into the water, completely nude. She took the orchestra with her. She had paid them to do it. The gondoliers had to rescue her.

'America is not pouring out those crazy people any more. They were very amusing. They had a sense of theatre. They were inventive, creative. Today Americans are not so amusing. *Va bene*. We will just have to amuse ourselves.'

Directly ahead of us in the canal lay the walled platform where the Fenice stored its cement mixers and other equipment. We drew up alongside the mural of the Fenice that had been painted on the plywood enclosure. De Luigi came out from under the *felze* and stood up. He was holding a can of red paint and a paintbrush. He looked up and down the Grand Canal.

'Does anybody see a police boat?'

'Not yet,' said Zucchetta. He and the gondolier at the stern swirled their oars to steady the gondola and keep it close to the mural.

De Luigi dipped his brush into the paint. Then, as he lifted his hand, he looked at me.

'You know so much about the fire,' he said. 'Where were the first flames seen?'

'Front façade, upper left window,' I said.

With broad strokes, De Luigi painted great tongues of brilliant red flames coming out of the window on the upper left. Then he painted them in the middle window, then the right.

A water taxi coming up behind us made a wide turn and pulled up next to us so that its partygoing passengers could get a better look.

'*Bravo! Fantastico!*' they called out. De Luigi turned and bowed. The wash from the taxi struck the gondola amidships and sent us rocking. Paint sloshed out of the can but fell into the water as De Luigi regained his balance. Then he turned and went back to work. He painted flames in the ground-floor windows and the main doorway, then he continued until all the portals on the front façade were filled with flames. They matched the flames painted on his dinner jacket. De Luigi's flaming jacket and the mural with its flaming windows had become an ensemble work of art. He was the torch setting the painted Fenice on fire.

Two more boats pulled up, then another and another. The gondola bobbed and pitched amid sounds of laughter, applause, idling motors, and sloshing water. De Luigi kept on painting. He was now standing in front of a cutaway view of the foyer and the Apollonian rooms, painting wherever his brush would reach. As he was painting flames on the ceremonial stairway, the mural was suddenly illuminated by a pulsing blue light. A police boat nosed through the flotilla around us. De Luigi, very much aware of its arrival, went on painting.

'What are you doing?' one of the policemen shouted.

De Luigi turned round, the incriminating paintbrush in one hand, the paint can in the other. 'I am telling the truth,' he said with triumphant defiance. 'The architect's commission for the new Fenice came out of the flames. I am turning his rendering into an honest statement.'

'Oh, it's you, Maestro,' the policeman said.

'Well, are you going to arrest me?' De Luigi asked.

'Arrest you? Again?'

'I have vandalized this mural,' said De Luigi.

'I'm not sure I'd call it that.'

'Am I not a public nuisance?' De Luigi looked bewildered.

'During Carnival, Maestro, everyone is a public nuisance. The rules are different. Come back and do this again next week. Then maybe we'll arrest you.'

12

Beware of Falling Angels

FROM THE TOP OF A SMALL BRIDGE, Lesa Marcello watched as workmen removed the last of the scaffolding from the five-hundred-year-old Church of Santa Maria dei Miracoli. The building had been wrapped in a cocoon of canvas for the past ten years while the restorers did their work, and now it stood revealed: a multicoloured, early-Renaissance jewel box sheathed in panels of inlaid marble and porphyry.

Like a gem itself, the Miracoli Church was set into a tiny niche at the heart of a maze of streets so intertwined and out of the way that one often came upon it by surprise. A small canal ran along one side, serving as a reflecting pool. The Miracoli was, in short, irresistible. Even John Ruskin, who detested Renaissance architecture, had to admit that it was one of the most 'refined' buildings in Venice. Small wonder that Santa Maria dei Miracoli – 'St Mary of the Miracles' – had been the church of choice for weddings as long as anyone could remember.

The restoration was financed by Save Venice, the American charity devoted to the preservation of art and architecture in Venice. As the director of the local office, Countess Marcello had been coming to the church several times a week for some years to check on its progress. She conferred with artisans, workmen, contractors, and city officials. At times she even climbed the scaffolding to get a closer look.

As with all such projects in Venice, the restoration of the Miracoli had not been a simple matter of putting up the money and telling the restorers to go to work. Venetian bureaucrats never shared the donors' sense of urgency. They could delay a project indefinitely if they felt the slightest challenge to their authority or their expertise. Understanding this, the officers of Save Venice had wisely hired Countess Marcello to run their Venice office. They had also elected several Venetian nobles to their board of directors, including Lesa Marcello's husband, Count Girolamo Marcello.

Countess Marcello was a woman of quiet, unassuming grace and had proved exceptionally valuable to Save Venice. She knew the local superintendents personally; more than that, she knew about the rivalries within the bureaucracy and was therefore able to manoeuvre deftly, without treading on toes. She was practised in the art of negotiation, Venetian style, which began with the understanding that one could accomplish more over a cup of coffee at Caffe Florian than across a desk in an office. In conversation Lesa Marcello raised issues obliquely. She compromised, and if there happened to be any impatience percolating among the officers of Save Venice, and there usually was, she never let the Venetians know about it.

'One always has to do these things privately,' she said when I came to see her in her office one afternoon, 'not in an official way. For example, if Save Venice pays to restore a painting, one of the art experts on its board of directors might want to come to Venice and say to the superintendent, "You know, you shouldn't use this chemical." The superintendent will think he's being criticized, so he replies, "But that's what we want to do." And then the project is stalled. I prefer to broach the subject by saying, "I've been asked if this or that might be possible." And then I would simply compare the two ideas rather than oppose one against the other. It's a very subtle difference, but it's important. It's our nature, our way of moving, of navigating. It's gentle, not aggressive. The superintendents are willing to discuss new ideas with other experts, but only if it's done in an evenhanded way. And, of course, only in private.'

'How do you mean "in private"?' I asked.

'One-to-one,' she said. 'If a third person is present, then it's no longer private. It's public, and the superintendent, being only human, would be embarrassed.'

Normally Save Venice selected restoration projects from a list drawn up by the superintendencies, but in the case of the Miracoli Church, Save Venice had originated the idea itself. It had not been on any of the usual lists. The church had become black with oily grime, inside and out. Save Venice proposed using experimental methods to restore it, and the superintendent of monuments was at first very much opposed. He wanted to conduct an exhaustive study of the whole building before allowing any work to start, and that could have taken decades. Finally Save Venice suggested proceeding in stages: open up a small portion of the walls, see what they found, and continue, or not, from there. The superintendent agreed, and the project went forward.

Save Venice had hoped to be finished in two years, by 1989, in time for the five-hundredth anniversary of the church. But even Save Venice's own experts insisted on preliminary research that consumed two years by itself. Technicians analysed samples of every structural substance in the building, made scale drawings with the aid of laser measurements, took soundings of the walls, and recorded humidity and temperature levels throughout.

When they detached the first marble panels from the brick walls, they discovered that salt from the canals had seeped up through the porous bricks and permeated the marble. The marble slabs had become 14 per cent salt. Many of them were on the point of exploding. Each piece of marble had to be removed and desalinated by soaking for months in specially built steel tanks filled with circulating distilled water.

The restoration had taken ten years, not two, and the cost had ballooned from an estimated $1 million to $4 million. But none of that mattered now. The completed Miracoli was already being hailed as a masterpiece of restoration and a model of co-operation all around. The project had been the most ambitious ever undertaken by any of the thirty private committees that were doing restorations in Venice. The spectacular results had occasioned an outpouring of goodwill towards Save Venice. Members of the prestigious Ateneo Veneto, the supreme council of the Venetian intellectual community, had voted to present their highest honour, the Pietro Torta Prize, to Save Venice and its chairman, Lawrence Dow Lovett.

Lesa Marcello had spoken with Lovett earlier in the day to let him know that the award had been confirmed. Lovett, a native of Jacksonville, Florida, had endeared himself to Venetians by buying a nineteenth-century palace on the Grand Canal, restoring it, and taking up residence in it. The palace was sumptuously furnished and had a spectacular view of the Rialto Bridge from its broad terrace, the largest terrace on the Grand Canal. Lovett frequently gave elegant dinner parties for twenty or more, catered by Harry's Bar and served by a squadron of white-gloved waiters.

Countess Marcello also sent word of the Torta Prize to the president of Save Venice, Randolph 'Bob' Guthrie, who lived in New York. Guthrie was a well-known plastic surgeon, one of two doctors who had invented the standard procedure for reconstructive breast surgery. He and his wife, Bea, lived in an Upper East Side Manhattan town house; their ground floor served as the headquarters of Save Venice.

Lesa Marcello was in high spirits as she walked back from the Miracoli to the Save Venice office. She knew that, in her own way, she had contributed to the success of the Miracoli restoration. At the office, she found a fax waiting for her. It was from Bob Guthrie. She read the first line. Then she read it again. 'The news that the Torta Prize has singled out an individual,' Guthrie had written, 'is shocking.'

She continued reading with a sinking heart. 'Please tell the head of the prize committee that the restoration of the Miracoli was the result of efforts by a great many people in Save Venice and that his committee's proposal to single out one individual is not acceptable to the Board of Save Venice. The award, if given, must go to Save Venice as a whole. Otherwise, Save Venice will formally request that the prize for its work not be given at all.'

Without ever mentioning Larry Lovett by name in the letter, Guthrie told Lesa to inform the committee that 'the person' they had selected to receive the award had not been the chief executive officer (in other words, the president) of Save Venice for nearly ten years and that, in any case, it would be presumptuous for one person to accept a prize for the work of so many others.

Guthrie's letter was blunt, peremptory, and unyielding. He closed by telling Lesa that unless the prize-committee members changed their minds, she was not to give them any information, photographs, or documents, or to co-operate with them in any way. 'I want there to be no mistake in Venice about how we feel.'

The reasons behind Bob Guthrie's fax were many and complicated, as Countess Marcello was well aware. But for the moment, the letter meant only one thing: that a panel of distinguished Venetians had voted to honour Save Venice and its chairman, Larry Lovett, with their most coveted award, and Bob Guthrie, the president of Save Venice, was prepared to fling it back in their faces.

Tension within Save Venice, between the chairman and the president, had been mounting for the last two years, since 1995. The first outward sign of it was so slight that few people even noticed: Bob Guthrie's name, as president, had appeared for the first time above Larry Lovett's at the top of a list of the Save Venice board of directors in a glossy journal put out by Save Venice and edited by Bob Guthrie. This sudden reversal of the pecking order had come as an unpleasant surprise to Lovett.

The roots of this burgeoning quarrel could be traced to the early 1960s, before the two men had ever met, when a retired American army colonel was overheard at a reception in Rome speculating that it might be possible to stabilize the leaning Tower of Pisa by freezing the subsoil under it.

The man doing the talking was Colonel James A. Gray. The person who overheard him was Italy's superintendent of fine arts and antiquities. The superintendent told the colonel that his idea of freezing the ground under the Tower of Pisa was ingenious and might be attempted if it was found to be viable. Gray went off to do research. Although the tower was eventually stabilized another way, Colonel Gray's investigations turned him into a passionate advocate for preserving the world's great art and architecture. Upon making enquiries, he found there was no private non-profit organization doing this kind of work, so in 1965 he created one. He called it the International Fund for Monuments, and he ran it from his apartment in the National Arts Club on Gramercy Park in New York. (Twenty years later, much expanded, Colonel Gray's organization would be renamed the World Monuments Fund.) Gray's selection of projects was a bit whimsical and far-flung – conservation of the mysterious stone heads on Easter Island and twelfth-century stone churches carved into hillsides in Ethiopia.

Then, on 4 November 1966, a combination of constant rain, strong winds, and seismic rumbling under the Adriatic seabed created exceptionally high tides that caused flooding across northern Italy and put Venice under five feet of water for more than twenty-four hours.

In the immediate aftermath of the flood, most of the attention went to Florence, where the Arno had overflowed its banks by more than twenty feet, killing ninety people and damaging or destroying thousands of works of art. Art lovers around the world formed committees to send aid and assistance. In the United States, the Committee to Rescue Italian Art was established, with Jacqueline Kennedy as its honorary president.

As for Venice, although no one had died and very little art had been damaged, it soon became evident that the situation was fundamentally worse than in Florence. Venice had been built on millions of wooden pilings driven into the muck at the bottom of the lagoon. Over the course of centuries, as the city settled into the earth and the sea level rose, the foundations became unstable. When experts took a closer look at Venice, they discovered that most of its buildings and almost all of its works of art were in desperate condition, owing to two centuries of neglect following the city's defeat by Napoleon. Paintings all around the city had become soot-blackened, mouldy, and brittle. Many of the most important were housed in churches, where they were unprotected from the elements because of holes in the roofs. At the same time, a great many buildings had eroding foundations and crumbling façades. It was a common hazard for chunks of walls, bricks, slabs of marble, cornices, and other decorative elements to come crashing down from on high. The whole eastern wall of the Gesuiti Church was in danger of falling into an adjacent canal. After part of a marble angel fell from a parapet of the ornate but sadly dilapidated Santa Maria della Salute Church, Arrigo Cipriani, the owner of Harry's Bar, posted a sign outside the church warning, 'Beware of Falling Angels'.

Recognizing a threat to the very existence of Venice, Colonel Gray established a 'Venice Committee' within his International Fund for Monuments. As the salvage operations in Florence were being completed, Gray enlisted the head of the Committee to Rescue Italian Art, Professor John McAndrew, to be the Venice Committee's chairman.

McAndrew, an architectural historian, was about to retire from his teaching position at Wellesley College. In an active and varied life, he had served as the architectural curator at New York's Museum of Modern Art after a Second World War assignment in Mexico as the State Department's co-ordinator of inter-American affairs. He was an expert on Frank Lloyd Wright and Alvar Aalto and had written frequently for scholarly journals.

In the 1970s, McAndrew recruited a group of intellectuals and art patrons for the Venice Committee, among them the Renaissance scholar Sydney J. Freedberg, chairman of Harvard's Department of Fine Arts; Rollin 'Bump' Hadley, director of the Isabella Stewart Gardner Museum in Boston; the Swiss art collector Walter Bareiss; and Gladys Delmas, an American philanthropist with a special interest in Venice. At the same time, similar organizations devoted to aiding Venice were being formed in other countries: in Britain it was Venice in Peril; in France, the Comité Français pour la Sauvegarde de Venise; in Sweden, Pro Venezia. Eventually there came to be thirty-three such private non-profit committees. The work of all these organizations was co-ordinated by a liaison office run by UNESCO called the Association of Private Committees.

In its first four years, the Venice Committee initiated more than a dozen important cleaning and restoration projects, starting with the elaborately ornate façade of Ca' d'Oro, a Gothic palace on the Grand Canal. To show their gratitude for the good works of Save Venice, the Venetian aristocrats did something extraordinary – extraordinary, that is, for Venetians: they invited the Americans into their palaces for cocktails. This seemingly modest gesture marked a social revolution in Venice. Traditionally Venetians invited no one into their homes but family and close friends. It was a virtual taboo to extend invitations beyond that close circle. This new hospitality was a measure of the high regard Venetians had for the Venice Committee; it was also the first of what would become increasing opportunities to gain entry to the magnificent inner sanctums that common tourists would never see.

Before long, however, a clash of personalities developed between the rough-hewn Colonel Gray and the highly sophisticated members of the Venice Committee.

Gray was a no-nonsense man of action, who possessed great charm but lacked social polish. He was an electrical engineer, a paratrooper who had made a hundred drops over Italy during the war, but he had no background in art. He used foul language when it suited him and would tell off-colour jokes at inopportune moments.

McAndrew, Hadley, and Bareiss were embarrassed by Gray and began to shy away from him. Gray, in turn, viewed them as a pack of dilettante socialites who attended parties on the Grand Canal and drank prosecco. When the Venice Committee proposed holding a fund-raising party in Boston, Gray rejected the idea as a waste of time. If you wanted to raise money, he said, all you had to do was to sit on the terrace of the Gritti Hotel at five o'clock, drink vodka, and talk to the rich people at the next table, and by the time you got up to leave, you had their cheque for ten thousand dollars in your pocket, earmarked for the Venice Committee. He had done it himself more than once.

In the opinion of the Venice Committee members, Colonel Gray was simply not their sort. Relations between them became increasingly hostile. Bump Hadley detested Gray and was barely on speaking terms with him. Finally McAndrew suggested to Gray in 1971 that the Venice Committee detach itself from the International Fund for Monuments and become an independent organization, devoted solely to saving the art and architecture of Venice. Gray did not object. 'Why don't you call it Save Venice?' he said.

With McAndrew as chairman and Bump Hadley as president, the Venice Committee transformed itself into Save Venice, Inc. It was a non-profit organization that consisted of a board of directors but no members. Instead of a membership it would have a mailing list of donors. Over the next decade, Save Venice undertook projects on a modest scale, restoring paintings and sculptures and making emergency repairs to roofs, walls, and floors of buildings. In the late 1970s, Bump Hadley approached Larry Lovett, a friend from his student days at Harvard, and asked him to join the Save Venice board as treasurer.

Larry Lovett was erudite, congenial, and, as an heir to the Piggly Wiggly grocery-chain fortune, rich. Having come to New York from Jacksonville with social aspirations, he had the good fortune to be taken under the wing of Mrs John Barry Ryan, a doyenne of New York society. He became chairman of the Metropolitan Opera Guild and, later, the Chamber Music Society of Lincoln Center. He had already been living several months a year in Venice when Hadley invited him to join the Save Venice board, and he accepted. Then, in 1986, Hadley handed the presidency to Lovett, and Lovett started looking for someone to take his place as treasurer.

Lovett had known Bob and Bea Guthrie for a decade or more. During his tenure as chairman of the Metropolitan Opera Guild, Lovett had worked with Bea Guthrie, who had been a volunteer in the development department in charge of 'high-end' giving. Bea Guthrie was a Phipps, a niece of society racehorse owner Ogden Phipps. She had graduated from Smith College *summa cum laude* in art history. The Guthries, like Lovett, were enthralled by Venice. But Bob Guthrie was a plastic surgeon with a full operating schedule, and he was reluctant to take on the job of treasurer. Lovett eventually talked him into it; then he sent Guthrie the Save Venice books, and Guthrie realized that the organization was in general disarray. And its mailing list was useless. More than half of the people on it had moved or were dead. From a list of thousands, Save Venice had only eighty-four active contributors and was collecting, at best, forty to fifty thousand dollars a year. Guthrie told Lovett that Save Venice was effectively dead.

But Lovett had an idea. Every year, at the end of summer, during the Venice Film Festival and the rowing regatta, a contingent of inter-national socialites descended on Venice – Nan Kempner, Deeda Blair, and their friends. Lovett knew many of these people, and he was certain that if Save Venice put on a lavish dinner-dance in a palace on the Grand Canal, they would come to it, and this core group would attract other people eager to be in their company. After much discussion, the idea grew to a four-day gala that would also include tours, recitals, lectures, and, taking advantage of the new willingness among Venetians to open their homes to the city's benefactors, parties in private palaces.

Energized by the idea of a high-society fund-raising gala in Venice, the board of directors agreed that they should turn Save Venice into something far bigger than anyone had ever thought it could be. Instead of restoring just a few paintings each year, Save Venice would raise much more money and restore entire buildings. They chose the Miracoli Church as their first major project and estimated they would have to raise a million dollars to do it.

The reorganization of Save Venice on this scale would require the services of a professional fund-raiser. Bea Guthrie agreed to become the executive director.

A year later, in 1987, the first Save Venice Regatta Week Gala drew four hundred people who paid a thousand dollars each for the privilege of attending. They were taken on private tours led by Gore Vidal, Erica Jong, and the British historian John Julius Norwich. They had lunches, cocktails, and dinners in five different private palaces. They were admitted to the Doge's Palace for the unveiling of Save Venice's most recent restoration, Tintoretto's monumental *Paradise*. They were taken in gondolas through winding canals to view the newest project, the as-yet-unrestored Miracoli Church. On the final evening, they attended a formal dinner-dance at the Palazzo Pisani-Moretta, where Peter Duchin and his orchestra played dance music on the ground floor and Bobby Short performed an evening of cabaret upstairs.

The high wattage of the assembled gathering was apparent at every turn. The official programme for the gala reminded people to bring their numbered tickets to events for reasons of heightened security, 'owing to the presence of a number of ambassadors, ministers and other public officials'. At any given function, one spotted the likes of Hubert de Givenchy, Prince Amyn Aga Khan, Evangeline Bruce, Michael York, the American ambassador Maxwell Rabb, and Their Royal Highnesses Prince and Princess Michael of Kent.

With many of the events underwritten by corporations in the luxury business – Tiffany, Piaget, Escada, Moët & Chandon – Save Venice netted $350,000 that year.

The Regatta Week Gala became a biannual, four-day event that continued to sell out, even when ticket prices climbed to $3,000 a person. On alternate years, Save Venice sponsored Mediterranean luxury cruises, always inviting historians and art experts to give lectures on board, lead tours, and in general lend the cruise an educational flavour. Gross receipts quickly climbed to a million dollars a year, and Save Venice became responsible for more than half of the restoration work undertaken in Venice by all thirty of the private committees combined.

Save Venice was a harmonious operation throughout the 1980s. The Guthries, along with a small staff, oversaw the day-to-day business operation on the ground floor of their town house, which they made available to Save Venice, rent free, as a headquarters. At Save Venice events, the gregarious Bob Guthrie circulated, introduced himself to people, and did his best to make sure everyone was having a good time. Bea Guthrie devoted considerable energy to the educational aspects of the activities planned for the galas.

For his part, Larry Lovett recruited titled Europeans, the ultra-rich, and the socially prominent, persuading some to join the board and others to come as honoured guests to its various events. As a result of his efforts, press coverage of Save Venice was invariably studded with names preceded by HRH, HSH, HE, Duke, Duchess, Count, Countess, Baron, Baroness, and Marchesa. The romantic allure created by these prefixes drew hundreds of people to Save Venice and its galas and balls.

In 1990, Lovett was beginning to find his presidential duties too time-consuming, and he asked Guthrie to take over the presidency while he became chairman. Guthrie agreed. By then Venetians had taken Save Venice to their hearts. Lovett continued to play the role of popular host on the social scene, and the Guthries were admired for their tireless efforts, all for the benefit of Venice. Bob Guthrie, in fact, had become a genuine hero, owing to the dashing role he had played in a harrowing and bloody accident involving a marchesa's face.

The marchesa was Barbara Berlingieri, one of the aristocrats Larry Lovett had cajoled into joining the board of Save Venice. She had been instrumental in opening the doors of Venetian society and Venetian palaces for Lovett and for Save Venice. And she had, in fact, become vice president of Save Venice as well. Barbara and her husband, Alberto, frequently had Prince and Princess Michael of Kent as house guests in their palace on the Grand Canal, and the Kents reciprocated. As the *Corriere della Sera* put it somewhat mockingly, the Berlingieris were practically living at Kensington Palace.

Barbara Berlingieri was one of the high-style beauties of Venice. She had a classic profile and lively blue eyes. She wore her blonde hair pulled back in a bun and tied with a black velvet bow. The Berlingieris' palace, the Palazzo Treves, was well known for its neoclassical interior and for a pair of huge marble sculptures by Canova, depicting Hector and Ajax, that stood on revolving pedestals in a columned hall built especially to accommodate them.

One afternoon immediately following a Save Venice four-day gala, Barbara Berlingieri was in her palace when the phone rang in an alcove at the far end of the long centre hall. Rushing to answer it, she slipped on the terrazzo floor and fell against a heavy curtain, crashing into the window immediately behind it. The window broke. A large piece of glass sliced through the curtain and slashed her face from just below her left eye to her mouth, cutting down to the cheekbone. With blood gushing, she screamed to her husband, 'Call Bob Guthrie!'

Guthrie was at that moment packing to leave for New York. He rushed over to the Berlingieris' palace.

'Barbara was in her bedroom,' he recalled. 'There was blood everywhere. Alberto was frantically spraying her face with an adhesive that dries like a cobweb and is meant for sealing small cuts. But this was a gaping wound, and all it did was make a thick white mat on her face with blood under it.'

Within minutes an ambulance boat picked them up and rushed them at top speed to the hospital at San Giovanni e Paolo. They were met by the head surgeon, who was going to perform the operation. He was not, however, a plastic surgeon.

'The cut on Barbara's face had created two serious problems,' Guthrie recalled. 'It had severed her smile muscle and had cut through the edge of her upper lip, which we call "the vermilion border". If the smile muscles were not sewn together correctly, Barbara would end up with a lopsided smile, one side drawn up, the other flat. And if the edge of the lip were sewn in a straight line, there would be a pucker at the vermilion border. You have to cut a slight jog there, a notch, in order to keep the edge of the lip smooth. But this surgeon had never done it before. Alberto told him who I was and said he wanted me to perform the surgery. The surgeon said unfortunately it would be illegal. I didn't have a licence to practise in Italy or at that hospital, and he couldn't let me do it. Alberto, who is normally a very mild-mannered man, seized the man by his necktie and said, "This is my wife! You will let Dr Guthrie perform the operation, or else!" I kept quiet, because I knew the doctor was right. He was a bit shaken, but he said, "Well, I see no reason why Dr Guthrie can't be in the operating room as an observer." So I got into green scrubs and washed my hands, and we went into the operating room. The doctor was about to start the operation when he turned to me and said, "Dr Guthrie, why don't you demonstrate your technique?" That sort of invitation was perfectly proper, so I performed the surgery, and it all went very well.'

After that heroic incident, Venice overflowed with goodwill toward Save Venice and everyone connected with it. Barbara Berlingieri proclaimed that Bob Guthrie had saved her face, indeed saved her life.

For the next four or five years, matters proceeded smoothly and happily. Given the overall success of the Save Venice projects, neither Guthrie, as president, nor Lovett, as chairman, chose to make an issue of certain irritations that started to crop up.

Guthrie discovered, for example, that Lovett was making pronouncements and commitments in Venice without informing him and that on occasion he countermanded positions Guthrie had already taken. In addition, because Lovett's name was at the top of the list of Save Venice board members, he alone received bulletins put out by the Association of Private Committees, the liaison office run by UN-ESCO. The bulletins contained crucial information relating to restorations in progress by Save Venice and the other committees. Yet for reasons that were never very clear, Lovett, according to Guthrie, would not share them. Guthrie was quietly piqued when Lovett accepted a medal for work done by Save Venice in St Mark's Basilica without inviting Guthrie to the award ceremony, or even informing him of it. Likewise, he was annoyed when Lovett put his name on a plaque commemorating the restoration of a baptismal font in the Church of San Giovanni in Bragora and then staged an unveiling ceremony, inviting members of the press and special friends, but not Bob Guthrie. It was the first time a Save Venice plaque had ever borne the name of a living donor, even though donors frequently earmarked funds for specific works of art, as Lovett had done in this case.

Lovett, for his part, did not raise objections when Bob Guthrie, after becoming president, began to exhibit autocratic tendencies, speaking for the board as a whole without first canvassing its members, or declaring that he, rather than Lovett, would address an audience at this or that event. Lovett cringed inwardly when Guthrie made overbearing demands of the Venetian authorities – insisting, for example, that Save Venice be allowed to use oversize motorboats instead of water taxis to ferry large numbers of people on the Grand Canal, even though the use of these boats was prohibited because of traffic congestion and because the waves could damage the foundations of buildings along the canal. (Permission in such cases was usually granted, because of the money Save Venice was spending on the city, but through clenched teeth.)

For a while, nonetheless, amity prevailed. The turning point came when Bob Guthrie learned that Larry Lovett had been making condescending remarks about him and Bea, referring to them as 'the hired help'. That was the moment when Guthrie put his own name above Lovett's at the top of the list of Save Venice's board of directors. It was the opening salvo in what would become an increasingly public, and increasingly nasty, battle.

Larry Lovett and Bob Guthrie could not have been more different in temperament or stature.

Lawrence Dow 'Larry' Lovett was a portrait of refinement in speech, manner, dress, and worldly surroundings. As a child, he had hoped to become a concert pianist and had toured South America at seventeen, performing before small audiences, but a debilitating stage fright forced him to give it up. He graduated from Harvard College and Harvard Law School. He worked in a succession of executive positions for companies owned by his father – oil tankers and a steamship line – but retired at the age of fifty, opting instead for a life of enjoyment and support of the arts and the cultivation of international society at its highest levels. He achieved his greatest social coup in 1995, when Diana, Princess of Wales, was in Venice for the opening of the British pavilion at the Biennale and came to Lovett's palace for lunch, trailing the usual swarm of reporters and television cameras.

Shortly after his triumphant lunch with Diana, Lovett opened his copy of the Save Venice Regatta Week journal and found his name topped by that of Bob Guthrie.

Randolph H. Guthrie Jr was a tall man. More to the point, he was massive in the sense that when he was walking, even very slowly, it seemed it might take him several steps to come to a complete stop. The son of a prominent New York lawyer (his father was the Guthrie of Richard Nixon's law firm – Nixon, Mudge, Rose, Guthrie, Alexander and Mitchell), Bob Guthrie was educated at St Paul's School until he was expelled for setting off a bomb behind one of the dormitories; he then graduated from Andover, Princeton, and the Harvard Medical

School. Guthrie was brilliant, assertive, motivated, highly focused, and possessed of a take-charge personality, which made him a natural leader. The downside was his tendency to handle disagreements in a confrontational, bullying manner, which had led to his departure from more than one corporate board. The slow pace of doing things in Venice vexed him, and more than once he had been heard to say that 'Venice would be better off without Venetians' and that 'Venetians are the world's biggest freeloaders'. He was also known on occasion to browbeat and humiliate subordinates in public.

In a face-to-face meeting with Guthrie, Larry Lovett objected angrily to Guthrie's reversal of their names. As Guthrie later recounted the conversation, he responded that Lovett had only himself to blame. He had been undermining Guthrie by giving contradictory instructions to the staff and making pronouncements and commitments on behalf of Save Venice without Guthrie's knowledge. Guthrie warned that he would put his own name at the top of the Save Venice stationery as well if Lovett persisted in this behaviour. Lovett threatened to resign if Guthrie did so, and Guthrie relented, feeling he had made his point. He then offered to return the presidency to Lovett, but Lovett said he did not have the time to do the work and did not want the legal responsibility.

'In that case,' said Guthrie, 'you're not going to have unilateral openings and unveilings, you're not going to give speeches, and you're not going to make commitments for Save Venice, or accept medals, or take credit for the work of Save Venice unless I agree to it in advance. I'd be delighted to step aside and let you be the boss again, but as long as I'm it, you're going to have to toe the line.'

Lovett glared at Guthrie. 'As chairman,' he said, 'I do have certain prerogatives!'

'Actually,' Guthrie replied, 'as chairman you have nothing.' Guthrie handed Lovett a copy of the Save Venice bylaws. 'Here, take a look at the bylaws. There's no mention of a chairman anywhere. It's very clear.

The president is the chief executive officer in sole charge of Save Venice. When you chose the title of chairman for yourself – you, who are so enamoured of titles – you titled yourself into oblivion. You don't exist.'

Few people noticed the chill between the two men six months later at the ball in the Rainbow Room the night the Fenice burned. The feud was still a private one.

However, relations worsened in the months that followed. In Venice, Lovett continued to represent himself as the head of Save Venice. He told Guthrie he would not 'demean' himself by informing UNESCO and the other private committees that Guthrie was in fact the CEO. 'Quite frankly,' Lovett told Guthrie, 'you are not liked in Venice. I am always having to clean up after you.' Guthrie again offered to return the presidency to Lovett, and again Lovett declined. Guthrie began making offhand remarks about Lovett's uselessness. He was lazy, said Guthrie; he did nothing. Why keep him on as chairman?

Matters took a more serious turn when, at a board meeting in New York in early 1997, board member Alexis Gregory raised questions about possible financial irregularities on the part of the Guthries. Gregory, an ally of Larry Lovett's, was the owner of Vendôme Press, an art-book publishing house; his brother was the actor/director Andre Gregory, best known for his film *My Dinner with Andre*. Alexis Gregory cited Bea Guthrie's $100,000 expense account and complained that the Guthries charged too many of their travel and dining expenses to Save Venice. He objected to the $50,000 yearly rent on the office in Venice. The office consisted of only two rooms; the rest of the space was a two-storey, three-bedroom house used as living quarters by the Guthries. Gregory pointed out that office space could be made available to Save Venice through UNESCO for only $5,000 a year. Larry Lovett accused Guthrie of 'a lack of clarity' in his handling of the finances. 'If you ask Bob Guthrie anything about financial matters,' said Lovett, 'he drops a pile of four hundred pages in front of you and lets you figure it out yourself.'

The auditors Ernst & Young were brought in to conduct a thorough audit of the books and found that every dollar was accounted for. Meanwhile members of the board searched for ways to settle a dispute that had become, as far as they were concerned, petty, degrading, and deeply embarrassing.

By mid-1997, however, the split in Save Venice was widening. At the May board meeting, Lovett took Guthrie completely by surprise by arriving with a handful of proxies and dominating the voting for key subcommittees, stacking them with people he perceived as loyal to him. It was the first time proxies had ever been used at a Save Venice board meeting.

A few weeks after that meeting, Barbara Berlingieri asked Guthrie to come to her palace for tea. She had been complaining for some time that Guthrie had undergone a change of personality since becoming president. 'We used to discuss things,' she said. 'But now he would say to us, "I am the president. I have total power. I tell you what I want, and I don't need to ask anybody." I would say, "Bob, why are there thirty board members? We are totally useless." He would say, "Ah, you don't understand, because you are Italian" – that was always his excuse – "because in America the president can decide for himself and doesn't need to ask or tell."'

Guthrie knew very well that the marchesa was Larry Lovett's closest ally. She was a formidable adversary, far more wily, in fact, than Lovett himself. It was Barbara Berlingieri who had collected the proxies for Lovett. She was a partner with another Venetian woman in a little business called Venezia Privata, which would organize tours and parties and arrange entrée into private palaces. For years she and Lovett had proposed letting the Venice office make all the arrangements for the biannual galas, rather than doing it from headquarters in New York. Guthrie opposed the idea, partly because he knew it was a power play and partly because he suspected that the marchesa saw a business opportunity in it for herself.

Barbara Berlingieri and Bob Guthrie sat in the living-room of the Berlingieris' *piano nobile*. Barbara came right to the point. 'Bob,' she said, 'you know we have enough votes right now to throw you off the board.'

Guthrie looked at her across the tea table. The light coming in through the windows along the Grand Canal illuminated the left side of her face, the side that had been slashed from her cheekbone to her upper lip, opening the wound he had closed so expertly that only the thinnest of hairline scars remained, so slight that no one who did not know it was there would notice it.

'But we won't do that to you,' she said, smiling, and her smile was perfectly symmetrical, not higher on one side than the other. The vermilion border of her lip was smooth and unpuckered.

Bob Guthrie sat looking at Barbara Berlingieri's still-beautiful face, admiring his own handiwork, and as he mused, he heard her say through the smile he had saved, 'This is what we're willing to give you. You can be the president of the Junior Committee. And when we create an advisory committee, we will make you president of that, too.'

Guthrie sat in silence for a moment, mulling over Barbara Berlingieri's purposely degrading offer and letting his mind wander a bit: what if he had stepped aside and let the surgeon at the hospital sew up her face instead of doing it himself? And what if the head surgeon, who had never performed plastic surgery before, had tightened the stitching of the muscles in her cheek a bit too much and left her with a sneer instead of her natural smile? What if he had sewn the vermilion border straight across, without first making a notch, so that it had a permanent pucker? No. It was better that Bob Guthrie had stepped into the breach. Because now and for the rest of her life, Barbara Berlingieri would look into her mirror upon rising, check her reflection as she passed shop windows, peer into her compact while refreshing her makeup, and in these and a dozen other ways every day confront her image and be reminded of Bob Guthrie's genius and of her own towering ingratitude.

'Barbara,' he said. 'You blew it.'

'I did what?'

'You wasted your proxies. You should have kept quiet about them and waited until the fall meeting, after the gala, when we vote on directors. That's the vote that counts. But by then, now that you've tipped your hand, I'll have proxies of my own. Then we'll see who really has the votes.'

More than three hundred people gathered in Venice for the Save Venice gala at the end of the summer of 1997. This year, as always, jewellers in St Mark's extended their hours, knowing that with the Save Venice crowd in town, they were about to have the best week of the year. Ten years had passed since the first gala, when Save Venice had set its sights on restoring the Miracoli Church. The unveiling of the church was scheduled for later in the autumn. In its first ten years, the organization had grown in stature and accomplishment. Its galas were always fully subscribed, despite the $3,000 ticket price, not including hotel and airfare. Its official masthead now sported thirteen titled individuals, not just half a dozen. And this year eight royals had come to the gala as guests of honour. The four-day programme included a tour of three vineyards on the mainland, parties in private palaces, and a full complement of culturally oriented treasure hunts, tours, and lectures. The Fenice opera company lent props and scenery for the décor at one of the dinners, and once again Peter Duchin and Bobby Short provided music at the formal ball.

As usual, the weather was sultry and the atmosphere a heady mixture of wealth, luxury, privilege, and power in the midst of the glories of Venice. But this year there was an undercurrent of gossip about the growing rift within Save Venice. The charges that the Guthries had their hands in the till, although proven groundless, were nonetheless heard around the Cipriani pool. Bea Guthrie noticed, or perhaps imagined, that certain people turned their backs when she approached. During a lunch party on the island of Torcello, Bob Guthrie greeted Princess Michael of Kent, who had been a frequent guest at Save Venice parties over the past decade. He addressed her, as he had always done, with her given name, Marie-Christine. The princess stiffened and said, 'You should call me "ma'am".'

At the board meeting immediately following the gala, both Bob Guthrie and Larry Lovett brought proxies, each hoping to shift the balance of power in his own favour. However, several members of the board were not ready for a showdown, and they abstained, depriving both sides of a majority. The duel of proxies ended in a compromise.

But a brand-new controversy had arisen. It had been discovered that Larry Lovett had quietly renounced his American citizenship some years before. He was now a citizen of Ireland and no longer paid American taxes. Several board members were incensed. 'If you want to be a philanthropist and lead a life of luxury, fine,' said one of them, 'but first you pay your taxes.' Terry Stanfill, the chairman of the nominating committee and wife of the former head of 20th Century Fox and MGM, told Lovett she could not in good conscience renominate him for another term as chairman. Lovett protested, but it was a losing battle. The board felt it was unwise for a tax-exempt American charity to be headed by someone the IRS might view as a tax fugitive. Lovett was elected instead to the new position of 'international chairman' of Save Venice.

This, then, was the state of affairs when Lesa Marcello received the good news that the Torta Prize was going to be awarded to Save Venice and Larry Lovett.

After reading Guthrie's fax demanding that the prize be given to Save Venice as a whole or not at all, Countess Marcello sat down to write him a reply. She explained that the Torta Prize was always given to an individual, and that if an organization was intended as a recipient, it would be given 'in the name of' someone who represented the organization, in this case Larry Lovett. She said she feared there was no way she could give Guthrie's message to the prize committee without insulting them and making it obvious that an embarrassing skirmish was taking place within Save Venice. She said she hoped the organization's internal problems could be resolved privately.

Guthrie was not mollified. He suspected from the outset that Barbara Berlingieri had arranged for Lovett to be singled out for the Torta Prize. Alexis Gregory had admitted as much by gleefully passing the word that 'Barbara engineered it all for Larry'. Guthrie saw it as yet another galling instance of Lovett's insatiable craving for recognition. He picked up the phone, called one of the members of the Torta Prize committee, and made his position unmistakably clear.

Word of Guthrie's phone call spread quickly in Venice. His manner was said to have been 'intimidating'. Lesa Marcello sent him another fax to say that members of the committee were 'extremely upset' by his call and dumbfounded that he would even consider refusing the prize. 'This is what I was anxiously hoping to avoid,' she said. 'The situation is very, very bad.'

The prize committee gave in to Guthrie, but grudgingly. They omitted Lovett's name from the award citation but included a photograph of him, along with words of praise, in the printed programme handed out at the award ceremony.

Guthrie was now convinced that Lovett and Barbara Berlingieri had 'subverted' Lesa, giving her the impression she was no longer answerable to New York. This would account, he thought, for her reluctance to convey his objections to the prize committee and for her explanation that the prize was always given to individuals, which was, in fact, the rule – but, Guthrie contended, there had been exceptions. Guthrie suspected that Lesa was being used by Larry and Barbara; she was passing information to them, spying on him. He decided to take action, and so, in a brief phone call one morning in mid January 1998, he fired her.

The phone call was in fact nominally made by Paul Wallace, chairman of the executive committee, but it had Guthrie's imprimatur stamped all over it. And although Wallace made the appropriate sounds – Lesa's work superb . . . Save Venice cutting costs . . . hope you'll accept six-month retainer as consultant . . . want to dedicate a Save Venice restoration in your name – the message was clear: Countess Marcello had been fired without notice and would kindly clean out her desk by morning. Guthrie sent a brief fax to the UNESCO office announcing the name of the new director of the Venice office, without even mentioning Lesa Marcello.

Within a day, news of Lesa Marcello's abrupt dismissal had spread through the immediate Venetian circles and beyond, to people who knew none of the principals and had only a vague notion of Save Venice. The story, as told in wine bars and food shops, was shorn of detail: an organization of rich Americans had fired a blameless Venetian countess. What had begun as a petty and ignoble private squabble had turned into a public insult to Venice and Venetians.

The firing deepened the split on the board of Save Venice. One board member resigned upon hearing the news – Professor Wolfgang Wolters, an art historian who had worked closely with Lesa Marcello on the Miracoli Church.

Girolamo Marcello, Lesa's husband and one of the Venetians on the board, did not resign. Instead he quietly made arrangements to come to New York for the next Save Venice board meeting. He had never before attended a board meeting in New York, only the ones in Venice. When he walked through the door of the University Club where the meeting was held, Bob and Bea Guthrie glanced at each other. Larry Lovett and Barbara Berlingieri were the only two people present who seemed to know what was about to happen.

But first the board heard detailed reports on eighteen Save Venice projects, including the restoration of a painting by Carpaccio and work in progress on the façade of the Scuola Grande di San Marco. The board then agreed to buy a thirty-five-foot cherry-picker for use in restoration projects, heard a proposal to fund a fellowship for a young conservator to work with leading restorers in Venice, and voted to share the cost of a microfilm reader/printer for the Venice State Archives.

Then Count Marcello took the floor. He handed out copies of an English translation of his prepared remarks, which he was going to read in Italian. 'My English is not so good,' he told me afterwards, 'and I was steamed up, so I would not have spoken very clearly.' He adjusted his reading glasses and then began.

'I have come here today to discuss a situation of grave concern to Venice and to you. In recent months, an unpleasant internal conflict within Save Venice has spoiled the delicate relationship between Save Venice and Venice itself. And it has to stop. The damage to the reputation and image of Save Venice is far worse than it may appear to you from New York.'

Count Marcello described as a piece of arrogance Bob Guthrie's threat that the board of Save Venice would refuse the Torta Prize. 'And as I am a member of the board of Save Venice, I know Bob Guthrie was speaking without board authorization.'

As for the firing of his wife, Lesa, Count Marcello acknowledged the right of management to dismiss an employee, but he objected to the manner in which it was done.

'You may not be aware,' he said, 'that in Venice the termination, with no notice, of a work relationship that has lasted for six years, invariably implies dishonesty by the person involved. This is what has been done to Lesa, and this is what I resent.

'To be Venetian,' Marcello went on, 'and to know how to live in Venice is an art. It is our way of living, so different from the rest of the world. Venice is built not only of stone but of a very thin web of words, spoken and remembered, of stories and legends, of eye-witness accounts and hearsay. To work and operate in Venice means first of all to understand its differences and its fragile equilibrium. In Venice we move delicately and in silence. And with great subtlety. We are a very Byzantine people, and that is certainly not easy to understand.'

Marcello cast a glance at his audience. Except for the two or three who were able to follow his Italian, they were reading along, and the mood was uniformly solemn. The board members of Save Venice, who thought of themselves as benefactors of Venice, knowledgeable and sophisticated in the ways of their adopted city, were receiving a dressing-down, as if they were no better than an unruly mob of litterbug tourists.

'I must tell you how the recent turmoil in Save Venice has been perceived in Venice. It is seen as evidence that a few members of the board do not consider Save Venice an association of friends who do good work for Venice but rather as a means to gain personal prestige and power. We Venetians regard our city with the same ancient civic sense with which we have built, governed, and loved it for centuries, and it is very painful to see it being used in this manner.

'As much as we are truly grateful for Save Venice's remarkable generosity in the past, we Venetians are loath to accept help from those who have so little respect for us.'

Almost as an afterthought, Marcello concluded his remarks with the comment, 'What course of action the board should now take is for you to decide, but I certainly feel that Dr Guthrie should be stripped of all powers.'

Upon his return to Venice, Marcello showed me his speech. It was a long speech, rambling at times, but unrelenting in its expression of restrained outrage.

'And how did they react?' I asked.

'Some shook their heads and said, "Finally!" But others were angry. One man said to me in Italian, "You have some nerve coming here and talking like that." And I said, "You know, when it's necessary to say such things, it's necessary also to have some nerve."'

I handed the speech back to him. 'Strong stuff,' I said, 'but you once told me that Venetians always mean the opposite of what they say.'

Count Marcello smiled. 'True, and when I told you that, I meant the opposite of what I said.'

The battle lines were drawn. Bob Guthrie's three-year term as a member of the board was due to expire four months later at the September 1998 board meeting in Venice. He would then have to stand for re-election and would need a majority vote of the twenty-nine board members to retain a seat on the board. Anything less would, in effect, throw him out of Save Venice altogether.

As the summer wore on, the board members discussed the crisis among themselves, and it became apparent that, in addition to the power struggle between Guthrie and Lovett, there was a subterranean issue that only now came to the surface. Certain members sympathetic to Lovett had begun to feel that Save Venice had lost its aura of exclusivity, that the Guthries had taken control of the invitation list with the result that many of the people buying tickets and showing up at parties and galas were . . . 'not our sort'. It was an echo of the social divide that had split Colonel Gray's old Venice Committee in the early 1970s and ended with a walkout and the creation of Save Venice.

One board member who would have been the first to admit that he might not be the Lovett 'sort' was Jack Wasserman, a New York international-trade lawyer who was an associate of corporate-takeover specialist Carl Icahn. Wasserman's attachment to Venice had grown out of his fascination, since college, with the life and poetry of Lord Byron. Wasserman was president of the Lord Byron Society of America and owned a major collection of Byron first editions. Although deeply devoted to Byron and Byron scholarship, he was by no means an academic. 'Byron was useful when I came to Italy for the first time on a student ship forty years ago,' he said. 'The first two lines of Byron's poetry got you laid every night.'

Wasserman was having a late lunch at a corner table in Harry's Bar when I joined him. He introduced me to a well-behaved black standard poodle sitting under the table, nursing a bowl of water. The poodle had been named after the British war secretary who had been Lord Byron's friend, travelling companion, and executor, John Cam Hobhouse.

'Save Venice was my first exposure to so-called high society,' said Wasserman. 'My wife and I had been going to the galas for years and meeting these fancy, type-A people. Or at least looking at them. So when they asked me to be on the board, because they didn't have a lawyer and they were growing very fast and legal questions were always coming up, I said, "Sure." I mean, I'm very impressed with myself! I'm on the board with Oscar de la Renta. That's very impressive people, I gotta admit.

'But these two guys, Larry and Bob, from my perspective – Larry is very glamorous, a wonderful social individual, and a very seductive man. You know, when you're in Larry's presence, you're always in a little bit of awe. He seems to have this halo around him. Bob doesn't have that. But Bob's background, his style of living, is so extraordinary that you always listen carefully to what he says.

'Bob and Bea Guthrie work from six o'clock in the morning till midnight, like dogs. Dogs! They'll talk to anybody. People call up: "I don't like my table, I didn't like where I was sitting last night." Bob and Bea take care of it. Happy to do it, no problem. Larry doesn't work on Save Venice on a daily basis. He doesn't work on a monthly basis. That isn't his function. His function is to be Mr Glamorous and, you know, get this fancy crowd to come to the party, so three hundred other people will pay to be in the same room with them. That's his job, and God knows it's valuable. But he doesn't work at the parties, not the way Bob does. Larry's aloof. *Aloof!* It's like talking to God! I mean, he always shows up, dressed to the nines, in the back of his private motorboat with some princess or something. He gets out and pronounces himself pleased that things are going well, and then he gets back in his boat with the princess, and off he goes. It's wonderful to watch. It's imperial. I mean, I'm in awe. It's like being with the fucking doge.

'But this whole thing with royalty. Somebody once told me the definition of a snob. You can be a snob upward by associating with people on a level above you or a snob downward by dismissing people below you. Larry has an obsessive, at times scary, commitment to people of title. I mean, scary! I think Larry really believes he was born to the purple. For example, during one of the gala weeks, somebody in the English royal family died, I forget who. I remember Larry saying, "The Palace has issued . . ." to me, talking to *me*, I mean, like I care. "The Palace has issued a decree saying that nobody is to go to parties." This was right before a Save Venice cocktail party. So I said, "But, Larry, you can go to a cocktail party. The decree isn't meant for you." And Larry said, "Oh, I couldn't do that. I mean, my friends. The king of Greece and so on." So he was not going to a cocktail party in Venice. He was going to sit home with Barbara Berlingieri because European royalty were not going to cocktail parties. I said to myself, "Whoa!"'

On the afternoon of the formal ball, I dropped in to see the Guthries at their red house at the foot of the Accademia Bridge. The interior was furnished with chintz-covered chairs and sofas and looked more like an apartment on the East Side of Manhattan than a Venetian dwelling. Bob and Bea Guthrie were sitting in the living-room surveying a large board propped up on an easel and covered with name tags pinned to circles representing tables.

'Ever seated a dinner party for three hundred and fifty people?' Guthrie asked. 'Try doing it when half a dozen people call up at the last minute, saying, "We simply must have so-and-so at our table," which means you have to do the whole thing all over again.'

'I suppose it would be especially difficult to do,' I said, 'if you were carrying on a really ugly personal feud at the same time.'

Guthrie was startled by my directness but recovered quickly. 'I guess that means you've heard,' he said with a laugh.

'Half of Venice has heard,' I said.

He looked again at the seating chart. 'Well, we're about done with this – for now. Want to go for a boat ride?'

We went outside to Guthrie's motor launch, a Boston Whaler, which was tied up at the edge of a small canal just beyond the gate. Guthrie stood at the wheel and backed out into the Grand Canal, then turned and headed in the direction of the Rialto. He spoke over the noise of the motor.

'On one level, sure, it's a quarrel between Larry and me. But it's really more involved than that. There are fundamental differences between most of our board members and the small group of dissidents who support Larry.

'Typically, members of our board are people of accomplishment. Save Venice is an avocation for them, not a principal activity in their lives. They enjoy each other's company, they love Venice, and it gives them satisfaction to help preserve the city. They contribute more to Save Venice in time and money than they get out of it. They're givers.

'The dissidents are quite a different breed of cat. They have money but no occupation of importance, no real accomplishments. Save Venice assumes too great an importance in their lives, because they don't have any other claim to fame. It's the horse they ride on. They introduce themselves using organizational titles. To prove their importance, they need to take credit for the organization's accomplishments, even though they do no work themselves. In fact, they refer to the people who put in long hours as "the hired help". They're takers.

'The dissidents use Save Venice to promote their own social lives, which is the only life they really have. They invite their high-flying friends and hoped-for friends to our parties and galas free of charge, and in return they get invited on cruises and to country estates for shooting weekends. These non-paying guests have become a problem. We're getting more and more of them, and the dissidents monopolize them. They hire limousines to take them to events in the countryside, while the rest of us travel on buses, and they pass by sitting grandly in the back seat. They arrive late and leave early. They all sit together at tables by themselves, snubbing the paying guests. And they really don't care how offensive it is to the other people.'

'I was under the impression,' I said, 'that these non-paying guests provide the sort of glamour that attracts the paying guests.'

'They do,' said Guthrie, 'but that was more important in the early years. Save Venice has become so well known that it's a draw in its own right. We don't need those people any more.'

We were just then passing the Palazzo Pisani-Moretta, where the ball was to be held that night. Caterers were unloading crates from barges at the water gate. Guthrie gestured towards the palace. 'It's the dissidents who always insist on being seated near the windows when it's hot or the fireplace when it's cold. They're very demanding, exigent people. Hell, I still practise surgery eighteen hours a day. I really don't need this.'

'Then why don't you quit?' I asked.

'Bea and I were on the verge of doing just that. We had already written our letters of resignation when the charges of financial improprieties started flying. That was the dissidents' big mistake, because it meant we couldn't quit. We could never leave under that sort of cloud. We had to stay and clear our names.'

A short distance past the Rialto Bridge, we turned in to a side canal. Guthrie cut the speed in half as we negotiated turns and edged past motorboats and gondolas going in the opposite direction. After several minutes, we passed under a small bridge and emerged looking up at the Miracoli. Its satin-soft marble exterior glowed in the afternoon light.

'This is what it's all about,' said Guthrie. 'We give parties so we can raise money to restore buildings like this one.'

'I think everybody would agree about that,' I said.

'Not at all,' said Guthrie. 'The dissidents have it the other way around. They think we're in the restoration business in order to give parties and mingle with royals.'

When I quoted Bob Guthrie's words to Larry Lovett later in the day, his reply was emphatic. 'That's absolute nonsense.'

On the morning of the September board meeting in Venice the week after the gala, both sides arrived at the Monaco Hotel armed with proxies. The Lovett forces were furious from the very start, because Guthrie had refused their request to reschedule the meeting for the afternoon so that three board members who were in New York could vote by telephone. As things stood, it would be 4.00 a.m. in New York when the vote was taken.

Ten positions on the board were to be filled, and the nominees would be considered one by one. As soon as voting began, the Lovett faction cried foul again. Guthrie had voted a proxy for a man who had resigned from the board months before. When the shouting died down, Guthrie explained that he had persuaded the man to withdraw his resignation, sign a proxy, and allow Guthrie to accept his resignation at the appropriate time. The appropriate time had not yet come. Lovett appealed to Jack Wasserman, who knew the bylaws better than anyone else, because he had helped draft new ones. Wasserman ruled the proxy valid.

The cry went up again when Guthrie produced signed proxies for two people who had just been voted on to the board as new members only minutes before. Guthrie argued that although the two had signed their proxies when they were not board members, the proxies were not used until they were. Wasserman ruled these proxies legal, too.

Lovett's proxies were not wholly above reproach either. One was signed by Countess Anna Maria Cicogna, the daughter of Giuseppe Volpi, Mussolini's finance minister, and half-sister of Giovanni Volpi. She was over ninety, and her mental faculties were known to be failing. Nevertheless, this was the third time in two years that the old woman's proxy had been obtained for a Save Venice vote. The first time, hers was one of the surprise proxies Barbara Berlingieri had gathered on Lovett's behalf a year and a half earlier. When asked about it afterwards, Countess Cicogna could not recall having signed it and doubted the signature was hers. For the next board meeting, not to be outdone, the Guthries got to her first. They tracked her down in the hospital where she was being treated for flu. But word of it reached Lovett partisans, who rushed to the countess and found her to be just as mystified by this proxy as she had been about the one she had signed for them. So they talked her into writing a letter to Bea Guthrie, asking to see a copy of what she had signed. 'As you know I have very little memory left,' Countess Cicogna wrote. 'I cannot remember exactly what document I signed at the hospital or to whom I gave my affidavit.' Another year had passed since that letter, and now, despite Countess Cicogna's rather plaintive admission of mental frailty, she had been persuaded to put her name on yet a third proxy. This time she had signed it for Lovett again, presumably without having any clearer notion what it was, or for whom, she was signing it.

However, even with Countess Cicogna's proxy, Lovett mustered only twelve votes. Guthrie had seventeen, including the proxy from the man on the verge of resigning, the two from the brand-new members, and the three from the abstainers who were asleep in New York and whose proxies, Wasserman ruled, could be cast for the management. Guthrie won re-election, and the vanquished took out their frustration on Wasserman. They protested that the voting had been rigged and that the whole affair had been a corrupt, hostile takeover. Alexis Gregory hurled imprecations in Wasserman's direction, including the words 'sleazy' and 'thug'.

'If you say that again, I'll deck you,' Wasserman shot back.

Terry Stanfill, who was re-elected to the board over Lovett's objections, left the room in tears, saying she could never work with people who had spoken of her so harshly.

At this point, Alexis Gregory leaped to his feet and declared, 'We're all leaving!' He then tendered resignations for himself and eight other directors, surprising virtually everyone in the room, including the directors whose resignations he had just volunteered and who appeared dazed that the endgame had been played so precipitately. A bit uncertainly, they rose to their feet and filed out of the room. They took a motor launch directly to Cip's, the new quayside restaurant at the Cipriani Hotel, to collect their thoughts, plan strategy, and partake of a long, four-star lunch with a view of St Mark's across the water, shimmering in the midday sun.

All that remained now was for the press to get wind of the walkout and have its fun. The *Gazzettino's* headline read, SAVE VENICE: THE ARISTOCRATS FLEE. Its story made it seem as if the quarrel had been a pitched battle between Venetians and Americans, although only four of the nine who quit had been Venetian (one was French, the rest American). 'It was a three-hour meeting around the same table but with increasingly divergent positions,' said the *Gazzettino*, 'the Americans taking one side, the Venetian nobles the other. The management of Save Venice was accused of being devoted more to parties than to the restoration of works of art. The departure of a small group of illustrious Venetians split the organization like an apple.'

According to the *Gazzettino*, the dissidents accused the management of 'using the city as a means of acquiring a position of prestige and as a stage on which to show it off. Save Venice, they claimed, had become a club restricted to "jet set society"'.

'My God! Those are the very things I would say about *them!*' art historian Roger Rearick, one of the board members who stayed, told the *Gazzettino*. 'Look, it's always been those people, the ones who quit, who think only about parties and VIP dinners. The truth is they care little about restoration. They left in the hope that they'd destroy Save Venice, but they've only fooled themselves. Save Venice will go on without them.'

By the time the last of the resignations had been submitted, no Venetians remained on the board of Save Venice. In all, fifteen people had left. Larry Lovett was said to be starting his own rival charity, and the dissidents predicted that the doors of Venetian palaces would slam shut on the Guthries and Save Venice. As the *New York Times* put it, 'access to titled Italians was owed to Lawrence Lovett, who was primarily responsible for opening the gates of Venice to Americans deemed socially worthy. But those gates could be closing.'

If that happened, Save Venice would find itself in a bizarre and highly improbable position – celebrated as the city's most generous foreign benefactor while at the same time shunned as a loathsome pariah.

The first arrivals at Larry Lovett's dinner party stepped out on to his terrace just after sunset, in that magical half-hour when the soft, dimming light turns the sky and water the same mother-of-pearl pink and palaces along the Grand Canal seem more than ever to be afloat.

Hubert de Givenchy, his back to the Grand Canal, sat on a cushioned banquette, chatting with New Yorker Nan Kempner. The Rialto Bridge rose dramatically behind them, illuminated against the darkening sky. A waiter with a tray of drinks approached the Marchese Giuseppe Roi just as he was making a lighthearted remark that elicited one of Countess Marina Emo Capodalista's distinctive, piping peals of laughter. 'Guess what!' cried Dodie Rosekrans, clasping Countess Emo's wrist. The wide-eyed San Francisco socialite and movie-theatre heiress had just arrived from a week on the Dalmatian coast. 'I've bought . . . a monastery!'

It was early September. A year had passed since the split in Save Venice. Lovett had launched his own charity after all and named it Venetian Heritage. He had gone about selecting a board of directors like a croupier scooping up blue chips, amassing a pile of aristocrats and royals in such quantity that the letterhead of Venetian Heritage read like a page out of *Debrett's*. Twenty-one of the fifty names on it had titles: one duke, one marchese, one marchesa, one baroness, the usual counts and countesses, and no fewer than six highnesses, both royal and serene. Save Venice, in contrast, was down to its last titled board member, a baroness. Lovett made gloating reference to that state of affairs in a letter addressed to Save Venice president Paul Wallace, noting that Bob Guthrie's upcoming Save Venice winter event in New York 'is under the patronage of a minor Savoia royalty, presumably as he is now lacking a major English one'.

Earlier in the summer, Venetian Heritage had played host to its first four-day gala. Lovett had scheduled it in June to coincide with the opening of the Venice Biennale, when the cream of the international art world descended on Venice. The gala, fully subscribed at $4,000 a ticket, had been a triumph, considering the select crowd it had drawn, the ultra-private doors in Venice that had been thrown open for it, and the money it had raised. Larry Lovett had every reason to be pleased. And he was. Nonetheless, the continued existence of Save Venice rankled him. And Save Venice, as he well knew, was far from dead.

At the time of the tumultuous split, the next Save Venice Regatta Week Gala had been less than a year away. It was going to become clear very soon whether private Venice would remain as accessible to Save Venice as it had been in the past. The Guthries were about to start reaching out and making calls when the telephone rang. Bea Guthrie picked up.

'It's Volpi!' the voice of Count Giovanni Volpi boomed at the other end. He was calling from his villa on the Giudecca. 'I hear those clowns are now saying the doors of Venice will slam in your face!'

'I've heard that, too,' said Bea Guthrie, 'but I don't really—'

'And the reason they give for walking out of Save Venice?' Volpi continued. 'Because you were throwing too many parties? This, coming from Venetians who always bitch about their seating – those free-loaders who never pay a penny for anything?' Count Volpi's famous contempt for his fellow Venetians burned through every syllable. 'Venice is like a courtesan who takes the money and gives nothing in return. Stingy, greedy, and cheap! They're nothing but scavengers! It wasn't enough that they slandered you all summer, calling you crooks. That kind of viciousness is intolerable. It was a moral lynching! They're lucky you haven't seriously sued them for it! And, frankly, I think you should.'

'Well, Giovanni, it's been a nightmare. But we—'

'Listen,' said Volpi. 'I'm calling because you've asked me in the past if you could use Palazzo Volpi for the Save Venice ball, and I've always said no. Well, I've changed my mind. If you think it would help, it would be my pleasure to lend the palace to you next summer for your ball.'

Palazzo Volpi, a magnificent sixteenth-century, seventy-five-room palace on the Grand Canal, was a palace and a half, actually. It had a courtyard garden and grand halls and salons. The lingering presence of one of Italy's most dynamic twentieth-century figures – Volpi's father, Count Giuseppe Volpi, founder of the Venice Film Festival, creator of Mestre and Marghera, Mussolini's finance minister, 'the Last Doge of Venice' – could still be felt throughout: the gilt-and-marble ballroom Volpi had built to commemorate his military victories as the governor of Libya in the 1920s, the full-length oil portrait of Volpi in diplomatic attire, the cannon sitting in the middle of the *portego*, furniture from the Quirinal Palace in Rome, a signed photograph of King Umberto di Savoia. For years Palazzo Volpi had been the setting for the glamorous Volpi Ball, which was given every September by Giovanni's mother. But the last Volpi Ball had been forty years ago, and since then the palace had remained largely unused – well maintained but not lived in.

Palazzo Volpi had been off-limits for so long that even the Venetians were curious to see it again. Knowing this, the Guthries made a shrewd political gesture. With Volpi's permission, they invited dozens of Venetians to come to the ball as their guests, including a number of people the cantankerous Volpi would never have invited on his own. Just this once, however, Volpi was delighted to let them come. It was his intention to demonstrate that no one could be frozen out of Venice just because certain 'clowns' decreed it. If welcoming Venetians into his palace enabled him to rub their noses in that fact, so much the better.

On the evening of the ball, the windows of Palazzo Volpi were brightly lit for the first time in recent memory. An armada of motor launches pulled up at the water gate, and hundreds of guests in evening gown and black tie alighted, dozens of Venetians among them.

The significance of the Volpi–Save Venice ball was understood well beyond the walls of Palazzo Volpi. It was, in fact, very clear to Larry Lovett, whose dinner party on his terrace was taking place that very night. It was widely assumed that the sole purpose of Lovett's party was to upstage Save Venice and deprive it of some of its Venetian guests. It was also assumed that Lovett had stressed 'business attire' for his dinner to prevent his guests going directly from his party to Palazzo Volpi without first going home to change into black tie. His friends conceded that, for Lovett, this dinner party was a rare *faux pas*; others saw it as a display of infantile spite that proved, once and for all, that Lovett was more concerned with his own prestige and prominence than with preserving Venetian art and architecture.

None of that mattered to Giovanni Volpi. While Peter Duchin played dance music in his father's ballroom and Bobby Short crooned his songs upstairs, Volpi stood at the edge of his courtyard garden, apart from it all, as usual.

'I don't know,' he said. 'Save Venice, Venetian Heritage – what's the difference? When you get right down to it, they're both really just glorified package tours. I don't know why Americans can't come to Venice and just have a good time, instead of coming here and beating their breasts. You know what I mean? It's this thing of having to come here on a mission. Why must they come to Venice to save it? It's nice, of course, the money they give. But it doesn't have anything to do with generosity. It means they want to look important. And, really, it's just a drop in the ocean. They should come and have a good time. Period. Right? Walk around. See some paintings. Go to some restaurants, like they do in other cities. Americans don't go to Paris to save Paris, do they? Right? When you see a five-hundred-year-old Venetian building, it may be a bit shabby and possibly even in danger. But you can't describe it as "decaying". It has *endured* five hundred years! The "decaying Venice" is all a big myth. That's what I mean about Save Venice. Forget it. Venice will save itself. Go and save Paris!'

13

The man who loved others

I FIRST NOTICED THE GRAFFITI — and there were several — as I was walking through the Rialto food market one winter afternoon. A few days later, I came across another one near St Mark's, and the next day a third outside the restaurant Osteria di Santa Marina. They were always written neatly in red spray paint and always on temporary wooden walls where they would do no harm. Their melancholy message was always the same: LONELINESS IS NOT BEING ALONE; IT'S LOVING OTHERS TO NO AVAIL (*Solitudine non è essere soli, è amare gli altri inutilmente*).

Unlike most graffiti, these had an author. They were signed 'Mario Stefani'. Stefani was a well-known character in Venice, a poet of some repute who appeared on a local TV channel, TeleVenezia, five days a week for a brief cultural commentary. He had a smiling, jowly face and a head of untamed hair. The first time I tuned in to his programme, it was quite by chance. He was delivering a casual, unscripted monologue that jumped from topic to topic.

'Venetians used to be great navigators and pirates,' he was saying. 'They stole things and brought them back to Venice to make the city more beautiful — carved marble from the East, gold, gems. Now people steal only for themselves. This is very sad.

'Signor Doge,' Mario Stefani went on, now addressing an imaginary guest, 'would you like a glass of water? You would rather have wine! I don't blame you. A glass of wine costs only a thousand lire in Venice today. Bottled water costs three times as much.'

Then he was on to something else.

'Signor Count,' he said, 'would you like to take a walk with me in St Mark's? No? You say you are not Moses and you cannot part the waters? Well, it is true that we have floods and high water more and more frequently. After twenty years of arguing about it, nobody can decide whether to build the system of dikes that would stop the flooding. I often hear it said that people who have a financial interest in postponing the decision are the ones who are causing the delay.

'Signor Doge, you seem hesitant to take a water taxi. Why is that? Because it costs a lot! True. And you have probably noticed that gondolas are expensive, too. And hotels. And restaurants. All the amenities that tourists pay for. Those are the people who have the power in Venice. No, no, no, not the tourists – I mean the taxi drivers, the gondoliers, and the hotel and restaurant owners. They run Venice, as anyone will tell you.'

Stefani's TV programme was a low-budget, single-camera, black-and-white production that ran at the most for about five minutes each time. It always opened with the musical theme from *The Pink Panther* and with Stefani looking straight into the camera and announcing, 'Venetian poisons and proclamations! Idle chatter!' Venice and Venetians were his basic theme.

'Venetians are creatures of habit,' he said on one broadcast. 'You always know you're early or late from where you see certain people in the street. If you are on time, you see them in such-and-such a *campo*. If you see them in the street before or after, you know you are late or early.'

Stefani lamented the passing of institutions and characters.

'All the cats have disappeared from the streets in Venice. That's because the old ladies who used to feed them are gone. I miss the old ladies who wore shawls and had delicate gold chains that got caught in the wool. One of my favourite old ladies used to come into the bar and order grappa. She would say, "Gimme two grappas. One for me and one for Franca." She would pay and drink hers, all the while looking around and saying, "Franca? Where's Franca? She must have gone to buy something . . . *Madonna*, I'm tired of waiting. I guess I'll have to drink hers, too." This scene would be repeated daily, and Franca never showed up. The old lady would always drink both grappas. Where is she now? I miss her.'

Stefani spoke of districts, especially his own, which was Campo San Giacomo dell'Orio, a lovely square in the Santa Croce area of town, safely removed from the main tourist route.

'The baker in our *campo* has printed a poem of mine on his paper bags — out of respect, not just for me but for poetry. So now people come in and ask for two rolls and a poem.'

Mario Stefani was a booster of his city. He had a generous, welcoming nature. 'Anyone who loves Venice is a true Venetian,' he said, 'even a tourist, but only if the tourist stays long enough to appreciate the city. If he stays only one day just to say he's been to Venice, no.'

Stefani taught literature at a school on the mainland, and his name appeared frequently in the *Gazzettino*. He wrote literary and art reviews and frequently took part in readings and other cultural events. He was probably best known in Venice for having made the often-quoted observation: 'If Venice didn't have a bridge, Europe would be an island.' That line was the title of one of his books of poetry.

During Carnival every year, Stefani took part in the erotic-poetry readings in Campo San Maurizio. Twenty per cent of his poems, he estimated, were erotic. They were also unrestrainedly homosexual. He made frequent reference in his poems to the muscles, the lips, the beauty, and the gaze of good-looking boys. He spoke of kneeling before them in adoration. He recalled a boy who pressed his groin against him on the bus, and others who met him late at night in the *campo*.

His erotic poetry ranged from playful to graphic, but he took his role as an acknowledged gay man seriously. 'Telling the truth is the most anti-conformist act I know,' he said. 'Hypocrisy is the consti-tutional basis and foundation of society. I have never led a double life. I have always declared my "cross and delight", which meant my desire for the male, for strong muscles and an adolescent body, a desire that has given me so much suffering and so much pleasure.'

Stefani's honesty earned him the respect and acceptance of Vene-tians. He had demonstrated his good faith, he said, and had overcome prejudice to the extent that mothers were willing to leave their sons and, more important, their sons' education in his hands.

From time to time, I saw Stefani in the street and in the wine bars around the Rialto. He was overweight, about sixty, and walked with a shuffling step. He dressed with a bit of flair – bright red braces, red sneakers, an ascot, and loose-fitting trousers – but his clothes were usually rumpled and soiled with food stains. He always carried two plastic bags bulging with books and groceries, one in each hand, making himself look like a vagabond. Every few paces he would call out an affectionate greeting, or stop to talk, or pop his head into a shop to exchange a few words or tell a joke. He liked to kiss women on the cheek, but several times I noticed that they surreptitiously wiped their faces afterwards. 'He's a dear, sweet man,' Rose Lauritzen said, 'and kind and generous. But I'm always of two minds when I see him headed in my direction, because he always kisses me and he *always* slobbers when he does.'

At the wine bars, Stefani came face to face with his own image. A local sculptor had made ceramic wine pitchers in the style of toby jugs that bore Stefani's likeness in the guise of Bacchus, with grapes on his head. The sculptor had produced an edition of one hundred and presented Mayor Cacciari with the 'author's proof' in a public ceremony. The presentation coincided with the publication of Stefani's new book of poems, *Wine and Eros*.

By the time Stefani's red spray-painted graffiti began appearing around Venice, it was clear to me that the man had a natural gift for self-promotion. His message – 'Loneliness is not being alone; it's loving others to no avail' – was perceptive and compassionate. It was also one of his better-known lines. Within days, the local press was running photographs of the graffiti accompanied by mood pieces and favourable mentions of Stefani. The publicity had cost him nothing. . When asked, Stefani claimed he had not written the graffiti. 'It wasn't me,' he said. 'It must have been a fan. I'm flattered, of course, and I'd like to meet whoever it was.'

A likely story, I thought.

And then, on Sunday, 4 March 2001, barely a month after the first of the graffiti had appeared, Mario Stefani hanged himself in his kitchen.

Suddenly the message in his graffiti took on a new meaning. It was no longer the wise observation of a sympathetic poet. It had been a cry of pain.

The news was received with disbelief across the city. 'But he was always smiling,' was the comment most often heard. 'He was such a popular man. He had so many friends.'

Carla Ferrara, a musician, saw it another way. 'In Venice loneliness is harder to notice. It's hidden, because when you leave the house, you have to walk. Everybody walks in Venice, so you see twenty people you know, and you have to say hello. But no matter how many people you greet, you can still feel lonely inside. That's the problem of a small city. You are surrounded by people talking to you and saying hello. In a big city, you don't find yourself talking to nearly so many people. The loneliness is more obvious.'

The disbelief was felt most deeply by Stefani's neighbours in Campo San Giacomo dell'Orio. 'None of us knew he was lonely,' said Paolo Lazzarin, the owner of Trattoria al Ponte on the ground floor of Stefani's building. 'He came in three times a day. We felt he was part of the family. He'd lost a little weight in the last few months, but he told us he was on a diet. We didn't know he needed help.'

The women who ran the restaurant La Zucca on the opposite side of the bridge in front of Stefani's house were also taken by surprise. 'We'd see him walking past with his plastic shopping bags,' said Rossana Gasparini. 'He'd drop in at least once a day, give us kisses, and say, "Have you heard the latest?" He was looking a little worn out lately, but we never would have imagined . . .'

The baker, Luciano Favero, said, 'He was always surrounded by lots of people, but maybe he had few real friends. He seemed pensive recently.'

Saturday night, the night before he died, Stefani had gone to Mestre for the opening of an exhibition by the painter Nino Memo, an old friend. 'He arrived early,' Memo said, 'and he seemed to be in a particularly good mood. He liked the show and even promised me he was going to write a favourable review of it. A lot of his friends were there – writers, painters, and academics – and he talked to everybody. I did notice one thing that was unusual, though: he stayed till the very end. That wasn't like him; he would usually leave a gathering like that before it was over. Afterwards he joined a group of us for dinner, and then we all came back to Venice. Before we parted at Piazzale Roma, he opened his shopping bag and showed us a roast chicken, already prepared. It was for his Sunday dinner. He said he probably wouldn't leave the house all day. He had a lot of work to do.'

On Sunday afternoon, a student friend of Stefani's, Elena de Maria, waited for him at the Trattoria al Ponte. He had said he would advise her on her thesis, but when he did not show up for their two o'clock meeting, she phoned him and got no answer. She kept trying all afternoon. Finally, around nine o'clock, she called the fire department. While the firemen went up to his apartment, she waited downstairs. Mario had been a family friend for many years, but in all that time he had never invited her up to his apartment – probably, she said, because it was a mess. An ambulance boat came ten minutes later, and the medics went up with a stretcher.

'When they came back down with the stretcher but without Mario,' she said, 'I knew he was dead. Then the firemen brought his body down in a sack. They weren't carrying him, they were dragging him down the stairs.'

Elena de Maria met me at Al Ponte to talk about Mario. 'Sunday is the one day of the week Mario would not have been missed so quickly,' she said. 'He liked to stay at home all day in his underwear. On any other day of the week, friends would begin to worry about him after a few hours if they hadn't heard from him. The baker would have missed him. The people at Al Ponte would have missed him. Most people would be dead for a week before friends would notice. Mario thought he was alone, but he wasn't.'

The public prosecutor in charge of Stefani's case, Antonio Miggiani, said police had found Stefani hanging from the banister of the stairs leading from the kitchen to the attic. He was wearing only a T-shirt. A suicide note was attached to a string tied round his neck. Police did not reveal its contents, but they said Stefani had listed a series of unhappy events that had led him to kill himself, including the recent death of his father. They said they had found no evidence of foul play.

In newspaper editorials and conversations, Venice searched its soul and wondered how it could have overlooked Mario Stefani's many messages of despair, especially the ones in red spray paint. A gathering at the Ateneo Veneto celebrated his life and poetry. However, the priest in Stefani's district provoked a bitter controversy when he refused to allow the use of the Church of San Giacomo dell'Orio for Stefani's funeral, because he had been a suicide. Ludovico De Luigi and other friends of Stefani's accused the priest of bias, saying he had invoked an old regulation that was no longer being enforced. They staged a protest demonstration in the *campo*. The impasse was resolved a week later, when the priest at the Church of San Giovanni e Paolo consented to have the funeral there. Hundreds of people attended.

I sat next to De Luigi at the service. He was in a caustic mood. 'All this week, Mario's been in the refrigerator,' he said, 'I'm disgusted with the public. They pay more attention to his homosexuality than to his poems and his heart and soul. Nobody can see past the physical aspect, because we live in a materialistic society. Everybody is explaining Mario's death through his asshole. They don't understand him. Today everything is tactile. We are back to the apes.' Ludovico shrugged. 'Me, I live in terror of the day they understand me, because it will mean I'm just like them. And that will be the end of my life, because all my life I've wanted not to be understood.'

Despite police assurances, some of Stefani's friends doubted that his death could have been a straightforward suicide. Stefani was physically inept, they said. He could not manage the simplest practicalities of daily life. As one friend put it, he would not have known how to hang a painting, much less himself.

Maria Irma Mariotti, a journalist who wrote for the cultural newspaper *Il Sole 24 Ore*, had known Stefani for thirty-five years and was perplexed that he had been found in a state of virtual undress. 'Mario was always concerned about his appearance,' she said. 'If he had planned this suicide himself, knowing that his body would be seen by any number of strangers, he would have wanted to be found in a more presentable state.'

Shortly after Stefani's death, his publisher, Editoria Universitaria, released a fifty-page book of his most recent poetry, *A Silent Desperation*. The cover image was a black-and-white photograph of Stefani looking weary, and the mood of the poems inside was equally grim. He spoke of having a smile on his face but a heavy heart. He was tired of living; life was an unbearable weight. Death was waiting for him at the end of a solitary train ride.

I found a copy of an earlier book of his poetry, *Secret Poems*. It had been published three years before his death, and even then his frame of mind could not have been more clear. 'I continue to live,' he wrote, 'but wish to die.'

It was obvious to me that most of the people who knew Mario had not read his poetry. I sat down and read for an afternoon. At least half of his poems were about life, death, searing memories, and the pain of love and longing.

At this point, I decided to pay a call on Stefani's publisher. I had assumed, from the sound of its name – Editoria Universitaria – that it was an august academic press, but I could not find it in the phone book. After many queries, I discovered that it was a one-man operation belonging to Albert Gardin, who ran it out of his wife's antique-clothing and costume shop in a narrow side-street, Calle del Scaleter, not far from Campo San Giacomo dell'Orio.

When I looked through the window of the tiny shop, I saw a floor-to-ceiling jumble of antique hats, dresses, coats, capes, scarves, umbrellas, dolls, and bolts of cloth – bunched, piled, strewn, draped, and hanging – but no sign of anything resembling a publishing enterprise. I stepped inside and asked a woman with light brown, shoulder-length hair if she could lead me to Albert Gardin. At that moment, a short, bearded man rose into view from behind a bunker of hats. It was Albert Gardin.

I introduced myself and said I was interested in learning more about Mario Stefani. Signor Gardin said he would be happy to tell me what he knew about his friend's poetry, which was plenty, and his death, which was not very much. He pointed to a stool, and I sat down.

'The police tell us nothing,' he said. 'We don't even know what Mario wrote in his suicide note. My best sources of information have been leaks. A friend in the fire department told me that Mario was found with a noose round his neck and his feet touching the floor. So he didn't die instantly from a snap of the neck but by a long, slow strangulation. His face had turned black. He used mountain-climbing rope, made of some sort of plastic, and it stretches. I think it's possible, though, that he died some other way and that his body was strung up afterwards to make it look like suicide.'

'You think it was murder?'

'It's possible. Maybe the autopsy will tell us something.'

'But the police say there is no evidence of foul play,' I said.

'Of course,' he said.

'They say there isn't any sign of robbery either. Money, paintings, and objects of value were all in their places.'

'They may have found money, paintings, and objects of value, as they say. But how would they know nothing was missing?'

'But weren't there plenty of signs that Mario Stefani was suicidal?' I asked. 'I mean, this new book you just published. It's almost a road map to suicide.'

'Mario talked to me about death and suicide more than once,' said Gardin. 'But I didn't think he was suicidal, and there are things about his death that don't seem right to me.'

'What sort?'

'The day before he died, he called to tell me to save the date of March thirtieth. He was planning an event on the Lido. I can't remember what — a reading involving children or old people. Whatever it was, he was enthusiastic about it. Why would he be making plans if he intended to kill himself?'

'Maybe the final urge came over him suddenly, without warning,' I said. 'I understand that can happen, especially to someone struggling with a suicidal impulse.'

Gardin shook his head. 'I knew Mario very well. Friendship meant a lot to him. I'm sure he would have come to see me one last time to say goodbye in person. That would have been more like him. Mario was—' Gardin caught himself. He closed his eyes. Then, after a moment, he blinked away tears. 'I'm sorry. I'm just not used to saying "Mario *was*". I was starting to say that Mario was a true friend, that's all. He'd been depressed, but he was not at the point of killing himself.'

'Why was he was depressed?'

Gardin paused and looked down at his hands before answering. 'I think he was being blackmailed.'

'Why?'

'Mario always prided himself on buying people drinks and dinner. He'd say, "I want to humiliate you with my wealth." Then, last summer, he stopped doing that. He would say that he was in financial trouble and could no longer pay, and if he did pay, it was only for his part of the bill. He'd see someone walking by a bar in a hurry and offer him a drink, knowing that the person would not have the time to accept.

'I knew there had to be a reason for his financial problems, and I became concerned. Finally I just asked him if he was being blackmailed. He said, "No, no, no!" But then he thanked me for asking the question and said, "Maybe one day I'll explain everything." '

'Why would somebody blackmail him? He was very open about his homosexuality.'

'Yes, but he kept that part of his life separate. He paid for sex. The boys were working-class, and some of them had criminal records. Some were drug addicts. They would come up to him in the street and say they needed money to pay the electricity bill, and he would say, "Come by my house tonight." To the boys, it was a matter of sex for money, but Mario would often fall in love, and it made him vulnerable. He'd give them whatever they wanted, and what they always wanted was money. That's the kind of blackmail I'm thinking of.'

Gardin was concerned about the disposition of Stefani's estate. 'Seventeen artists drew portraits of Mario, including Giorgio de Chirico. Mario told me he wanted all his paintings, his writings, and his collection of thousands of books to go to the Querini Stampalia Foundation museum.'

Gardin was especially worried about the fate of Stefani's un-published poetry. 'He was always jotting down poems,' said Gardin. 'There have to be dozens of them in notebooks, on scraps of paper, finished, unfinished. To the untrained eye, they might not look like anything. They could get thrown away.'

It was assumed at first that Stefani's heir would be his closest relative, a distant cousin who knew him only slightly. She had made his funeral arrangements and was the sole person allowed by the police to enter his apartment. But soon after his death, two non-profit organizations came forward, both claiming that Stefani had told them he had named them in his will as beneficiaries – a cancer-research organization in Milan and the Waldensian Church in Venice. The Waldensian Church bequest was the more recent, and therefore it seemed to be the valid heir.

A month later, however, a headline in the *Gazzettino* trumpeted, 'The Mystery of the Third Will'. The police had found a third will in Stefani's apartment, and it bore a later date than the other two. They would not reveal the identity of the beneficiary, except to say that it was someone not named in either of the two previous wills. There was one catch, however: this third will was only a photocopy, so it was not valid by itself. The original would have to be found. The public prosecutor said he would interrogate Stefani's notary to determine whether the original copy of the will had been suppressed, hidden, or destroyed.

The most surprising revelation in this news story was that Stefani's estate included not only his house but six rental apartments in Mestre and two *magazzini* in the Rialto. The total worth was more than a million dollars.

The next day, Stefani's notary found the original of the third will stuck into a book of poems that Stefani had given him several months earlier. He also found a fourth will in the book, dated a month later, which simply reiterated the terms of the third. The identity of the heir was still not divulged.

The story took another unexpected turn six weeks later with the surprising announcement that the heir was a one-year-old girl. Stefani had adored the child as if she were his daughter. According to the

Gazzettino, Stefani had made the girl's father his heir because the girl was a minor, and if he had left his estate in her name, the courts would have taken control until she was eighteen. Still the names were not revealed. The girl's parents were described as working-class people who were amazed and incredulous at the bequest.

This latest development mystified everyone who knew Stefani, especially Albert Gardin. Toward the end of June, I was walking by his storefront and saw the top of his head behind a pile of hats. I went into the shop.

'Have you found out anything more about the little girl?' I asked.

'There is no little girl,' he answered.

'What?'

'Mario left everything to a thirty-two-year-old man. That's all it says in his will. No mention of a baby girl.'

'How did you find that out?' I asked.

Gardin reached into a drawer and took out a single sheet of paper. It was a copy of Mario Stefani's third will. It was handwritten, as all Italian wills are required to be. The 'sole and universal' heir was listed as Nicola Bernardi.

'Who is he?'

'A fruit-and-vegetable dealer,' said Gardin. 'He works in his family's shop in St Mark's. He and his wife have a baby girl. Her name is Anna. Mario wrote a poem about her.'

I remembered then that I had heard Stefani speak twice on his television programme about a beautiful baby girl who had helped him come out of a deep depression. Gardin handed me a copy of Stefani's last book of poetry and opened it to the poem about her. Anna had given him hope, he wrote, and the will to go on living.

'The *Gazzettino* got something else wrong, too,' said Gardin. 'They said the notary found the will in a book of poems. But when the notary registered the will, he reported that it was *given* to him by Nicola Bernardi's lawyer, Cristina Belloni. I've got the registration documents, too.'

'What do you make of it?' I asked.

'I am more suspicious than ever. Let me show you something *really* strange. Look at the wording of the will. It's full of grammatical errors. Mario would never have written anything like this. For example, he switches from the first person to the third, then back to the first: "*I,* Mario Stefani, being in full control of *his* mental faculties, leaves all *his* worldly goods and properties and all *my* financial assets . . ."

'If it isn't an outright forgery, then Mario had to be under tremendous strain at the time he wrote it. It might have been dictated to him. If Mario wrote this will intentionally, then he committed suicide a second time – a literary suicide. I mean, what does this fruit-and-vegetable dealer know or care about poetry? How will he know the difference between a piece of paper with a poem scribbled on it and a piece of paper that can be safely thrown away? Will he be making decisions about literary rights and translations? Will he negotiate with publishers?'

'Speaking of which,' I said, 'how does this affect you as Stefani's publisher? I notice that in his books Editoria Universitaria is identified as the holder of the copyright.'

He shrugged. 'Who knows?'

'What are you going to do about it?'

'First I want to have this mystery cleared up. I'm going to petition the public prosecutor to launch an honest, open investigation, and I'll send copies to the newspapers.'

A week later, Gardin did just that.

The following day, the *Gazzettino* duly reported that Gardin's petition 'puts in doubt the news published here about the suicide of the Venetian poet'. The newspaper quoted Stefani's will verbatim, including the grammatical mistakes, but omitting Bernardi's name. It was clear that no baby girl had been mentioned. The paper also cited Gardin's complaint that in registering the will the notary said it had been given to him by an attorney, not that he had found it between the pages of a book, as the *Gazzettino* had reported. The paper gave no reason for the discrepancies.

Two days after this story appeared in the *Gazzettino*, my telephone rang shortly before noon. It was Gardin. He sounded shaken.

'Something very serious has happened,' he said. 'Can you come to the shop? The police have already been here.'

'Are you all right?' I asked.

'Yes, yes,' he said. 'You'll see.'

Fifteen minutes later, I was standing in front of Gardin's office, which is to say outside his wife's clothing shop. Scrawled with a blue felt-tip marker on the shop window was the warning DON'T GO BREAKING BALLS OVER MARIO STEFANI'S WILL.

Once I had read and absorbed it, Gardin wiped it off with a rag. 'The *Gazzettino* and *La Nuova* were here an hour ago,' he said. 'They took pictures. I've filed a complaint with the police.'

'Whoever this fruit-and-vegetable dealer is,' I said, 'he must be awfully dense not to realize he'd be the obvious suspect.'

'It could be him,' said Gardin. 'Or a friend of his, or a member of his family.'

The next day, both newspapers published stories about the threatening scrawl accompanied by photographs of Gardin standing next to the window. 'Someone is not happy about my petition to the public prosecutor,' Gardin told *La Nuova*, 'but I intend to get to the bottom of this.' He had filed a petition with the police asking for increased nighttime patrols around his wife's shop. Still neither paper revealed Bernardi's identity.

That happened three weeks later, at the end of July, when Nicola Bernardi stepped forward publicly and identified himself as Stefani's heir. Through his lawyer, Cristina Belloni, he said he intended to safeguard Mario Stefani's legacy by donating all of his manuscripts, books, correspondence, and paintings to the Querini Stampalia Foundation. He had hired specialists to catalogue everything in Stefani's house by the end of summer.

Belloni insisted that there was no mystery behind the will. Her client found out that he was the heir only after Stefani's death, when he was summoned by the police.

Albert Gardin was not satisfied. Three days later, he held a news conference in the lobby of the Sofitel Hotel and introduced sensational new charges. 'The last relationship of Mario Stefani,' he said, 'turned into a dangerous erotic game that got out of control and cost him his life.

'I would describe his death as *pasoliniana*,' he went on, referring to the brutal murder in 1975 of the film director Pier Paolo Pasolini for which a hustler was convicted. 'Mario paid for sex with the boys he wrote about in his erotic poems. The police should investigate Mario's bank account, because there was movement in it right before his death, and when he died, the account was empty.'

A reporter pointed out to Gardin, 'Many people think you have a personal motive for calling attention to this case even though it seems to be resolved.'

'It is absolutely *not* resolved,' Gardin replied. 'Only the lawyer for the heir thinks it is.'

The next morning, a second warning appeared on Gardin's shop window. This one, like the first, was written with a blue felt-tip marker: HAVEN'T YOU READ THE NEWSPAPERS? THERE'S NO MYSTERY ABOUT STEFANI'S WILL. IF YOU KEEP TALKING, THERE WILL BE TROUBLE FOR YOU.

Gardin filed another complaint against persons unknown, once again asking the police for night-time surveillance.

I stopped in again at his shop to look at the writing on his window. Gardin and his wife were both inside. He came out into the *calle*. 'My wife is terrified,' he said under his breath. 'She wants me to abandon my campaign.'

But he did not. Instead, he organized a posthumous sixty-third-birthday party for Stefani the following Sunday in Campo San Giacomo dell'Orio. He sent out invitations entitled 'Poets Never Die', addressed to 'My Friends', and signed 'Mario'. The *Gazzettino* said that the invitation was in dubious taste. 'It is right to remember the poet,' the paper declared, 'right that his friends (the real ones) gather, but let us not exploit his death. Leave Mario in peace, as he wanted.'

The party took place outdoors in the *campo* and was attended by about forty people. It began as a tasteful homage to Stefani's poetry but quickly turned into a platform for denunciations of the police and speculation about what had really happened.

Stefani's long-time friend, the journalist Maria Irma Mariotti, proposed the most extreme scenario, in line with Gardin's. 'In my opinion, Mario was murdered,' she said in a raspy, smoker's voice. 'I won't exclude the possibility that he was the victim of an erotic game, one that involved asphyxiation with a bag over his head or a rope round his neck, followed by a staged hanging.'

Mariotti said that she had been with Stefani at an art exhibition a year before he died, when he suddenly broke down in tears, trembling uncontrollably, and told her he was desperately in love with a young man who was threatening never to see him again unless Mario paid him ever-increasing sums of money. 'He's ruining my life,' Stefani had said, 'but I can't turn back.'

'I warned Mario to break off this relationship,' she said. 'It sounded dangerous. But he said he had already written the man into his will.

' "Tear it up," I told him.

' "But if he finds out, I don't know how he'll react."

'When I heard that,' said Mariotti, 'I told Mario, "If you don't end this affair in a hurry, you'll be signing your own death warrant." When I left him that evening, not only did I beg him to drop this gold-digger, I swore I wouldn't see him again until he did. Some time later he called and said, "Relax, it's over," but to tell you the truth, I didn't believe him.'

The *Gazzettino* published an account of the party, including a summation of Mariotti's suspicions. Ten days later, Mariotti submitted a detailed, three-page report to the *carabinieri*, and two days after that a third warning appeared on the window of Gardin's shop. Once again, it was written with a blue felt-tip marker and in the same handwriting as before: YOU ARE THE ONLY ONE TALKING BULLSHIT ABOUT EROTIC GAMES SAYING MARIO STEFANI WAS MURDERED. HE COMMITTED SUICIDE. UNDERSTAND??? WE'LL BREAK YOUR ASS. LAST WARNING.

For the third time, Albert Gardin filed a complaint against persons unknown and repeated his request for night-time surveillance.

That was where matters stood when I went to see Aurelio Minazzi, the notary who had purportedly found Mario Stefani's will in a book of poetry. Minazzi was youthful and likeable. He said he had known Stefani for thirty-five years, having met him through his father, who had been secretary to the editor of the *Gazzettino*.

'Did you really find the third will tucked into a book of poetry?' I asked him.

'Yes,' he said.

'Then, when you registered it, why did you say Cristina Belloni had given it to you and asked you to file it?'

'That was a legal formality,' he said. 'The law requires that someone *request* that a notary register a will. I could not have done it on my own. I could have taken the will to another notary and asked *him* to register it. So when I found the will, I called Cristina Belloni and said, "Yes, I've found it." Then she came here with Bernardi. I handed the will to Bernardi. Bernardi gave it to Cristina Belloni, and then she gave it to me and asked me to publish it.'

'Why didn't you mention in your report that you found it in a book?'

'Because it's irrelevant. It makes no difference where it was before it was registered. Mario could have put it in a bank vault, or given it to his publisher, or left it in his desk drawer. He didn't have to leave it with a notary.'

'Then why did the judge immediately point the finger at you and launch an investigation into why you hadn't turned over the original?'

'Because at the top of his will, Mario had written "For the notary Aurelio Minazzi". So naturally the judge assumed I had the original.'

'Fair enough,' I said, suddenly remembering that indeed Minazzi's name had been at the top of the will Albert Gardin had shown me.

'But why would you keep a will in a book of poems?'

'Mario wrote many wills,' Minazzi said with a smile. 'He kept changing his mind. It was – I won't say a mania, but it was his way. He would give me a will, and then he would call and say, "I'm not happy with it." And then he'd write a new one.

'When Mario died, I checked the registers and found a will Mario wrote in 1984, leaving everything to the Association for Cancer Research. I also had a note he sent me later on, saying he wanted to leave everything to the Waldensian Church. But he never actually wrote that will. So when he died, I told the judge that Mario had disavowed the last will he'd made without formally writing another one, as far as I knew. That's when the judge sent the police back to the house to look for anything else written by Mario, and they found the photocopy of the will leaving everything to Bernardi.

'The judge called me and asked if I had the original. My secretary and I tried to recall Mario's last visit. Then we remembered he'd dropped in without an appointment, as usual, and brought a plant, some chocolates, and a book of poems. That's when we found the two Bernardi wills.'

'How many wills did he write?'

'To tell you the truth, I'm not sure. In fact, after Mario died, another man brought me a copy of a will leaving everything to *him*. He's a fireman. Mario had written that will back in 1975, before I was a notary. I had to tell him his will was invalid, that there were others after his.

'Mario had his problems,' said Minazzi. 'Perhaps changing wills was his way of solving them.'

Cristina Belloni agreed to see me in her office in Campo Santo Stefano. An attractive, fashionably dressed brunette, she came right to the point.

'My client, Nicola Bernardi, received a summons from the public prosecutor for information relating to the suicide of Mario Stefani. The prosecutor told him it would be only an informal chat, but it turned out to be an interrogation. Nicola came here to my office straight afterwards, upset. He said they told him Mario Stefani had made him his sole heir. He had not the slightest idea about this bequest. But then they told him that the will was a photocopy and therefore not valid. So Nicola was shocked twice, first because there was a will and then because maybe it was worthless.

'I had to move quickly, because I thought someone might have found the original will and destroyed it. It had been reported in the newspapers that a gift-wrapped package had been found on Mario's kitchen table. It had Nicola's phone number on it, and it was a birthday present for Nicola's daughter, Anna. So I immediately went to see the prosecutor and asked him if he had opened the package. He said no. I asked him if by chance he had thought the original copy of the will might be inside it. He said no. I insisted it be opened, and I warned him I would do everything a lawyer could do. I would petition the chief prosecutor to at least give the package to the person it was intended for – Anna. The prosecutor answered me angrily, saying that he had the authority to drag out the investigation another thirty days and would do so if I interfered in any way.

'Now I had to take the offensive. I sent Mario's notary a certified letter, and rather than saying I knew he didn't have the will, I played it just the opposite. I wrote, "I wonder if you, a friend of Mario Stefani, could be holding his signed will. Give me confirmation, and if you have it, file it immediately, because I am the lawyer of the person named in the will." Twenty-four hours later, the notary called me and said, "I found it." '

'Do you believe he found it in the pages of a book,' I asked, 'or that he was hiding it for some reason?'

'That's not for me to believe one way or the other. I was interested only in protecting my client. The notary said to me, "I cannot register it yet, because I must have various certified documents." I said, "Notary, tomorrow morning you will have them. And then you *will*, tomorrow morning, file them for me!" '

Cristina Belloni's aggressiveness was startling, and slightly off-putting. She confirmed what Minazzi had told me about the route the will took: Minazzi handed it to Bernardi, Bernardi gave it to Cristina Belloni, and then Cristina Belloni gave it back to Minazzi and asked him to publish it.

'I got a certificate from the notary,' she said, 'and, with that in hand, I went to the prosecutor and told him, "Now unseal everything immediately." He tried to delay a little, and after forty-eight hours I got a court order for him to release Mario's house from sequestration.'

'How did the story get out that Anna was the heir?' I asked.

'Nicola sells fruit and vegetables – he's a simple person, socially unsophisticated. He could have been hounded by the press, and he was frightened. So I made an agreement to keep his nomination secret, for a while at least, to permit him to absorb the shock. It takes about twenty days for the registration of a will to become public, and then anybody can see it.'

'Your secrecy plan seems to have made people more suspicious,' I said.

'The media have reported a lot of malicious things about Mario and Nicola, things that were not true. I advised Nicola not to respond; otherwise it would have got even worse. So we waited until the inventory of Mario's work was under way and the gift to the Querini Stampalia was arranged, and then he gave a press conference.'

'What about the speculation that Mario had been blackmailed? That he'd been hounded for money?'

'I found out that Mario was being sued by some woman in Mestre who was demanding restitution for water damage coming from a leak in the apartment he owned above hers. It was a lot of money, and apparently he was very worried about it.'

'The accusations and suspicions have persisted,' I said.

'Yes, from Albert Gardin, who presents himself as Mario's publisher. I did research on him at the Chamber of Commerce. Gardin has had many careers in his life, but his publishing house doesn't exist. It has no address. There was a contract in 1991, but after that it closed. I became suspicious of him when he published a collection of Mario's poetry after he died without making any effort to contact Mario's heir. He sells books without a bar code, so there is no way of tracking the number of copies sold. He seems eager for publicity.'

'Do you think Nicola or any of his friends wrote those messages with the blue felt-tip marker on Gardin's window?'

'Absolutely not.'

'Who would have done it, then?'

'Maybe Gardin did it himself.'

Even before Nicola Bernardi was identified by the press as Mario Stefani's heir, his name and whereabouts circulated among Stefani's friends, and a steady stream of curious people filed by his family's shop to get a glimpse of him. Some took photographs, pretending to be tourists; some went into the shop and bought a kilo of tomatoes. They compared notes. Bernardi was tall and plain-looking. He had a lean build; close-cropped, thinning hair; and a long, equine face.

'He has small eyes,' one of Stefani's friends, a woman, reported, 'and they move very quickly, like a lizard's. His smile, in my opinion, is too eager. It's forced, like the sudden smile you see on beggar children in Morocco, Mexico, and India, when they want money. The mouth opens unexpectedly. Children of the rich have more restrained smiles. They laugh less often – only when it comes naturally.'

A Korean journalist, also a woman, recalled that in the past, on several occasions, Stefani had insisted that she accompany him to Bernardi's fruit-and-vegetable shop. 'He was irresistibly drawn to the place,' she said, 'but he was afraid to go there alone. When we arrived at the shop, Mario would pretend we just happened to be in the area. I was surprised by the reception he received. It was not at all friendly, and it made me uncomfortable. They barely spoke to him. There was no communication, not even a laugh or a smile. The young man, Nicola, went about his business and pretended not to know him. If anything, he seemed annoyed by Mario's presence.'

Nicola Bernardi lived with his wife and daughter in a one-room, ground-floor apartment near the Frari. It was a tight space, four hundred square feet at most; the front door opened directly into the living-room. I paid them a visit a year after Mario Stefani's death, having got in touch through Cristina Belloni. I took a seat on the couch opposite Nicola, who was wearing jeans and jogging shoes. Francesca had auburn hair, a luminous complexion, and calm, cool eyes. She was helping Anna into a pink jumper. Anna was blonde and now two years old.

'We got to know Mario,' said Nicola, 'because he used to come to our shop all the time to buy fruit and vegetables and visit my parents, my brother, and me. His bank was nearby. He was such a good customer we offered him a discount, but he never took it. He'd say, "*Mamma mia*, what a job you have! You all get up so early. So I don't want a discount."'

This recollection of warmth and friendliness among the fruit and vegetables did not square with the Korean journalist's account of indifference verging on hostility. But whose version was the accurate one? Francesca, too, like Nicola, remembered Mario as a virtual member of the family.

'Mario came to the hospital when I had Anna,' she said. 'He was at the christening, too. We had invited him to Anna's first birthday party, and he said he'd try to come, but he killed himself before that.'

'Did he ever come here?'

'He'd call and say he was close by,' said Nicola, 'and that he had a gift for Anna or a set of pots and pans for us. If we weren't at home, he'd leave presents on the windowsill and close the shutters. He was like that. We'd come home and find the stuff. In fact, we finally had to put a stop to it. I said, "Mario, you can't keep giving us gifts. We don't need anything."'

It had been agreed that I would meet the Bernardis at their house and from there walk over to Mario's apartment. Francesca put Anna into a push-chair and handed her a teddy bear.

'Anna,' she said, 'who gave you this teddy bear? Remember? Uncle . . . Uncle . . . Uncle who? Uncle Mario! You remember Uncle Mario?' Anna did not respond.

On the way to Stefani's house, Anna got out of the push-chair and walked over each of the four bridges. Nicola and I went on ahead.

'It's been a year now,' I said. 'How has your life changed since you became an heir?'

'We don't have money problems any more,' said Nicola. 'If an electricity bill comes, we don't worry about it. And if I want to keep the air-conditioning on all summer, now I can. But the work is just the same. I still get up at four thirty and take the boat to buy fruit and vegetables and bring them to the shop. The only difference is that I don't take any money from my parents for it now.'

'You work without pay?'

'Nobody is making me do it. I really don't have to work at all, but I feel I have a moral obligation to my parents and my brother. It's right that we continue to work together.'

Bernardi spoke with casual ease and without any apparent guile. He had a relaxed charm and flashed a disarming smile every so often, which was remarkable, I thought, under the circumstances. He had been accused, after all, of having had a secret relationship with Mario and of somehow having been involved in his death. And here we were, walking towards the supposed scene of the crime. Nicola had every right to be uneasy, whether the accusations were true or wholly made up. But he appeared to be completely untroubled.

'Have people asked you for loans?'

'No, but Francesca and I, we're the ones who can offer now. And as soon as we can, we're going to renovate Mario's apartment and move in. We haven't started yet, though. It's still the way it was when Mario lived in it, except that the papers and the books have been taken away to be sorted.'

'Had either you or Francesca seen Mario's apartment before he died?'

'We didn't even know where he lived. I went there for the first time with Cristina and the police. The door was chained shut. We had to be let in by the officer. We found a gift for Anna inside and some money, but the apartment was a mess. Books were everywhere, and stuff was piled up and lying around. It was disturbing.'

'Have you read any of Mario's poetry?'

'I've never been a great reader. When I walked to school, I used to pass the saint in the wall in Calle Bembo and put a coin in the box, so I wouldn't get bad marks. But I did read the poem about Anna. It was something serious. Then I recorded some of Mario's stuff on TV.'

'What do you think about all that speculation over Mario's suicide and his will and your part in it?'

'I was really angry. People were saying I forced him to write his will and that I was having an affair with him. That shit really got to me. I wanted to answer back, but everybody told me not to, because then it would only be in the *Gazzettino* again.'

'Of course.'

'And who are those people? They're supposed to be Mario's good friends. But they were standing up in public saying terrible things about him – that he was paying for sex and playing dangerous sex games. In the end, what I discovered about Mario was that he was everyone's friend and at the same time no one's friend.'

'What about the threats written with the blue felt-tip marker on Albert Gardin's window?'

'Why would I do something crazy like that? One of those things even appeared when I was up in the mountains.'

At Campo San Giacomo, we waited for Francesca and Anna. Then the four of us went up to Stefani's apartment. At the top of a steep flight of stone steps, a pair of heavy wooden doors opened on a scene of musty gloom. The apartment had high ceilings, tall windows, heavy oak furniture, and wallpaper that was stained and peeling. Framed pictures, including several pen-and-ink portraits of Stefani, were hung haphazardly on the walls. We walked from room to room.

'Anna! Look!' said Francesca. 'Whose apartment is this? You know who! Uncle Mario!' It crossed my mind that these evocations of Uncle Mario might have been meant as much for my ears as Anna's. Nicola was a lucky fruit-and-vegetable dealer, that much was certain. But his million-dollar windfall had come at a price: the lingering suspicion that he had earned it through some secret, nefarious dealings that he and his family would for ever be at pains to deny.

In the kitchen, I looked at the narrow stairs leading up to the attic and at the wooden railing where Stefani had tied the rope that had choked him to death. A poster taped to the wall halfway up the stairs showed two young, lighthearted soldiers kissing; it was captioned 'Make love, not war.'

'We haven't started working on renovating it yet,' said Nicola. 'We'd never sell this apartment. It's Mario's.'

We came into the dining room. On a sideboard, I noticed a glass sculpture that appeared at first to be in the shape of a plant, but upon taking a closer look, I saw it was a phallus. Next to it was another phallus-shaped object, this one made of marble. On the floor, there was a box that contained a variety of penises, more in the nature of tawdry jokes than pornography – penis candles with wicks coming out of the end, clay penises fashioned into pipe smokers' pipes, salt-shaker penises, ceramic penises lying in ceramic ashtrays, door-knocker penises.

'I guess these objects aren't going to be included in Mario's permanent archives,' I said to Nicola. His laugh was light, easy, and, as far as I could tell, completely genuine.

A year later, the Mario Stefani Collection opened at the Querini Stampalia, a library and museum housed in an exquisite sixteenth-century palace. Stefani's life's work had been rescued from the squalid disorder of his house and installed in a place where it would be preserved for future study. The collection included his writings, his paintings, portraits, memorabilia, and his correspondence with such people as Alberto Moravia, Giorgio de Chirico, Pier Paolo Pasolini, and others. Strangely, however, there were no unpublished poems among the papers donated. This only fuelled fears among Stefani's friends that Bernardi might have mistaken Stefani's jottings for trash and thrown them out before the controversy over the estate became public and forced him to hire experts to cull the material with a professional eye.

The librarians at the Querini Stampalia, however, were quite content with the acquisition of Stefani's library of sixty-eight hundred books, most of which were works by lesser-known local poets. The collection was the largest of its kind. As for Stefani's own poetry, librarian Neda Furlan said that it would be difficult to assess its standing since the poems had not yet been the subject of academic study. 'He was very well known locally and nationally, and some of his poetry is truly beautiful,' she said, 'but during his lifetime he was never considered exceptional. Perhaps it is too soon to say. The distance of time will be needed for an objective interpretation of his work.'

Meanwhile Stefani's heir, after two years, was still working gratis for his parents at the fruit-and-vegetable shop, still rising at four thirty, and still living in the same one-room apartment as before – but with a wife and *two* children now. The renovation of Mario's apartment had not yet begun.

'Nicola is taking care of things a little at a time,' Cristina Belloni told me. 'He paid for the experts who worked on the inventory, and because of what they found, they have been able to reconstruct the figure of Mario as a poet, as a writer, as a critic, and as a homosexual who was one of the first to have the courage to admit it openly – even reconstructing his collection of erotic literature.'

Some time after being recognized as Mario Stefani's legal heir, Nicola Bernardi ordered a gravestone placed on Stefani's burial niche on the cemetery island of San Michele. Then he asked the cataloguers of Stefani's papers to look for a suitable quotation to use as an epitaph. They found one in the text of a speech Stefani had given, and Nicola had it engraved on the stone: 'Even more than as a poet, I would like to be remembered as one who loved others.'

Albert Gardin's protests and accusations about Mario Stefani's sad end eventually subsided to a murmur. By 2003 he had become involved in a clamorous public debate over an eight-foot statue of Napoleon that was being given to the city by the French Committee to Safeguard Venice. One side favoured accepting the statue on the grounds that Napoleon was part of Venice's history, for better or for worse. The other side, for which Albert Gardin was a prominent spokesman, was vehemently opposed, calling Napoleon a terrorist, a plunderer, a traitor, a barbarian, and a vandal. The anti-Napoleon side was preparing to haul Napoleon before a posthumous Nuremberg-style ad hoc tribunal.

I was walking along Calle del Scaleter when it occurred to me to drop in on Gardin and have a chat about the Napoleon controversy. As I approached his wife's antique-clothing shop, I saw the top of Gardin's head poking up behind a pile of hats and boxes, as usual. But when I put my hand on the door, I caught sight of something that stopped me cold. The words 'Vintage Clothing, Special Sale on Hats and Shawls' had been written on the window to the right of the door – with a blue felt-tip marker.

14

The Inferno Revisited

L AURA MIGLIORI STOOD in one of the Fenice's formal reception rooms and stared at the soot-blackened walls. It was January 2000, four years after the fire, and the Fenice still had no roof. The theatre hall was a muddy pit. Signorina Migliori knew that beneath the grime on the walls of this room – the Dante Room – lay the remains of a frescoed panel depicting, of all things, the *Inferno*. As an art conservator, she had been hired to restore what was left of the six frescos in the room, all scenes from *The Divine Comedy*.

'It was not just the flames and the smoke that did all the damage,' she said. 'The firemen had to use shallow, low-tide water to put out the fire, so the frescos were blasted for hours with muddy salt water. Then you have to remember that without a roof there has been nothing to protect the walls from years of rain.'

'Where do you begin?' I asked. The blackened walls were covered with an oily film.

'The first thing we'll have to do,' she said, 'even before we wash the mud off, is to secure the fresco. It's become detached from the wall in places; there's about a one-centimetre space between parts of the fresco and the wall behind it. So first we'll cover it with a thin Japanese paper to keep pieces from falling off. Then we'll inject tiny amounts of plaster through the fresco to fill in the space and bind it to the wall. When that's done, we'll remove the paper and take colour samples. Then we'll begin the cleaning process by gently patting it with pads soaked in distilled water mixed with various substances. No one really knows what we'll find, because for the past twenty-five years the frescos have been covered by Virgilio Guidi oil paintings that were mounted on top of them. No one has seen them in all that time, and the only photographs we've found for reference are old and blurry.'

Laura Migliori could not begin the restoration immediately. Work on the Fenice had come to a complete stop in February 1998, when the court cancelled the contract won by Fiat's Impregilo eight months after they had started. The contract was then given to the second-place bidder, Holzmann-Romagnoli, but the resumption of work was delayed by the purchase of the privately owned apartments, approval of plans, and tangled contractual negotiations. It was not until sixteen months later that construction finally started again, and it went badly from the first day.

Disagreements arose over money, scheduling, and changes in the structural plan mandated by the city. Then, in November 1999, barely five months after work had resumed, Holzmann, the German half of the Holzmann-Romagnoli consortium, announced that it was on the edge of bankruptcy.

Philipp Holzmann AG was one of the biggest construction companies in Europe, and news of its looming insolvency drove its stock price down 90 per cent on the German stock market. Panic hit Venice. Chancellor Gerhard Schroeder held emergency meetings with the German parliament and put together a $50 million bailout for Holzmann. This calmed nerves in Venice, but only slightly. The pace of work continued to lag behind schedule. The deadline was extended once, then again. Archaeological discoveries under the Fenice – two ancient wells, an arch, and a pillar – resulted in further delays. Holzmann-Romagnoli demanded more money and an even later deadline, but the Comune refused.

In May 2000, with work halted once again because of problems installing a new crane, Mayor Cacciari chose not to stand for re-election. Venice elected a new mayor – Paolo Costa, an economist of national stature, who had served as Italy's minister of public works and as rector of Ca'Foscari University. White-haired, bespectacled, and deceptively bland in appearance, Mayor Costa boldly took charge of the Fenice morass. He made the unprecedented move of asking to be appointed commissioner in charge of rebuilding, which made him responsible for the success or failure of the project. Costa was putting his job and his reputation on the line, and he discovered soon enough that the odds were not in his favour. Shortly after becoming mayor, he made a surprise inspection tour of the Fenice and found only one person on the job.

Costa had been in office six months when a contingent of two dozen Fenice employees boarded a large transport boat and came down the Grand Canal in a noisy protest. It was 29 January 2001, the fifth anniversary of the fire. The demonstrators were singing, chanting, and waving a banner that read COM'ERA, DOV'ERA, IN QUALE ERA? ('As it was, where it was, but when?' – or, literally, 'but in which era?', the Italian *era* meaning both 'it was' and 'era', the same as in English). They tied up in front of the town hall, Ca' Farsetti, where they were joined by a hundred more demonstrators with whistles, horns, bells, and a cardboard model of the Fenice with special-effects smoke pouring out of it. Opera music blared from loudspeakers. The crowd sang the aria 'Di quella pira' from Verdi's *Il Trovatore*, in which the tenor sings, 'The horrid flames of that pyre consume me. Cowards, put it out, or I will extinguish it with your blood . . . To arms! To arms!'

Costa reviewed the status of the Fenice: sixty per cent of the allotted time had elapsed, but only five per cent of the work had been done. The foundations had not even been completed, and Holzmann-Romagnoli was still asking for more time and more money. Costa was convinced that unless he took action, he would still be arguing about money and deadlines in five years. He told Holzmann-Romagnoli he was terminating their contract. They were fired. They had thirty days to remove their equipment, or the city would seize it.

Costa tried to assure a doubtful public that, as absurd as it might sound, this was the fastest, cleanest way to get the job done. He was speaking now as a former minister of public works. He was saying, Trust me. The whole process would have to start all over again with a new call for competitive bids. The boldest part of Costa's action was to declare that Venice, not Holzmann-Romagnoli, owned Aldo Rossi's architectural design and that Venice was going to build it, working with Rossi's associates in Milan but not with Holzmann-Romagnoli. Costa was confident he would prevail in any court battle.

Holzmann-Romagnoli writhed and thrashed and refused to leave the work site until Costa sent the police to roust them out. On 27 April 2001, Venice once again had custody of the Fenice, but work had come to a virtual halt. A single company stayed on the job, working on the foundations, while Costa looked for a new contractor.

Eight construction companies responded to the new solicitation for bids. One letter, however, arrived fifteen minutes after the deadline, and Costa rejected it. He was in no mood to tolerate lateness.

From the assembled bids, Costa chose the Venetian construction company Sacaim, an outfit well accustomed to operating in the difficult environment of Venice. Sacaim had worked on a great many important Venetian buildings, including Palazzo Grassi and the Malibran Theatre. Nor was it a stranger to the Fenice: Sacaim had been the principal contractor for the renovation in progress the night the Fenice burned.

In early March 2002, after a hiatus of eleven months, Mayor Costa erected a large digital clock outside the Fenice to keep the workers and the public informed of the number of days remaining until Sacaim's 30 November 2003 deadline. When Sacaim took physical possession of the Fenice on 11 March, the clock read 630 days.

The count was down to 614 when I put on a hard hat and joined Laura Migliori in the Dante Room. It had been two years since she had first taken a look at the blackened walls, but only two weeks since she had been able to begin work. She and her assistants had already removed the overlay of mud and soot from the frescos. Now, with further treatment, they would erase some of the deeper stains and bring out the colours. In five of the six panels, only fragments of the frescos remained. However, two-thirds of the *Inferno* panel had survived. There were three figures in the foreground. A man in a red robe was fully intact, but only the lower halves of the other two were left.

'I'm pretty sure the one in red is Dante,' said Laura, 'and we think one of the others is Virgil. When we do colour testing, we hope to find out which. We'll be looking for traces of green, because he wore a laurel wreath.'

Much of the work on the Fenice would be completed away from the site and then brought to the theatre to be installed. Guerrino Lovato, the owner of the Mondonovo mask shop, had been hired to make the models for all the three-dimensional ornaments for the theatre hall. He rented a *magazzino* across the street from his shop to use as a studio where he would sculpt the clay models for the satyrs, nymphs, sylphs, caryatids, angels, animals, flowers, vines, leaves, lattices, shells, horns, scrolls, suns, moons, masks, swags, and swirls that would adorn the parapets of the boxes and the walls and ceiling of the theatre. From his originals, sculpted in clay, his assistants would make the negative plaster moulds in which ornaments would be cast in papier mâché and plaster by craftsmen in Mogliano; his assistants would make positive moulds to be copied by wood-carvers in Vicenza. To make sure that the ornaments would fit snugly on to the curving contours of the theatre, which did not yet exist, Lovato checked his work against a full-size model of half the theatre that had been erected in a warehouse in Marghera.

Laura Migliori and her two assistants would have to restore the *Inferno* frescos right where they were, in the midst of workmen putting large structural elements in place, installing air-conditioning ducts and electrical cables, and carrying out such other tasks as painting, plastering, welding, soldering, applying gold leaf, and laying floors of terrazzo and parquet. She would be working, in other words, surrounded by chaos – and happily.

'We all have a feeling of exhilaration,' she said. Her efforts, like those of everyone else, would be part of an attempt to re-create the Fenice as it was designed after the 1836 fire so that, as the architect Giambattista Meduna put it at the time, 'no part will be diminished in flamboyance [and] those who see it will say that the magnificence of the decorations of Versailles are no more splendid'.

As to whether the former opulence, magnificence, and flamboyance could be regained, Laura Migliori would say only, 'We've made a start. We've got the mud off.'

The opera music blasting out of the protesters' loudspeakers on the fifth anniversary of the Fenice fire carried across the Grand Canal to the Palace of Justice, where, as it happened, prosecutor Felice Casson was making his closing remarks in the arson trial of Enrico Carella and Massimiliano Marchetti. The charge of attempted murder had been set aside in an earlier session.

Casson sat alone at a table in the high-ceilinged chamber wearing black robes over a collarless shirt and facing a panel of three judges. He spoke for five hours, detailing the case against the two electricians. The defendants and their lawyers sat at tables behind him. Enrico Carella wore a dark suit, a silk tie, and polished black shoes; Massimiliano Marchetti was dressed in a sports jacket, corduroy trousers, a plain tie, and work shoes. Both were subdued. Carella shifted nervously in his chair.

Casson told the story of the fire in a meticulous, spellbinding narrative – the workers leaving the theatre at the end of the day, Carella pouring solvent on a pile of planks of wood upstairs in the *ridotto* in preparation for setting the fire later on, Carella and Marchetti hiding as the last of the workmen left, Carella using a blowtorch to ignite the fire while Marchetti stood lookout, the fire creeping, then roaring, through the theatre. Casson's narrative was accompanied by a computerized, three-dimensional re-enactment shown on four large television monitors placed around the courtroom.

In the course of his recitation, Casson made it clear that he had placed the two young electricians under near-constant, almost obsessive surveillance.

In one conversation, taped after a lengthy interrogation at police headquarters, Carella and Marchetti had got into their car unaware that it had been bugged. Their behaviour at this moment, Casson said, was significant:

'They get into the car, and you would think that after what they'd been through they would blurt out, as any normal, innocent person would, "They're crazy! This is madness! What do we have to do with the Fenice?" Instead Carella says, "Mauro better get his story in line." They were worried about somebody named Mauro. They were hiding him. Then Massimiliano tells Enrico that he didn't mention Mauro's last name to the police, and Enrico answers, "Good, perfect!"'

The recording was the first time Casson had heard mention of Mauro Galletta, a fishmonger who lived near the Fenice. According to Casson, Carella and Marchetti wanted to keep his existence unknown for two reasons. First, a few hours before the fire, Galletta had come to the Fenice at Carella's request to take photographs of the electrical work that Carella's company was doing at the time. Those photographs, once they came to light, proved that Carella was way behind schedule and faced a penalty charge, which Carella had repeatedly denied. The prospect of a penalty was central to Casson's explanation of a motive; it was just as important to Carella's defence to prove he was not facing a penalty. Second, after leaving the Fenice, Carella and Marchetti had *not* gone directly to the Lido as they had said; they had gone to their friend Mauro Galletta's house to smoke marijuana and eat pizza. According to Galletta, they arrived at his house a little after nine o'clock. This would have made it impossible for them to have reached the Lido by nine fifteen, as they had claimed.

Casson now estimated that it was not until ten o'clock that Carella and Marchetti had left for the Lido, where Carella claimed he had received the call telling him about the fire.

'By the time they were crossing the lagoon on the way to the Lido,' said Casson, 'the sky was all lit up. How could they *not* have known about the fire?' Carella had offered an absurd explanation, said Casson: they had been sitting with their backs to Venice.

Casson's surveillance picked up two virtual confessions from Carella and Marchetti. A plainclothes man sitting behind them on a *vaporetto* overheard Marchetti say to Carella, 'Don't worry, I won't rat on you.'

Then, in a conversation taped after a particularly gruelling police interrogation, Marchetti was heard to say, 'We're both going to jail,' to which Carella replied, 'They've got us. They've really got us.' Casson read these two quotes to the court, adding drily that he had omitted the profanities from both remarks.

One of the most damaging blows to Carella's credibility came from an unexpected source: his father, Renato Carella. When Renato Carella was asked how he had heard about the fire, he said his son had called to tell him at 10.10 p.m. That was twenty minutes before the first mention of the fire on television, but Enrico Carella had claimed that *he* had learned about the fire from someone who had just seen it on TV. Was Renato Carella sure about the time? Yes, he said, he was positive.

In fact, Renato Carella had become the mystery man in the case. He had set up his son's company for the sole purpose of receiving the electrical subcontract from Argenti in Rome. Renato Carella was then hired by Argenti to serve as its liaison at the Fenice. When Casson announced his original list of defendants in 1998, Renato Carella had not been among them. But Casson had named three suspects who were still under investigation. Two were Mafia bosses from Palermo. The other was Renato Carella. The Mafia bosses had since been dropped as suspects, but Carella remained in Casson's sights even at this late date, and Casson intended to keep him there indefinitely.

'I'd like to know more about Renato Carella myself,' said Giovanni Seno, Massimiliano Marchetti's lawyer, during a one-hour break in Casson's closing remarks. I had gone downstairs to take a walk in the Rialto food market and found myself in step with Seno. We started talking. Seno still had his air of cocky confidence, but I could tell he was worried. Casson had built a strong case, and Seno no longer argued that the fire had been caused by negligence. He now claimed that the hapless Marchetti was in the dark 'about what was going on that night'. He did not say the same for Enrico Carella, and he admitted that he had suspicions about Renato Carella. As we spoke, he kept looking round as if to make sure he was not being overheard.

'Look,' he said, 'I'm going to tell you some things you may not know. About how contracting and subcontracting work in Italy. Behind these big contracts – and this is just between you and me – there is almost always favouritism, some politics, and maybe a little bribery. I'm not saying that's what happened in this situation, but it would be unusual if it didn't. The way it works is this: a big company like Argenti wins a contract and then dumps all the work on to subcontractors who do the job as cheaply as possible. The big company doesn't do any of the work themselves. It doesn't send labourers. It does nothing. It gets the contract for, say, seven hundred fifty million lire [$375,000] and then turns around and hands out jobs to subcontractors for maybe six hundred million [$300,000]. The company makes a profit without lifting a finger. It goes on all the time, and it's not illegal. Now, in this case, certain people suspect that maybe – just maybe – it was Renato Carella, the lowly foreman, who secretly won the contract for Argenti.'

'How?'

'Maybe he had inside information. Maybe he knew the costs or what other competitors were bidding, but since he wasn't a registered contractor, he couldn't bid for the job himself. So he passes this valuable information to Argenti. Argenti tailors its bid to fit Renato's information and wins the contract. To show their gratitude, they throw some money Renato's way by subcontracting part of the work to a company Renato sets up for his son – a company that, bear in mind, didn't exist before, that had no track record. And then Argenti hires Renato as the foreman. Have I explained myself?'

Seno leaned a little closer. 'The way I figure it, Renato Carella, my client's uncle, was the one in control, the one who had the real power. It's not clear to me exactly how. I don't have specific information, but this guy is an operator. Right after the fire, even though he was under suspicion for arson, Renato Carella got another big public subcontract, this one at the Arsenal. He took Enrico along on that job, too.'

'But what has this got to do with the Fenice fire?'

'I'm giving you the broad picture. Renato Carella is a man with connections to lots of companies. Not just Argenti.'

'I understand,' I said.

'But inside that broad picture, there are some very curious specifics. We know, for instance, that at the time of the fire, the son had debts of a hundred and fifty million lire [$75,000]. Mysteriously, seven months after the fire, Renato Carella gives him the money to pay off the debts. That's on the record. If he's only a foreman, how can he afford to do that? Where did he get the money?'

'So you think,' I said, 'that the money might have come from whoever paid Carella to set the fire, assuming somebody did.'

'No, no!' Seno raised his right hand, as if swearing an oath. 'Don't misunderstand. I'm not saying that! I never said that! You'll have to draw your own conclusions.' He looked round again. 'But here's another curious fact: Renato Carella hired one of the most expensive attorneys in Italy, a guy who works for Prime Minister Berlusconi.'

'No kidding,' I said.

'This was for his own defence,' said Seno.

'And for his son?'
'Nothing.'
'What about his nephew?'
'Even less.'

At the end of his summation, Casson asked the court to find Carella and Marchetti guilty of arson and send them to prison for seven years. As to the possibility that the fire was ordered and paid for by others, he said an investigation was continuing and would perhaps lead to another trial later on.

Before the judges would issue their verdict, the trial would go into its second phase: charges against eight defendants for negligence and dereliction of duty.

Casson opened by arguing that convictions for arson did not automatically rule out criminal negligence.

'Attacks on works of art,' he said, 'especially theatres, are unfortunately not unusual in the Italian panorama. Since October 1991, when the Petruzzelli Opera House in Bari burned, there have been a dozen instances of damage to theatres and art galleries by arson. Therefore, in 1996, a fire at the Fenice was within the realm of possibility, and those responsible for its security should have known this. But nobody gave a damn.'

He read the names of the defendants and the prison terms he had selected for each. The list was headed by ex-mayor Massimo Cacciari: nine months in jail. A sentence of that length was purely symbolic, however, since any jail term of less than two years was automatically suspended. The only other of the eight to draw a proposed sentence of less than two years was the Fenice's caretaker, Gilberto Paggiaro. Casson considered Paggiaro's absence from his post on the night of the fire to be negligence of a less serious nature, because it had not contributed to the hazardous conditions at the theatre before the fire. Casson asked that Paggiaro, who had suffered two heart-attacks and depression since the fire, be given a sentence of eighteen months.

The other six were charged with a long list of derelictions and malfeasances, from failure to control the handling and storage of flammable materials to allowing the fire-extinguisher system to be dismantled before a new one was installed.

The most serious offender, in Casson's view, was the chief engineer of the Comune of Venice, who was the top executive in charge of the theatre's renovation. For him, Casson proposed a four-year prison term; for his two assistants, two years; and for the top management of the Fenice, the general manager and the secretary-general, three years.

Arguments for the defence all had one theme in common: the denial of responsibility. Officials at the top pointed sideways and downwards. Those at the bottom pointed up.

The most novel defence was offered by the lawyer for Gianfranco Pontel, the Fenice's general manager. Pontel's attorney claimed, at great length and with a straight face, that his client was responsible for the safety and security of the Fenice theatre and that when the Fenice was not putting on productions, it ceased to be a theatre and became a mere complex of buildings for which his client had no legal obligations at all. The theatre had vanished, at least where Gianfranco Pontel was concerned, and would reappear only when productions once again were mounted on its stage. The lawyer's speech drew laughter from the gallery and could have fitted seamlessly into *Alice in Wonderland* or any number of Gilbert and Sullivan operettas. Gianfranco Pontel had been a political appointee, one who was always thought to have been an odd choice as general manager of the Fenice, as he had no musical background and spent most of his time in Rome. In any case, since the fire, Pontel had moved on to become secretary-general of the Venice Biennale.

When the second phase of the trial was finished, the judges retired to consider all the evidence. At the end of the month, the presiding judge read the verdicts to a crowded courtroom:

Enrico Carella – guilty of arson, seven years in jail. Massimiliano

Marchetti – guilty of arson, six years in jail. All eight negligence defendants – not guilty. Arson had been the sole cause of the fire.

Giovanni Seno was incensed. 'The verdict was written by the end of the first day in court!' he told reporters. Carella, who had not been present at the reading of the verdict, gave a statement to the *Gazzettino*, proclaiming his innocence. Marchetti said nothing. The two would remain free, pending appeal.

Two months later, the judges filed the *motivazione*, their explanation of how they reached their verdict. Their report contained a chilling revelation:

'Carella and Marchetti were not alone,' the judges said. 'They were surrogates for others who remained in the shadows, people with financial interests of such magnitude that, by comparison, the sacrifice of a theatre would have seemed a small thing.'

The judges had put the weight of their authority behind the notion that the arson had been paid for by persons unknown. 'For the judges,' the *Gazzettino* reported, 'what had once been merely an investigative theory has now become a certainty.'

A presumptive spotlight fell on Renato Carella. But three months later, Renato Carella was dead of lung cancer. I called on Casson at his office in the Tribunal building to ask what effect this would have on the investigation.

'It's over,' he said simply. 'Renato Carella was the focus of our investigation. We thought he might have been the link between the boys and the money. He had contacts with a number of companies outside Venice. We were investigating him and also looking into every contractor and subcontractor that was hired to work on the Fenice, but we were never able to come up with any concrete evidence. And now, with his death, all trace has been lost.'

'What about the boys?' I asked. 'Have they shown any inclination to talk?'

'On several occasions, they told us they would give us further

THE CITY OF FALLING ANGELS

information about him, but they changed their minds every time. And, unfortunately, we have a huge number of cases that demand our attention. Until there is something new — like a statement from Carella or Marchetti — the case won't be reopened. We simply don't have the time to pursue it.'

'The father's dead, the trail goes cold, and the mystery lingers on,' said Ludovico De Luigi with a chuckle. 'It's all about money, as usual. Not love — money. The perfect ending, for Venice.'

De Luigi was sitting in his ground-floor studio in front of an unfinished painting of a jewelled dress floating against a barren landscape, as if it were being worn by an invisible woman.

'I'm painting a portrait of Peggy Guggenheim's self-esteem,' he said. 'It's the gold evening gown she was wearing in the famous photograph Man Ray took of her in the 1920s. It's a Poiret dress.' The photograph had appeared on the dust jacket of Peggy Guggenheim's autobiography, *Out of This Century*, which De Luigi had tacked to the side of his easel.

'Why a perfect ending?' I asked. 'Things are left hanging.'

'Yes, but this is the sort of ending Venice can live with, happily and for ever.' He daubed gold paint on the canvas. 'Look what the story offers: a great fire, a cultural calamity, the spectacle of public officials blaming each other, an unseemly rush for the money to rebuild the theatre, the satisfaction of a trial with guilty verdicts and jail sentences, the pride of the Fenice's rebirth, and' — he lifted his brush and looked up — 'an unsolved mystery. Money secretly changing hands. Unnamed culprits hiding in the shadows. It stimulates the imagination, gives people the freedom to make up any scenario they want. What more could anyone ask?'

The digital clock outside the Fenice stood at 537 on the day Laura Migliori found traces of green paint exactly where she had hoped to find them, meaning that the truncated figure in the foreground *had* been Virgil after all. At one o'clock that same day, an appellate court in

Mestre upheld the guilty verdicts of Enrico Carella and Massimiliano Marchetti. Lawyers for the two young men announced they would take their case to a higher court, the court of *cassazione* in Rome, for the second and final appeal.

A year later, in midsummer 2003, the theatre resembled a life-size plywood model of itself: bare ceiling, bare walls, and five tiers of bare wooden boxes. It seemed impossible that the Fenice would be finished in four months, but construction managers assured the press that the rebuilding was still on target. Shortly after noon on day 140, word came from Rome that the *cassazione* court had rejected the final appeal of Carella and Marchetti. They would go to jail.

The police arrived at Marchetti's house at 4.00 p.m. and led him away in handcuffs to begin serving a sentence of six years.

'That *cassazione* court really busted my balls,' said Marchetti's lawyer, Giovanni Seno, when I called him a week afterwards. 'They usually give a person a couple of days to get his affairs in order before they finalize the sentence and lock him up. Ball-breakers! Last year I had a guy sentenced to nine years for drug trafficking, and they let a month go by before they arrested him. But that's nothing. My associate has a woman defendant who's a drug addict/robber/prostitute, and she's still free after a year and a half, because they can't find the paperwork from the appeals court, so they haven't finalized her sentence. Marchetti they grab in a couple of hours! Tell me, where was he going to run off to with a newborn baby girl and a wife? But *Carella!*'

Enrico Carella had not been home when the police came to get him, nor did he turn up later on in the day, or the next day. In an interview two months earlier, he had told Gianluca Amadori of the *Gazzettino* that if his appeal failed, he would serve his term. Carella's defence attorney said shortly after the appeal was rejected that he had already spoken with Carella and that he would surrender himself soon. On the third day, the Venetian authorities pronounced Carella 'missing' but not 'in hiding'. At the end of the week, they declared him a fugitive.

'So who forfeits the bail money?' I asked Seno. 'And how much was it?'

'What bail?' he said. 'We don't have a bail system in Italy. We had one for two or three years, but there weren't any bail bondsmen, like you have in America, so only the rich defendants were able to get off. It became a social issue.'

'Do you think the police are still looking for him?'

'I know they are, because obviously it's a humiliating defeat for them. They didn't catch the one they should have caught. In my opinion, Carella behaved like someone who was going to take off. He prepared for it. Even the interview he gave the *Gazzettino* was part of the set-up, saying he'd serve his term if the *cassazione* went against him.

'It's not over yet. I've been in this business thirty years, and I'm not used to losing cases. I haven't shelved the file. I have it all on computer. And I promise you that if something happens, I'll let you know. I haven't told you everything. I have to be honest with you. I haven't told you everything.'

Whatever it was that Giovanni Seno was holding back from me, it could not have been much comfort to Massimiliano Marchetti, who was serving time in a jail in Padua – the same jail Seno's old Mafia client, Felice 'Angel Face' Maniero, had broken out of a few years before.

I went to Solzano to see the Marchettis. We sat in their kitchen drinking Coke from a plastic litre bottle, as we had on my first visit.

'Because of "Angel Face" Maniero,' Marchetti's father said, 'they keep the prisoners locked in their cells all day now.'

Although the Marchettis were careworn and depressed, I sensed they felt some relief knowing that the countdown to a conclusion of their nightmare had already begun. With good behaviour, Massimiliano could be out in two years and eight months.

'But they still find ways of torturing him,' said his mother. 'Last week they sent him a formal letter telling him his sentence had been miscalculated and that he would have to serve an additional fourteen days.'

'Then they sent him a bill for court costs,' said his father. 'Two thousand five hundred eighty-two euros.' Signora Marchetti shook her head.

'Have you heard anything about your nephew, Enrico Carella?'

'No,' said Signora Marchetti.

'What has your sister said about his disappearance?'

'I haven't spoken to her,' she said.

'Really? Since when?'

'It's been about three months, ever since Massimiliano went to jail. She stopped talking to me. She hasn't called.'

'And you haven't called her?'

'No. She's the one who should call.'

'Is this because you feel that Enrico is responsible for all your troubles?'

'We just wish he'd never offered Massimiliano the job,' said her husband.

When I came back to Venice, I went to the Giudecca to see Lucia Carella, Enrico's mother. She had not heard from her son since the day he vanished.

'I prefer not hearing from him,' she said, 'because hearing from him means something has happened. When I don't hear anything, I think he's okay. Maybe. As okay as a runaway can be.'

'Do you assume your telephone is tapped?'

'Telephones, cell phones, his ex-girlfriends' phones, everybody's phone. They're hoping he'll call me. I hear strange noises when I'm on the phone.'

'In his interview with the *Gazzettino*, Enrico said he thought Massimiliano's parents blame him for everything. Why did he think so?'

'The way they acted.'

'Did they say anything directly to Enrico?'

'No, absolutely not.'

'Your sister tells me the two of you haven't spoken in about three months.'

'She called the day Massimiliano was arrested, but I haven't heard from her since. My mother lives with me, and that means she hasn't spoken to her mother either. And since I am eight years older – and my mother, by the way, is eighty – I think it should be her to call us, or at least call her mother.'

'So that's the way it stands.'

'She has always been the smallest one and the most spoiled. She thinks I'm the one who should call, and I think she's the one who should call. It's stupid, but the longer it goes on, the worse it gets.'

'It's sad.'

'Yes, it's sad. But maybe suddenly I'll just pick up the phone and call her. That's the kind of person I am.'

'Your sister is probably a little distracted at this point.'

'Yes, she is distracted, but I am more distracted than she is. At least she knows where her son is. I don't.'

15
Open House

T HE NARROW CANAL BETWEEN THE Gritti Hotel and Palazzo
Contarini was the only route along which boats could ferry
building materials from the Grand Canal to the Fenice. The first
cargoes had been disassembled cranes and scaffolding, then bricks,
beams, pipes, and planks – the building blocks of the theatre. Now,
after some twenty thousand boatloads, came the refinements: the gilded
ornaments, the painted canvases, the lighting fixtures, the chairs
upholstered in rose-coloured velvet. The day-counting clock in front
of the Fenice was down to two digits, and work was still on schedule,
give or take a few days.

When at long last the Fenice shed its scaffolding and wooden
barriers, the gloom lifted from Campo San Fantin. The Ristorante
Antico Martini came out from the shadows and basked in the glow of
the Fenice's freshly cleaned façade. 'We left a few streaks of discolora-
tion here and there so it wouldn't look too new,' said Franco Bajo, the
chief construction engineer. 'That's the complaint we expect to hear
most often, that the Fenice doesn't look old enough.'

Inside the theatre, the auditorium was once again becoming an
Arcadian forest glade. Vines, flowers, woodland animals, and mythical
creatures climbed the walls and parapets towards the ceiling, where
bare-breasted nymphs bathed in the gilded swirls of a sylvan stream.

As it turned out, none of the thousands of colour photographs of the
theatre's interior had been much use in determining its true colours.
The silk lampshades on the sconces around the hall had cast a
distorting yellow glow. Only one source could be trusted: the opening

343

scene of Luchino Visconti's 1954 *Senso*, the first Italian feature-length film shot in colour. Visconti had been meticulous in re-creating the look of Italy in 1866. He removed the Fenice's lampshades to make it appear as though the theatre was lit by gaslight and, by doing so, achieved near-perfect colour reproduction.

It was decided that the Fenice would open with a week of orchestral concerts rather than full-scale opera; the backstage crew had not yet been trained in the use of the computerized scenery-moving machinery. Operas would begin a year later. For the grand opening night, Riccardo Muti would conduct the Fenice's orchestra and chorus.

To cope with the rush for tickets, the Fenice held an auction on the Internet, with prices ranging from $750 to $2,500 at first, then dropping each day, as tickets were sold. It was a game of box-office chicken: the longer one waited, the cheaper the seat but the more limited the selection. Wait too long and the concert might be sold out.

That was not the entire story, however. It was no secret that hundreds of opening-night seats were being given away to celebrities and the well-connected. Only fools and the truly desperate would buy a ticket. Since this was a pageant I felt obliged to witness, however, I gritted my teeth and bought a seat in the third tier on the last day of the auction, for $600.

Mayor Costa had done his best to promote the evening as a world-class, star-studded event. His staff leaked the names of likely to attend celebrities, including the actors Al Pacino, Jeremy Irons, and Joseph Fiennes, all of whom were in the throes of making *The Merchant of Venice* – but not in Venice. The movie was being filmed on the cheap in Luxembourg. Mayor Costa, all but down on his knees, promised that if they came to the opening, he would fly them back to Luxembourg by private jet immediately after the concert, in time for filming the next morning.

As dignitaries began arriving two days before the concert, security tightened around the Fenice. Streets were blocked off. Police and firemen were more than ever in evidence, although for different reasons. The police were protecting the VIPs from terrorists; the firemen were staging noisy demonstrations over a contract dispute, hoping to embarrass Mayor Costa.

When the president and first lady of Italy, Carlo and Franca Ciampi, arrived from Rome, the local and national media chronicled their every move. The *Corriere della Sera* reported that the Ciampis had passed up a high-society luncheon, to be given in their honour by Larry Lovett, in favour of a sentimental lunch at Taverna La Fenice, where they had dined on their honeymoon fifty-nine years before. According to the *Gazzettino* the Ciampis ate baby shrimp and polenta, creamed cod, pasta with artichokes and scampi, scalloped sea bass, and Venetian pastries along with prosecco and Tokay.

As the hour of the inaugural concert approached, I recalled the mask-maker Guerrino Lovato's explanation of the opera-going experience as a gradually unfolding ritual that began at home with the opera-goer getting dressed. That being the case, my night at the opera started at about the time I was inserting my shirt studs with one hand, holding the telephone receiver with the other, and listening to Ludovico De Luigi pronounce the evening an ignoble farce.

'It will be an exercise in vanity, vulgarity, and self-congratulation,' he said. 'Costa has been boasting that the reopening of the Fenice means "the city still has a pulse". It means no such thing. Sadly, Venice is already dead. Everything is based on the exploitation of the corpse – the shameless exploitation of the corpse.' De Luigi would not be attending the opening. The temptation to pull off another *scherzo* would be too great, he said, and the police were already on edge, what with the protesting firemen complicating security. There would be zero tolerance for any sort of spontaneous artistic expression tonight. Anyway, De Luigi had not been invited, and he had no intention of buying a ticket.

My opening-night ritual unfolded further as I stepped on to the

Number 1 *vaporetto* for the ride down the Grand Canal. It had been reported a few days earlier that Enrico Carella had been briefly sighted on a *vaporetto*. I spoke with Felice Casson afterwards.

'I doubt that the police are really looking for him,' Casson said. 'If he were a terrorist or a Mafia boss of a certain importance, then special search teams would be set up, with either the *carabinieri* or the police, and then it would be only a matter of time. They have methods that work very well. But they probably don't think Carella is worth the effort. Other, more dangerous cases have higher priority.'

It crossed my mind to pass this information on to Lucia Carella, who would probably have taken it as welcome news. But that would be meddling; besides, Casson was far too clever. If I repeated what he had told me, Signora Carella might let down her guard and play right into his hands. It was none of my business. In any case, Enrico Carella was not on board the Number 1 *vaporetto* the night of the Fenice reopening.

Bright white television lights illuminated Campo San Fantin and the red carpet cascading down the steps of the Fenice. Ahead of me, President Ciampi entered the theatre, all but hidden inside a phalanx of praetorian guards wearing ceremonial helmets topped by horse tails that arched and fell, like fountains of white hair.

I went directly upstairs to the Dante Room, which was now the bar, curious to see how the *Inferno* fresco had turned out. Laura Migliori and her crew had revived the colours in the surviving segment, sketching the missing figures in outline against a plain background. I was looking at the sketch of Virgil and his laurel wreath when I felt a tug at my elbow.

I turned and confronted a vaguely familiar, florid-faced man, who was smiling as if he knew me. It was Massimo Donadon – the Rat Man of Treviso. I had not seen him since the Carnival ball in 1996.

'Signor Donadon!' I said. 'How's the rat-poison business?'

'I'm just back from the Netherlands,' he said. 'I have new customers.'

'What's your secret ingredient for Dutch rats?' I asked.

'Salmon and cheese,' he said.

'No Dutch chocolate?'

'A little, not much.'

Donadon's expression suddenly turned serious.

'Something very strange is happening in Italy,' he said. He motioned for me to move towards the corner of the room, where we could hear each other better.

'I've noticed,' he said, 'that in the past few years Italian rats have begun to prefer eating plastic to Parmesan cheese.'

'Really!'

'My entire business, if you remember, is based on the idea that rats eat what people eat.'

'Yes, of course I remember.'

'But people don't eat plastic!' he said. 'I thought, "My God, I'm ruined! What am I going to do? Rats are beginning to eat food that human beings don't eat! This cannot be true!"'

Then, just as quickly, Donadon's face perked up again.

'At last it came to me!' he said. 'Plastic is a non-food. True?'

'Yes, absolutely,' I said.

'And I realized: *people eat non-food, too.*'

'We do?'

'Yes! We eat fast food! Fast food is non-food! Plastic is the rats' equivalent of fast food! It means that all is well: rats are still imitating the eating habits of people, and, like people, they are losing their taste for natural food. They are going for junk food.'

'What are you going to do about it?' I asked.

'I've already done it!' said Donadon triumphantly. 'I've put granulated plastic in my Italian rat poison!'

'Does it work?' I asked.

'Like a dream,' he said.

I congratulated Donadon on his new success and started working my way towards the auditorium and the stairway to the third tier. On the stairs, I encountered Bea Guthrie. She had flown over from New York

THE CITY OF FALLING ANGELS

for the opening, accompanied by the new president of Save Venice, Beatrice Rossi-Landi. Save Venice had been a major donor to the Fenice, contributing $300,000 for the ceiling.

I took my seat and looked out at the five gilt-encrusted tiers of boxes. They were dazzling, but the colours were noticeably brighter and fresher than they had been in the old theatre. The gilt, in fact, looked new. I expected, however, that when the lights were dimmed for the concert, it would all tone down a bit. For now anyway, the bright lights made it easier to see the details and look at people.

There were no movie stars in sight, nor would there be. Pacino, Irons, and Fiennes were fogbound in Luxembourg.

Downstairs on the orchestra level, Princess Michael of Kent, tall and blonde: a coronet twinkling in her hair, stood in the centre aisle, chatting with the ballerina Carla Fracci. The princess's hostess, the Marchesa Barbara Berlingieri, hovered close by her side, turning when the princess turned, pausing when the princess paused. Larry Lovett approached to say hello. Lovett's new Venetian Heritage had been a great success. He had wisely chosen a somewhat different mandate from that of Save Venice by funding restorations not only in Venice but throughout the old Venetian Republic — in Croatia, Turkey, and elsewhere. Although Venetian Heritage had not contributed to the rebuilding of the Fenice, Lovett had been given two choice seats in the orchestra, on the aisle. That might account, I thought, for the look of displeasure on Bea Guthrie's face as she climbed higher and higher towards *her* complimentary seat, all the while coming closer and closer to the Save Venice-sponsored ceiling. Whether her seat assignment had been the result of a consensus within the Fenice hierarchy or the work of a lone antagonist, the insult could not have been more obvious. Larry Lovett was clearly still the favourite among Venetians with power.

A hush came over the audience as members of the Fenice orchestra took the stage and began tuning up; the chorus filed in behind them. I looked around the hall and recognized a man sitting in a box directly across from me. He was scanning the crowd through a pair of opera glasses, and it occurred to me that he might have been looking for Jane Rylands. Mrs Rylands had recently taken people by surprise by publishing a book of short stories set in Venice. Some of her fictional characters appeared to be based on real people, or certain aspects of real people, or combinations of real people. The man with the opera glasses had discovered a number of uncomfortable similarities between himself and a character who was the butt of a particularly vicious satire in Jane's book. Jane insisted that all of her characters were total fabrications. However, at a recent Guggenheim reception, Philip Rylands had engaged the man in conversation, and at one point lightheartedly referred to an innocuous detail of the man's ancestry, not realizing that this detail had been invented by Jane as part of her character's thin disguise.

The man stared icily at Philip.

'That's true, isn't it?' Philip asked, referring to the ancestral detail.

'Only in your wife's book!' the man replied.

Jane Rylands had wisely steered clear of any character or plot-line that would remind anyone of Olga Rudge or the Ezra Pound Foundation. But one of her most belittling caricatures bore a twisted resemblance to a woman who had been among her most vocal critics at the time of the Ezra Pound Foundation imbroglio. This and other unsympathetic portraits created the impression that Jane Rylands had used the stories as a score-settling device.

As for the now-defunct Ezra Pound Foundation, one of its would-be assets, the Hidden Nest cottage of Ezra Pound and Olga Rudge, was currently providing a substantial rental income for their daughter, Mary de Rachewiltz. Pound memorabilia had been increasing in value. In 1999, Mary de Rachewiltz had offered for sale, through Glenn Horowitz Bookseller in New York, 139 of her parents' books, which had been stored for years in Brunnenburg Castle. They included signed first editions of the *Cantos* and books by other authors, many with marginal notations by Pound and Rudge. Horowitz's asking price came

THE CITY OF FALLING ANGELS

to a total of over $1 million, prompting people to wonder what the 208 boxes of Olga Rudge's papers, sold to the Ezra Pound Foundation for $7,000 in 1987, and later to Yale for an undisclosed sum, might now be worth on the open market.

Riccardo Muti strode on to the stage, his glossy black hair falling into his eyes. He bowed, raised his baton, and led the orchestra in the Italian national anthem. The audience, rising to its feet, turned towards the royal box at the rear of the hall and saluted the presidential couple with a sustained ovation. Standing at the Ciampis' side in the royal box were the patriarch of Venice, Cardinal Angelo Scola, Mayor and Maura Costa, and former prime minister Lamberto Dini, whose wife, Donatella, had broken the news of the fire at the Save Venice Ball in New York eight years earlier.

My gaze drifted up to the lion of St Mark's, mounted atop the royal box like a burnished diadem in exactly the spot once occupied by the insignias of France and Austria. It reminded me of what Count Ranieri da Mosto had said about the royal box: 'It's not Napoleon's royal box any longer, nor is it Austria's. It's ours.'

The gift to the city of an eight-foot statue of Napoleon had sparked an intensely emotional debate over whether to accept it. The statue had been commissioned in 1811 by Venetian merchants who were grateful to Napoleon for turning the city into a free port. It had stood in St Mark's for two years until Venice fell to the Austrians in 1814. After that, it was lost for two hundred years and had only recently surfaced at Sotheby's in New York, where the French Committee to Safeguard Venice had bought it for $350,000 in order to make what they had assumed would be a welcome gift for Venice.

The moderates, including Mayor Costa and the director of civic museums, Giandomenico Romanelli, argued that Napoleon and the statue were simply part of Venice's history and therefore worthy of being displayed. The anti-Bonapartists, whose ranks included Count Girolamo Marcello, Count da Mosto, and most of the centre right,

OPEN HOUSE

countered that on those grounds one could argue that the bronze bust of Mussolini in storage at the Correr Museum should be displayed as well.

The debate rang with endless recitations of Napoleon's thefts, desecrations, and other outrages against Venice. Virtually everyone took one side or the other. Peter and Rose Lauritzen were vocal anti-Bonapartists. I dropped in on a lecture Peter was giving to a group of English students in the Accademia. The first words I heard him say were, 'Napoleon saw to the suppression of forty parishes in Venice and the destruction – *razed to the ground!* – of one hundred and seventy-six religious buildings and more than eighty palaces, all of which were decorated with paintings and other works of art. In addition, Napoleon's agents saw to the listing for confiscation of twelve thousand paintings, a great many of which were sent to Paris to enrich the collections of something called the Musée Napoleon. I trust if any of you have been to Paris you have been to the Musée Napoleon. Today it's rather better known as the Louvre, and of course it is the single greatest monument to organized theft in the history of art!'

A poll conducted by the *Gazzettino* showed the public to be twelve to one against accepting the statue. Nevertheless, Mayor Costa did accept it, and in the dead of night it was smuggled into the Correr Museum, where it was installed in a niche behind a protective shield of Plexiglas. Months later the anti-Bonapartists brought Napoleon before an ad hoc Nuremberg-style tribunal and found him guilty as charged.

At the height of the controversy, the leaders of the anti-statue coalition sent two menacing letters to Jerome Zieseniss, the head of the French committee, advising him to get out of town. Zieseniss expressed his outrage, and city officials hastened to condemn the letter writers. Though tempers had since cooled, the gift of the statue was still widely resented as an insult to Venice. In spite of all that, however, Zieseniss had been given two excellent seats at the Fenice's reopening. He was

351

sitting in the orchestra beside the chairman of the World Monuments Fund, Marilyn Perry.

The concert opened with Beethoven's 'Consecration of the House', which was, of course, an apt choice. It put me in mind of the comment Robert Browning made in 1890 to his son, Pen, upon learning that Pen and his rich American wife had bought the enormous Palazzo Rezzonico on the Grand Canal. 'Don't be a little man in a big house', Browning warned. Henry James, visiting the Curtises at Palazzo Barbaro a bit farther down the Grand Canal, wrote to his sister about the news, '[Palazzo Rezzonico] is altogether royal and imperial – but "Pen" isn't kingly and the *train de vie* remains to be seen. Gondoliers ushering in friends from pensions won't fill it out.' Three years later, James wrote to Ariana Curtis, 'Poor, grotesque little Pen – and poor sacrificed little Mrs Pen. There seems but one way to be sane in this queer world, but there are many ways of being mad! and a palazzo-madness is almost as alarming – or as convulsive – as an earthquake – which indeed it essentially resembles.' Pen Browning had not filled out Palazzo Rezzonico in any memorable way. In fact, it was Robert Browning himself, ironically, who stole the honours from his son by dying in the house and being remembered by a plaque attached to the façade.

The Curtises had 'filled out' Palazzo Barbaro admirably for over a century. And, now that the Barbaro had passed into the hands of Ivano Beggio, the proprietor of the motorcycle-maker Aprilia, Venice was watching to see how well the Beggios would fill it out. Beggio had wasted no time in seeing to the cleaning of the Barbaro's double façade. He removed important paintings from the *piano nobile* for cleaning and restoration.

But then . . . nothing. Months, then years, went by. The windows of the *piano nobile* remained boarded up. The Beggios were rarely seen in Venice. Specialists hired to work on the restoration were utterly perplexed. Speculation abounded that the Beggios had hoped that their ownership of Palazzo Barbaro would lead to their acceptance in Venetian society and that they had been disappointed when it did not.

Then the truth emerged. Ivano Beggio was broke! The phenomenally successful Aprilia motorcycle company was facing bankruptcy. Palazzo Barbaro was once again for sale – but not for the $6 million Beggio had paid the Curtises for it. The new asking price was said to be $14 million. No offers had yet been made, and, tragically, none would be forthcoming from the young, idealistic Daniel Curtis – the only Curtis in five generations to have any Venetian blood in his veins. Daniel had died suddenly from an aneurysm at the age of forty-seven. For a full week after his death, loving notices had appeared in the *Gazzettino*. One in particular captured the spirit of all the others: DANIEL. 'A friend for ever, *a great Venetian.*'

The Fenice's house lights did not dim when the music started, because the evening was being televised, which meant that the baroque hall would be as bright as a TV studio all night. The theatre's subtleties would be lost, at least for now. I closed my eyes and listened to the music. After Beethoven came Igor Stravinsky (buried in Venice), Antonio Caldara (born in Venice), and Richard Wagner (died in Venice). I concentrated on the sound. Were the acoustics a success? The experts had said they were. But, of course, for people sitting in boxes, especially towards the rear of the boxes, the sound quality would never be as good as it was for people sitting out in the open.

The most distinctive sounds in Venice, however, were not really the ones inside the Fenice. Jürgen Reinhold, the Fenice's master acoustics engineer, had put his finger on it when he expressed surprise at having discovered that the ambient nocturnal sound level in Venice was a very low thirty-two decibels. Forty-five decibels was typical of most other cities. The absence of automobile traffic, of course, accounted for the difference. 'All this Venetian quietness has me bewitched,' Reinhold had said. 'When I came back to my house in Munich, the noise was unbearable. But it was only the usual traffic sounds.'

I, too, had been bewitched by the peacefulness of Venice, and by much more about Venice besides. What had at first been largely an attraction to the city's beauty evolved into a more generalized enchantment as time went on. From the very start I had kept Count Marcello's cautionary words in mind: 'Everyone in Venice is acting . . . Venetians never tell the truth. We mean precisely the opposite of what we say.'

I knew that in Venice I had been told truths, half-truths, and outright lies, and I was never entirely sure which was which. But time often clarified matters. Only a few days before the Fenice reopened, for example, I had come upon a revealing piece of information while I was walking along the arcade of the Doge's Palace. I noticed a plaque with the name 'Loredan' inscribed on it. I thought immediately of Count Alvise Loredan, the man I had met at the Carnival ball, who had held up three fingers as he told me, more than once, that there had been three doges in his family.

That much was quite true.

Count Loredan also told me that a fifteenth-century Loredan had defeated the Turks and thereby prevented them from crossing the Adriatic and wiping out Christianity. There was, in fact, a well-known Pietro Loredan who had defeated the Turks in the fifteenth century. But the man commemorated on the plaque at St Mark's was a *seventeenth*-century Loredan named Girolamo, a coward who had been exiled from Venice in disgrace for having abandoned the fortress of Tenedos to the Turks, 'to the great detriment of Christianity and [his] country'.

Alvise Loredan had been under no obligation to wash his family's dirty linen in front of me. His deception was harmless enough, and I accepted it as part of the act, part of the perpetual myth and mystery of Venice.

When the concert was over, I came out into Campo San Fantin, where I noticed a man with two scarves draped round his neck – one white silk, one red wool – standing at the centre of a burst of flashbulbs. It was Vittorio Sgarbi, the art critic who had made himself persona non grata at the Courtauld Institute in London by walking out with two rare books in his satchel. Sgarbi was posing for photographers with one arm slung round Signora Ciampi and the other clasped round the waist of a woman wearing a cap of pearls. Sgarbi had *not* been made Italy's minister of culture, as it had been rumoured he might be; he had been named under-secretary of state for culture, a lesser but still prominent position – and a surprising one, under the circumstances.

At the edge of the *campo*, a dozen silk-stockinged men in black capes and tricorne hats were waiting to escort the eleven hundred members of the audience to boats headed for the Arsenal and a great celebratory banquet. Teams of party planners had been working on the decorations for weeks. The *Gazzettino* had scheduled an early printing of the next day's newspaper – 15 December 2003 – so that as guests took their seats at the banquet, they would be greeted by a glorious, full-colour photograph of the Fenice splashed across the paper's front page. World events had intervened during the day, however, and as a consequence, tonight's guests would sit down instead to a page-one photograph of a grubby and bewildered Saddam Hussein, who had been captured in Iraq only hours earlier. But no matter.

Having dinner with a thousand people did not appeal to me especially, and anyway I had other plans. I left Campo San Fantin and walked along Calle della Fenice towards the rear of the theatre, then over a small bridge to the house on Calle Caotorta, where I paid a visit to Signora Seguso, now the widow of the maestro Archimede Seguso, the 'Wizard of Fire'.

We stood at the window where Signora Seguso had seen smoke rising from the Fenice eight years earlier, and from which Archimede Seguso had watched the fire all night. Signora Seguso said she did not care to look out of the window at the Fenice any more, because in spite of all the talk about '*com'era, dov'era*,' the Fenice was definitely not 'as it was' before the fire – not from her window, at any rate. The Fenice's north wing, thirty feet across the canal, had been rebuilt several feet taller than it used to be, and an array of metal ducts, pipes, and fences had been mounted on top, making the view look more like the industrial landscape of Marghera than the lovely vista of terracotta rooftops that she and her husband had enjoyed before.

No smudge, no scar, no trace or telltale sign of the fire remained anywhere in sight, except for the swirling, spiralling chips of colour embedded in the tall black vase on Signora Seguso's bedside table. This vase had been the first of the more than a hundred 'Fenice' pieces that Archimede Seguso had made as his unique, eyewitness account of the fire. He had brought this one home as a gift for his wife.

And where were the others?

Signora Seguso sighed. It had been ten years since she had spoken to her younger son, Giampaolo. Her husband's estate was still the subject of a legal battle, four years after his death, and the 'Fenice' bowls and vases were at the centre of it. Until a court could decide their fate, those creations of love and fire would remain locked in a storeroom at the glassworks – seen by no one, gathering dust.

GLOSSARY

Italian words are defined the first time they appear in the text. The following words occur more than once:

acqua alta
   High water, i.e., high tide.

altana
   An open rooftop deck, usually wooden.

buongiorno
   Hello, good day.

calle
   A narrow street; plural: *calli*.

campo
   An open square or plaza; plural: *campi*.

capito
   Understood.

carabiniere
   The national police, or policeman; plural: *carabinieri*.

cassazione
   Appeals court.

ciao
   Hello, also goodbye. Used in the familiar.

'com'era, dov'era'

'As it was, where it was.' The slogan adopted for the rebuilding of the Fenice Opera House, exactly as it had been before it burned.

comune

Municipal government.

doge

The head of state of the former Venetian Republic.

lira

Italian monetary denomination, before introduction of the euro; plural: *lire*.

magazzino

Storeroom, warehouse.

marchesa

Marchioness, ranks above a contessa, below a duchess; the masculine is *marchese*.

palazzo

Palace.

piano nobile

The principal floor of a palace.

ponte

Bridge.

portego

The central hall of a palace.

prosecco

Sparkling white wine, produced in the Veneto region.

putti

Babies, children, or cherubs in paintings and sculpture.

ridotto

Lobby, foyer.

rio

Canal in Venice; elsewhere, a stream, a brook.

salone

Large drawing room.

scherzo

A joke.

stucchi

Sculpted plaster decoration.

tu

You, the familiar form.

vaporetto

Water bus.

PEOPLE, ORGANIZATIONS AND COMPANIES

Argenti
A Roman construction firm that subcontracted electrical work to Viet for the renovation of the Fenice Opera House.

Aulenti, Gae
Architect associated with the Impregilo consortium and architect Antonio (Tonci) Foscari in their bid to rebuild the Fenice Opera House.

Berlingieri, Marchesa Barbara
Vice president of Save Venice.

Bernardi, Nicola
Fruit-and-vegetable dealer. Friend of poet Mario Stefani.

Cacciari, Massimo
Mayor of Venice, philosopher, university professor.

Carella, Enrico
Owner of Viet, a small electrical contracting company working at the Fenice Opera House.

Carella, Lucia
Mother of Enrico Carella, housekeeper at the Cipriani Hotel.

Carella, Renato
Father of Enrico Carella, foreman of his son's work site at the Fenice.

Casson, Felice
Prosecutor.

Cicogna, Countess Anna Maria
Board member of Save Venice; daughter of Giuseppe Volpi, who was finance minister under Mussolini and founder of Venice Film Festival; half-sister of Giovanni Volpi.

Cipriani, Arrigo
Proprietor of Harry's Bar.

Corriere della Sera
Milan-based daily newspaper.

Costa, Paolo
Mayor of Venice after Massimo Cacciari, former rector of Ca' Foscari University and Italy's minister of public works.

Curtis family
(American) Owners and residents of Palazzo Barbaro since 1885. First generation, originally of Boston: Daniel and wife, Ariana; second: Ralph and wife, Lisa; third: Ralph and wife, Nina; fourth: Patricia, Ralph, Lisa; fifth: Daniel, son of Patricia.

da Mosto, Count Francesco
Architect, associated with the Holzmann-Romagnoli consortium and architect Aldo Rossi in their bid to rebuild the Fenice Opera House. Jane, his English wife.

da Mosto, Count Ranieri
Patrician, father of Francesco.

De Luigi, Ludovico
Artist, surrealist, provocateur.

de Rachewiltz, Mary
Daughter of Ezra Pound and Olga Rudge. Her son: Walter.

Donadon, Massimo
The Rat Man of Treviso.

FitzGerald, Joan
(American) Sculptor, friend of Ezra Pound and Olga Rudge.

Foscari, Count Antonio (Tonci)
Architect, associated with the Impregilo consortium and architect
Gae Aulenti in the bid to rebuild the Fenice Opera House. University
professor, lives in Palazzo Barbaro with architect wife, Barbara.

Gardin, Albert
Publisher of Mario Stefani's poetry.

Guggenheim, Peggy
(American, 1898–1979) Collector of modern art; lived in a palace
on the Grand Canal, now a museum: the Peggy Guggenheim
Collection.

Guthrie, Bea
(American) Executive director of Save Venice, wife of Bob Guthrie.

Guthrie, Dr Randolph (Bob)
(American) President of Save Venice, plastic surgeon, husband of
Bea Guthrie.

Holzmann-Romagnoli
A German-Italian consortium bidding to rebuild the Fenice
Opera House in association with architect Aldo Rossi.

Il Gazzettino
Daily newspaper in Venice. In written and spoken English, it is
often referred to simply as 'the *Gazzettino*.'

Impregilo

A consortium headed by Fiat Engineering bidding to rebuild the Fenice Opera House in association with architect Gae Aulenti.

Lauritzen, Peter

(American) Author of books about Venetian art, architecture, history, and culture; husband of Rose.

Lauritzen, Rose

(English) Owner of apartment I occupied; wife of Peter Lauritzen.

Lovato, Guerrino

Artist, sculptor, master mask-maker, owner of mask shop Mondonovo.

Lovett, Lawrence (Larry)

(American) Chairman of Save Venice, formerly chairman of Metropolitan Opera Guild, shipping and grocery-chain heir. Living on Grand Canal.

Marcello, Count Girolamo

Board member of Save Venice, husband of Lesa.

Marcello, Countess Lesa

Director of the Venice office of Save Venice, wife of Girolamo.

Marchetti, Massimiliano

Electrician, worked at the Fenice Opera House for the electrical contracting company Viet owned by his cousin, Enrico Carella.

Meduna, Giovanni Battista, and Tommaso

Brothers who designed the reconstructed Fenice Opera House after the original burned in 1837.

Migliori, Laura

Art conservator working on the restoration of frescos depicting scenes from Dante's *Divine Comedy* at the Fenice Opera House.

Moro, Mario
Soldier, sailor, marine, fireman, policeman, airman, *vaporetto* conductor, electrician, and resident of the Guidecca.

Pound, Ezra
(American, 1885–1972) Poet, critic, expatriate; lived in Venice with his companion of fifty years, Olga Rudge, in a cottage Pound nicknamed the Hidden Nest.

Rossi, Aldo
(1931–1997) Architect associated with Holzmann-Romagnoli consortium and architect Francesco da Mosto in the competition to rebuild the Fenice Opera House.

Rudge, Olga
(American, 1895–1996) Poet Ezra Pound's companion of fifty years, violinist, Vivaldi scholar.

Rylands, Jane
(American) Vice president of the Ezra Pound Foundation, wife of Philip.

Rylands, Philip
(English) Director of the Peggy Guggenheim Collection, husband of Jane.

Sacaim
The Venetian construction firm that rebuilt the Fenice Opera House.

Save Venice
An American organization devoted to raising money for the restoration of Venetian art and architecture.

Seguso, Archimede
Master glassblower, founder of glassworks Vetreria Artistica Archimede Seguso.

Seguso, Giampaolo
  Son of Archimede, proprietor of Seguso Viro.

Seguso, Gino
  Son of Archimede and president of the family company, Vetreria
  Artistica Archimede Seguso.

Seno, Giovanni
  Lawyer for Massimiliano Marchetti.

Sherwood, James
  (American) Proprietor of Cipriani Hotel in Venice, Orient-Express
  railway, board member of Save Venice, trustee of the Guggenheim
  Foundation.

Stefani, Mario
  Poet.

Viet
  An electrical subcontracting company under contract to Argenti for
  renovation of the Fenice Opera House. Owned by Enrico Carella.

Volpi, Count Giovanni
  Son of Count Giuseppe Volpi di Misurata, who was founder of
  Venice Film Festival, creator of the port of Marghera, finance
  minister of Italy under Mussolini. Also, half-brother of Countess
  Anna Maria Volpi Cicogna.

NAMES OF BUILDINGS AND PLACES

Accademia Bridge
   One of three bridges that cross the Grand Canal.

Apollonian rooms
   Formal reception halls in the neoclassical entrance wing of the
   Fenice Opera House.

Ateneo Veneto
   An ornate, neoclassical palace facing on to Campo San Fantin,
   across from the Fenice Opera House. Now a meeting hall for the
   intellectual academy of the same name.

Ca' Farsetti
   Palace on the Grand Canal, the town hall of Venice. *Ca'* is the
   abbreviation for *casa*, meaning house or palace.

Campo San Fantin
   The small square in front of the Fenice Opera House.

Cannareggio
   One of the six *sestieri*, or districts, of Venice. At the western
   end.

Cipriani Hotel
   Luxury hotel on the Giudecca Island, owned by James Sherwood.

Doge's Palace
   Fourteenth-century Gothic palace on St Mark's Square, seat of

government for the former Venetian Republic and residence of its head of state, the doge.

Dorsoduro

One of the six *sestieri*, or districts, of Venice.

English Church

St George's Church, on Campo San Vio.

Fenice

(pronounced feh-NEE-cheh) Gran Teatro La Fenice, an opera house.

Frari

Refers to the Santa Maria Gloriosa dei Frari Church.

Giudecca

Long, narrow island that forms part of the city of Venice. Residents are called Giudecchini.

Gritti Hotel

The Palazzo Gritti converted into a luxury hotel.

Guggenheim Museum

See: *Peggy Guggenheim Collection*.

Harry's Bar

Bar and restaurant near St Mark's, owned by Arrigo Cipriani.

Hidden Nest

The name Ezra Pound gave to the cottage at 252 Calle Querini where he and Olga Rudge lived together, off and on, from the late 1920s until his death in 1972.

Lido

Barrier island between the Venetian lagoon and the Adriatic Sea.

Malibran Theatre

Seventeenth-century theatre, restored by architects Antonio and Barbara Foscari.

Marghera

Shipping port at the mainland end of the bridge from Venice; part of the municipality of Venice.

Miracoli Church

See: *Santa Maria dei Miracoli.*

Mestre

Town on the mainland, part of the municipality of Venice.

Monaco

Reference to the Monaco and Grand Canal Hotel, on the Grand Canal near St Mark's.

Murano

Island in the Venetian lagoon, to the north of Venice, site of glassblowing factories.

Padua

A university city twenty-five miles west of Venice.

Palazzo Barbaro

A double palace on the Grand Canal, built in the fifteenth and seventeenth centuries and owned since 1885 by the Curtis family, originally of Boston.

Palazzo Pisani-Moretta

Fifteenth-century palace on the Grand Canal, available to rent for parties. Often illuminated exclusively by candlelight.

Peggy Guggenheim Collection

Paintings and sculpture assembled by the American collector of modern art Peggy Guggenheim (1898–1979), housed in her former residence – an unfinished palace on the Grand Canal.

Piazzale Roma
Large parking area and bus depot in western Venice at the foot of the bridge to the mainland.

Rialto
Area around the Rialto Bridge, one of three bridges that cross the Grand Canal. Name derived from Riva Alta, meaning 'high riverbank'.

St George's Church
The English Church, on Campo San Vio.

St Mark's
Refers to both St Mark's Square (Piazza San Marco) and St Mark's Basilica. San Marco is also the name of one of the six *sestieri*, or districts, of Venice.

Salute Church
See: *Santa Maria della Salute.*

Santa Maria dei Miracoli
Fifteenth-century church, restored by Save Venice.

Santa Maria della Salute
Baroque church on the Grand Canal, in Dorsoduro, opposite St Mark's. Since its domes are visible from great distances, it is an orienting landmark.

Strada Nuova
A main thoroughfare in the Canareggio district of Venice.

ACKNOWLEDGMENTS

O F MY BRILLIANT EDITOR, Ann Godoff, I will say simply that when she left the publishing house that brought out my first book and came to the house that has published this one, I followed without a moment's hesitation, and I would do the same again. My literary agent, Suzanne Gluck, also moved, from one agency to another, and I went along with her just as readily and for many of the same reasons.

In addition to the people whose co-operation is made clear in these pages, there were a great many others who were enormously helpful. In Venice there was, above all, Pamela Santini, whose cheerful assistance was invaluable to me — whether helping out when my knowledge of Italian was inadequate, cutting bureaucratic red tape, or providing research assistance.

Among the Venetians, first a fond thank-you to the late Alessandro Albrizzi, who in the early 1970s, and with great good humour, was the first to invite me through the invisible door that leads from the public to the private world of Venice.

I would also like to thank, for various reasons, Robert Beard, William Blacker, Atalanta Bouboulis, Carla Ferrara, Joan FitzGerald, Fiora Gandolfi, Geoffrey Humphries, Antonio Leonardi, Jim Mathes, William McNaughton, Randy Mikelson, Aurelio Montanari, Ewa Morgan, Robert Morgan, Sergio Perosa, Pete Peters, Tim Redman, Stefano Rosso-Mazzinghi, Jeremy Scott, Toni Sepeda, Holly Snapp, and Hiram Williams. For their unstinting efforts at The Penguin Press, I am much obliged to Liza Darnton, Tracy Locke, Sarah Hutson, Darren Haggar, Claire Vaccaro, and Kate Griggs.

For their many helpful comments on the manuscript, I am indebted to Carol Deschere, John and Ginger Duncan, Annie Flanders, Sue Fletcher, Linda Hyman, Rhoda Koenig, Deborah Mintz, Joan Kramer, and Marilyn Perry. Throughout the research and writing of this book, Sean Strub has been a source of support and encouragement, as well as a perceptive and much valued sounding board.

In the course of my research, I consulted a great many published sources. Among them, I found Gianluca Amadori's coverage of the Fenice fire and its tangled aftermath for *Il Gazzettino* especially helpful. His reports are assembled and reworked in his excellent book *Per Quattro Soldi* (Editori Riuniti, Rome, 2003).

The superb catalogue for the exhibition mounted by the Isabella Stewart Gardner Museum in Boston in April 2004, *Gondola Days: Isabella Stewart Gardner and the Palazzo Barbaro Circle*, was enlightening on the subject of the Boston Curtises, Palazzo Barbaro, and Henry James, as was Rosella Mamoli Zorzi's informed commentary in *Letters from the Palazzo Barbaro* (Pushkin Press, London, 1998).

I am grateful as well to the Marciana Library for making the diary of Daniel Sargent Curtis (1825–1908) available to me, to the Beinecke Rare Book and Manuscript Library at Yale for providing access to the Olga Rudge Papers, and to the authors of the indispensable *Calli, Campielli e Canali* (Edizioni Helvetia) for enabling me to find even the most cleverly hidden, impossibly out-of-the-way places in Venice.

ABOUT THE AUTHOR

JOHN BERENDT IS A JOURNALIST and former editor of *New York* magazine. His first book, *Midnight in the Garden of Good and Evil*, was an international bestseller and a finalist for the 1995 Pulitzer Prize in general non-fiction. He lives in New York.